THE GIRLS

SUNY series in

Modern Jewish Literature and Culture

Sarah Blacher Cohen, editor

The Girls

———•◆•———

Jewish Women of Brownsville, Brooklyn,

1940–1995

Carole Bell Ford

STATE UNIVERSITY OF NEW YORK PRESS

Published by
State University of New York Press, Albany

© 2000 State University of New York

For information, address State University of New York Press,
State University Plaza, Albany, NY 12246

Production, Laurie Searl
Marketing, Frank Keneston

Library of Congress Cataloging-in-Publication Data

Ford, Carole Bell, 1934–
    The girls : Jewish women of Brownsville, Brooklyn, 1940–1995 /
Carole Bell Ford.
        p.   cm. — (SUNY series in modern Jewish literature and
culture)
    Includes bibliographical references and index.
    ISBN 0-7914-4363-9 (hc. : alk. paper). — ISBN 0-7914-4364-7 (pbk.
: alk. paper)
    1. Jewish women—New York (State)—New York—History—20th
century. 2. Jewish women—New York (State)—New York Interviews.
3. Jews—New York (State)—New York—History—20th century.
4. Jews—New York (State)—New York Interviews. 5. Brownsville (New
York, N.Y.) Biography. I. Title. II. Series: SUNY series on
modern Jewish literature and culture.
F128.9. J5F84 2000
974.7′1004924—dc21   99-20745
                                                                        CIP

10   9   8   7   6   5   4   3   2   1

For Momma and the Cherry Sisters

—Brownsville "girls"—

Contents

Reclaiming our Past

Jewish women have fared no better than their gentile sisters in history.

—Baum, Hyman and Michel,
The Jewish Woman in America

There are almost no women mentioned in the two histories that have been written about Brownsville, a neighborhood in Brooklyn, New York, that was almost completely Jewish until mid-century. This is the story of women who came of age there—and then.

Today, Brownsville is one of the most destitute communities in New York City, perhaps rivalled only by the South Bronx for its problems. It was never affluent. From the start, in the late nineteenth century, it was a poor working-class community, which had the attraction of being a suburban haven from the Lower East Side of Manhattan, where immigrants from Eastern and Southern Europe settled when they first came to America. It was founded soon after bridges and improved transportation to Manhattan made commuting from eastern Brooklyn possible.

Brownsville began where Crown Heights ended, reaching down from the Eastern Parkway, its northern border. It stretched eastward toward the New Lots, which had been acquired for sale by enterprising real estate brokers. Its eastern boundary was demarcated by the BMT train tracks at Junius Street, on the other side was East New York. To its south and west, Brownsville merged with the more affluent neighborhood of East Flatbush.

Like the women I am writing about, not incidentally, I was born in Brownsville in the midst of the Depression. Brownsville is my old neighborhood. The tracks of the elevated subway, the IRT El, ran right beside the windows of our second-story flat, above Abramowitz's grocery store on the corner of Livonia Avenue and Barrett Street.

Because of my closeness to the subject, I walk a narrow line between objectivity and subjectivity. A participant-observer, I mingle my voice with the voices of the women I write about. At the same time I try to provide the objective and analytical "voiceover" of the historian. At a recent international conference of historians, the balance between narrative and objectivity was discussed. It was concluded that the historian should not, of course, fall into total subjectivity, but should find a "middle ground" that connects with historical "reality."

In the first comprehensive history of Jewish women in America, Charlotte Baum, Paula Hyman, and Sonya Michel wrote that the time had come to reclaim our past, as "Jewish women have fared no better than our gentile sisters in history." If researchers asked new questions and looked in new places, they suggested, a great deal of rich material could be unearthed. It has been. Since 1975, when Baum, Hyman, and Michel published *The Jewish Woman in America*, research on Jewish women has proliferated among historians and other scholars. It is hoped that the stories of "the girls" will add to the ever-growing history of Jewish women in America.

For this study I conducted lengthy interviews with more than forty women and briefer, informal interviews with many others. This process has enabled me to let the women, as Paula Giddens said in *When and Where I Enter*, "tell a story largely untold." But, above all, the women *are* the story. The women define and explain their lives: their meaning and connection to the lives of their foremothers, their partners, and their children. I have synthesized the information and provided some of the historical background necessary to fully appreciate the story (with additional information in detailed endnotes). I have also offered my interpretation of how so many of these Jewish women prevailed in spite of the severe limitations imposed upon their full emotional and intellectual growth.

In order to understand the Brownsville "girls" and to recognize parts of ourselves, our sisters, and our mothers in them, it is necessary to locate them not only in their historical time and place but also, primarily, in their Jewish-immigrant cultural milieu: one that was dominated (not only for the observant but for those who did not practice the rituals) by the norms, values, and attitudes of the orthodox Ashkenazic, that is, Eastern European Jewish culture. Recognizing this context enables us to understand their perceptions and their reality, their actual freedom of choice and limitations within which they made choices, the contradictions they faced, and how—and why—they were able to overcome the limitations imposed on them.

Alter Landesman's was the first and, for almost twenty years, the only history of Brownsville. Landesman was an important local figure, a rabbi and director of the Hebrew Educational Society, who represented Brownsville on more than twenty civic organizations. Recently, another history of Brownsville was written, this one by historian Gerald Sorin the Director of the Jewish Studies program at SUNY, New Paltz, and a Brownsville boy.

Landesman compiled an important record but wrote a nostalgic and sentimental history. In one chapter (which is one of the self-congratulatory listings often found in histories of this type) Landesman names almost four hundred notables who were born, raised, or spent some time in Brownsville. There are writers and scientists, doctors and lawyers; almost no women appear among the hundreds of names. He lists singers, dancers, and actors; there are a few women here. He lists sports figures; of course no women are mentioned. Finally, he cites education, the field in which women dominated and in which they were able to achieve a measure of professional status. Of the twenty-five educators he found worthy of mention, Landesman found only *one* woman to name, an administrator. Not a single outstanding female teacher's name remained of the thousands who taught school there—although he did find enough for a section on Jewish boxers!

Gerald Sorin is a close friend and colleague of mine; we first met twenty years ago when he supervised my master's thesis. His most recent published works are on Jewish history. Among them is *The Nurturing Neighborhood: The Brownsville Boys Club and Jewish Community in Urban America, 1940–1990*, a social history that triggered my interest in writing this account. For very different reasons, Sorin's history of Brownsville, like Landesman's, does not take the experiences of women into account.

Alter Landesman, it seems, was oblivious to women's contributions to the community. His criteria for choosing who to include on his list was the traditional historical definition of "important" people. Inevitably, the people he included had made some mark in the public realm, from which women, and certainly Jewish women dominated by an orthodox tradition, were excluded. Landesman was a chronicler, not a critical historian. Sorin, on the other hand is a historian who, in other works, has written with sensitivity about women and women's issues. *The Nurturing Neighborhood,* however, is about the Brownsville *Boys* Club. Sorin shouldn't be faulted for the focus of his history, only for drawing conclusions and formulating generalizations from his history of the boys (men) of Brownsville as if they applied to both men and women. The experiences of the Brownsville girls was unlike that of the boys in many significant ways.

Together with Landesman's and Sorin's, this study completes the comprehensive history of Brownsville. Since the story of the men has already been so well elaborated, this study also provides an opportunity to examine and compare gender issues in a Jewish-American community through listening to voices that have not been heard before now: the voices of the women of Brownsville.

If both Sorin's and Landesman's are histories of only half of Brownsville, this is the story of the other half.

Acknowledgments

In the preparation of this manuscript I am indebted to so many people: first, to my friends and colleagues at SUNY, Empire State College, with thanks especially to David Porter and Steve Lewis. I am also grateful to the administrators who gave their support to this project, particularly Dean Jim Case. Deborah Dash Moore took the time from her extremely busy schedule not only to read my proposal but to make suggestions and pose questions that were invaluable to me in thinking through and clarifying what I wanted to say. My son Gregg and my daughter Julie, others in my family, and many friends suffered through my earliest grapplings with the subject matter and content. My big brother, Joe Bell, shared his earliest memories of growing up in Brownsville with me. My good friend and neighbor, the biographer and poet, Robert Polito, helped by suggesting revisions. But there are three people without whom I doubt I would have persisted through the more than eight years of research, interviews, writing and rewriting. Gerald Sorin not only encouraged this project but facilitated my work at every step. Myra Sorin read every word, more than once, spotted misspelled words and misplaced semicolons, was sensitive to inferences and nuance, and offered consistent support and encouragement while she gently suggested changes. And finally, thank you, Steve. My husband, Steve Ford, may have been baffled by my desire to take on such a project at this point in my life and career but he listened to my endless reports and discussions. He found inconsistencies in my arguments but used his excellent teaching skills in leading me to find my own answers, and he read everything from the roughest drafts through to this final version.

They Still Call Themselves "the Girls"

Profiles of Two Brownsville Women

> The gradual evolution in women's roles came about because of a painful awakening in each woman's awareness that maybe she could do more.
>
> —Adrienne Baker,
> *The Jewish Woman in Contemporary Society*

Among the teenagers who were growing into adulthood in Brownsville in the 1940s and 1950s were Terry Apter and Ruth Kesslin. I am beginning the story of "the girls" with Terry and Ruth because their personal histories contain almost all of the elements that make them representative of their contemporaries and because, through their stories, I can bring the key points I will be making about Brownsville women into focus.

Terry Apter is a slender, handsome, stately but warm, gentle, and soft-spoken woman. Terry and I had talked on the phone a number of times before I met her in southern Florida in 1991. A number of former Brownsvillians had gathered in Florida at that time because of an upcoming dinner-dance: the annual reunion of the Brownsville Boys Club Alumni Association, an organization of men which, ironically, plays an important role in this history of women.

I was there to meet and interview women who, after retirement, had either settled in Florida or spent part of each winter there; Terry was one of the latter. She and her husband Al spent most of the year in a retirement community in New Jersey but also owned a condo in Delray Beach. "I lost my best friend," Terry told me, when Al passed away recently.

Terry is typical of her generation of Brownsville women, now in their late sixties and early seventies. This is the group I call the "forties women," although *they* still call each other "the girls" (as in, "I really have to run. I'm meeting 'the girls' at the gym").

Terry is like most of the other women I've interviewed whose parents, or grandparents, were immigrants. (Only one of the interviewees, Raye Cohen, was born in Europe.) Terry is typical of the women who were born into struggling, working-class Jewish families in Brownsville and the adjacent community, East New York. Terry, like her contemporaries, grew up during the Great Depression and came of age in the 1940s, graduated from high school during the war years, and married soon after the war ended. All of the women married Jewish men, and, as Terry did, many married boys from Brownsville. As Gerald Sorin wrote in *The Nurturing Neighborhood*, quoting an alumnus of the Brownsville Boys Club, it was inevitable that many marriages would be between men and women from the neighborhood, "after all, who had carfare?"

Like her Brownsville friends, Terry set about becoming a *baleboste*, an accomplished homemaker and a model for her daughters. Like the other women of her generation, she established a "Jewish home." Terry defines this as a home in which Jewish values were perpetuated in which *Yidishkeit*, the Jewish culture, was preserved by "keeping kosher," observing the high holy days, and sending sons to Hebrew school to prepare for their *Bar Mitzvah*; a home that was child-centered, in which the highest value was family.

Like many of her friends, Terry moved from Brownsville to Canarsie when she was able to afford a "better" neighborhood. She stayed home to raise her children and then, like almost all the others, she returned to work outside the home once her children were in school. Terry worked at a clerical job. Others returned to college, completing the unfinished business that had been interrupted by marriage and children. Quite a few achieved successful careers.

Today, Terry lives in a retirement community, surrounded by extended family and lifelong friends. She lives among women who enjoy their grandchildren but don't depend on babysitting to occupy their time. In fact, many of their children live great distances away and the women are busy leading their own active lives. One of the reasons the Brownsville women carry on so well in their "empty nests" is that they suffer from little self-recrimination. They say that they did their jobs, and they believe they did them well. They're entitled now to reclaim their lives. "Now it's time to do something for myself."

Like all of the women in this study, Terry is a product of the Jewish and Jewish-American culture that evolved during the Depression, the war years, and the Cold War. Her "typicalness" doesn't detract from the fact that her story is uniquely her own. Although it seems a contradiction, by being both the same as they and different, she exemplifies her Brownsville contemporaries, the other forties women—the girls—whose individual stories are told here within a larger, collective biography; they are all the same while they are all different.

Terry was the child of eastern European Jewish immigrants; her parents married in Russia and left their families behind when they came to America. Once settled, they "brought over" her aunts and grandmother; most of Terry's paternal family, however, had already been lost in a *pogrom*, the periodic organized slaughter of Jews in eastern Europe.

Terry's father had been schooled in Europe as a mathematician and engineer but was unable to find professional work in this country; instead, he read blueprints. Terry's mother worked at home "doing sewing" and (like my own mother, who knew only Yiddish and some Russian) went to night school to learn to read and write English.

Like most working-class families, Terry's family, the Gubermans, fell upon hard times during the Depression and moved repeatedly back and forth between Brownsville and East New York, taking advantage of "concessions," that is, two or three months of free rent offered as enticements by desperate landlords. At different times Terry lived on Linwood and Sutter Avenues, Sackman Street, Blake Avenue, Bristol Street, and Pitkin Avenue.

During World War II, which the women call, simply, "the war," Terry's mother ran a shop, a grocery-general store, as did the mothers of many of the girls. But wartime, a boon to many people, was a struggle for the Guberman family. Terry's father fell ill, and although her brothers were in the service, their government allotment checks were not enough for the family to live on. It was Terry who "became responsible for her mother" and "had to grow up quickly"; she got a job at a bridal shop and worked every day after school, and on weekends, for six dollars a week.

A small number of the girls took academic courses in school, hoping
to become teachers, the one acceptable, and attainable profession in the
1940s for a woman from a Jewish working-class family. But, like the
majority of her female classmates, Terry graduated from Thomas Jefferson High School with a commercial diploma. She was hired as a secretary
in a defense plant, at the respectable salary of eighteen dollars per week.

Terry remembers the war years, especially the pictures of "fellows"
in uniform displayed in the windows of their homes. She wrote to some
of them. "But we had no social life," she says about that time, "so many
of the boys were away." Soon after the war, when he returned from the
service in 1946, she married Al Apter. Their first daughter was born, in
Brownsville in 1947.

In the 1950s, Terry, and many of her friends, moved from
Brownsville to Canarsie, a community that was developing on the flat-
lands near Jamaica Bay; others moved to Queens, Long Island, and New
Jersey. "We all enjoyed being home; we did it together," she says of her
years as a young housewife and mother. But "we got tired of playing
cards and Mah-Jongg. We wanted to do something worthwhile."

Terry and a small group of women formed "Pals for Palsy" under
the auspices of the national cerebral palsy organization. The Brownsville
Boys Club provided them with an office for their philanthropic work.
They became formally organized, "chartered," and began to learn fund
raising. By doing this, Terry and the others were fulfilling a primary cultural imperative: *tsedakah,* a basic principle of Jewish life. A Jewish
woman was expected to express *tsedakah* (literally, righteousness)
through charitable activities, "giving to the community" through phil-
anthropy or service.

Jewish cultural messages concerning charitable and other obligations had been transmitted to the women in sharp and clear tones. They
were expected to avoid idleness and to engage in meaningful, goal-
directed work. When her children got older, and homemaking no longer
felt to her like "meaningful work," Terry held several different jobs, and
eventually found a career at one the New York City Board of Education's school district offices. As secretary to the Supervisor for Special
Education, Terry finally had a job that made her "feel important."
Teachers asked for her advice; she was a "problem solver." Being part of
the school system felt right to her. Terry thinks she might have "gone for
teaching" if she hadn't been so poor and been needed to help support
the family.

For similar reasons, because they sought meaningful activities, other "forties women" returned to paid work and resumed careers, the unfinished business that had been interrupted by marriage and children. A few went back to school but most, like Terry, achieved success without the benefit of a formal education.

With some misgivings, Terry retired in 1987 because Al had retired and, "it wouldn't have been fair for him to be alone." After twenty-seven years in Canarsie, they decided to move to New Jersey, near their daughters and other relatives. For the first year after her retirement, Terry was unhappy; she missed her job and her colleagues. But then she got busy. She became involved with "Deborah," a Jewish philanthropic organization, helping raise funds for a heart and lung machine for a nearby "Deborah" hospital. Terry had never been able to be idle. She never stopped to dwell upon her empty nest; instead, she has filled her life in her retirement with important relationships and meaningful activities.

Like almost all of the Brownsville women, when she compares her own life to her mother's and her daughters', Terry feels that she "had it the best." Her mother was "old before her time," she says. "Her whole life was her family, she had no life outside." Her daughters "have a lot more but their lives are very stressful," Terry says.

> Our children have a different way of life. They grew up having a lot but they compete with others who had more. They have to borrow; it's rough to pay back. They need two incomes. Can you imagine them doing what we did? We went partners with my brother and sister-in-law on our first car!

Still, Terry would not tell her granddaughter to be "just a housewife":

> We did it because we didn't know better. We didn't have options, we didn't have babysitters and day care. I would tell her, "get married but first get a degree, have a career to go back to."

Like the other Brownsville women I've interviewed, Terry has come a long way from her impoverished beginnings. She feels, and believes, that she has been successful: she "married the right man"; she has daughters who are "good wives and mothers"; she is able to "feel for people who are in trouble or who are sick"; she has successful relationships.

It was in Brownsville, within that exclusively Jewish community, that Terry internalized the values that enabled her, like her contemporaries, to become successful in her personal life, using as measures of success strong lifelong friendships, good relationships with her children, and a fulfilling long-term marriage. As men were nurtured in the Jewish tradition to achieve through education and hard work, women were nurtured to achieve through dedication to their domestic roles. Immersed in the traditional eastern European, orthodox Jewish culture of Brownsville, Terry learned to value not only the importance of family but also meaningful work, a goal-directed life, a sense of obligation to the community, and a social consciousness. Brownsville was a nurturing neighborhood for the women of Terry's generation, the forties women, as it was for the men—with respect to their traditional, gendered roles.

The women of Terry's generation were not nurtured, however, to develop their full potential beyond feminine roles. For their lives to be less limited—to become educated, to pursue professional careers, to become independent persons—the women had to struggle not only against Jewish tradition but against the values of the broader American society, which were congruent with, and which powerfully reinforced, Jewish norms.

Both the 1940s and the 1950s, had their idiosyncratic features, so that the women who came of age in the fifties entered a different world from that of the previous decade. As Terry Apter is typical of her generation, Ruth Kesslin is of hers—the fifties women.

It's hard to imagine Ruth as she describes her past self: "I was under a rock for sixteen years," she says. Today she is elegant and attractive. She is slim, stylish, well groomed, bright, and articulate. She is easy to talk to; it seemed as if we were old friends catching up with each other, as we sat in her smartly furnished apartment on Manhattan's upper East Side.

Like almost all of the women in the fifties group, Ruth was a homemaker for most of the time that her children were in school. It wasn't until she had given sixteen years to her marriage and children that she, like other fifties women, left the shelter of her exclusively domestic life, went to college, established herself in a career, and managed both it and a successful marriage that has lasted forty years. It wasn't done without a struggle.

Because Brownsville did not prepare its women to succeed in the public realm, the fifties women had to dig deeply within Jewish culture to unearth and claim rights for themselves that were traditionally reserved for men, particularly the right to an education and a choice of careers. And Ruth and the women of her generation also had to overcome attitudes instilled by what historians have, aptly, termed the "cult of domesticity," which had prevailed in American society in the early years of the Cold War. Fortunately, the fifties women were aided just as they were returning to the workforce, by liberalizing attitudes and expanding opportunities.

Ruth's parents were American-born but, as was still common in Brownsville, they shared a two-family house with her orthodox grandparents who had emigrated from Poland and Russia earlier in the century. They lived on Strauss Street, between Sutter and Pitkin Avenues. Like many second-generation Jewish women, Ruth's mother kept a kosher home, lit candles on *shabes*, the Sabbath, and was moderately observant of her religious obligations. Ruth studied Hebrew at a local *shule* and also at the Hebrew Educational Society (whose director was Alter Landesman, the Brownsville historian). The H.E.S., as it was known, was where many of the Brownsville girls went for Hebrew lessons, or music lessons, or to socialize. Ruth often met there with her clubmates, the girls of "Club Diablos," who wore blue and grey sweaters that signified the in-group identification that was—and still is—so important to adolescents.

"It was a difficult household," Ruth says, "my mother was an angry woman and I had to give up my brain for my father. He was very traditional." He was an attorney, but "wasn't able to get into a practice and didn't establish one of his own." Later, he became ill and couldn't go out of the house to work. But he was a scholar, he studied languages, translated books, and wrote at home. Consequently:

> Money was always an issue. We always knew we were poor. There was always food, but just enough; we were well dressed, but in second hand clothing.

In fact, Ruth's mother supported the family with a secondhand clothing store during the war. "It was the *shtetl* model," Ruth says, referring to small town or village life in eastern Europe, in which the wife worked to support her scholar-husband and her family.

Ruth has many recollections of her teen years. Some flash through as images, such as the death of F.D.R. ("walking in the street, aimlessly, my grandmother crying, feeling as if the whole ground had fallen away"), the end of the war, the establishment of the state of Israel, which was very important to her because she "worked" for a Zionist group.

Ruth's relations with her mother had never been good, but they got worse. Ruth had skipped a year in elementary school and, like a number of the girls, had been in the rapid advance track in junior high. She chose the academic, college-bound course in high school, "but," she says, "my mother made me change my course. Actually, she went up to school and changed it. There was no discussion." Her mother insisted that Ruth had to be prepared to work.

And so she did. Ruth took an after-school job as an assistant book-keeper while she was still in high school and continued to work until her marriage in 1956, five years after her graduation. She didn't return to the workforce until 1972. "What started my journey," Ruth says,

> was financial hard times. The children were on their own,
> pretty much. I did some real estate, sold jewelry, got a job as
> a secretary and went . . . into a depression. I didn't know who
> I was. I knew I was a wife and mother, but who was *I*?

When she was about forty-five, Ruth enrolled in a Bachelor of Social Work program at Kean College in New Jersey. It was 1976.

> My life had been put on hold. I began developmentally again
> and I blossomed in those years. I said, "I'm doing my adoles-
> cence now." I began singing lessons, I picked up where I
> dropped off.

Ruth graduated *summa cum laude*, won a grant to do her master's at New York University, and then enrolled in a two-year postgraduate program in advanced clinical social work, followed by a certificate program in psychoanalysis and comprehensive psychotherapy at the National Institute for Psychotherapies in Manhattan.

Ruth had grown intellectually, but then found that she also had to "grow up" in her relationship with her husband. He was very support-ive, "unique for his generation," Ruth says, but neither he nor Ruth were prepared for the shifts in their traditional relationship. He was con-flicted about her growing and changing; she "didn't want to give up the perks, didn't want to be powerful, wanted to be taken care of." But both adjusted. They renegotiated their relationship. As Ruth describes the process, he relinquished his role as the dominant, paternalistic authority figure; she gave up her dependence and submissiveness. Their goal became "an integration of the traditional masculine and feminine dichotomy," their "ideal became interdependence."

Ruth's development was not a direct result of the women's move-ment, in which she was not involved. She did not even read feminist literature. However, she believes that she was profoundly touched by the changes feminism brought about for the fifties women, which had just missed the women of the forties. And she believes that there was another difference between the two groups: she was born into a generation that was not enveloped by the collective cultural and emotional depression "that came out of the actual Depression" and overcame the older women. "They felt it was too late," but Ruth's generation came to believe they could be "more than they had been"; they developed what Ruth explains as, "possibility thinking, a positive risk factor."

In spite of the limitations they experienced, both Ruth and Terry believe that life has been better for them than it was for their mothers, or can be for their daughters and the women of their daughters' generation. Ruth believes that life is much harder and more complicated for young women today. There are "no set expectations." Because of this, "life is very confusing for the next generation. Even those who become powerful in their professional lives have a longing to be dependent, traditional in their relationships." Ruth thinks that what may be better for women might be "worse for the family."

The life chances of the Brownsville women were proscribed both by Jewish cultural norms and by the fact of their gender. Although most of Brownsville was not religiously observant, orthodox culture dominated the community throughout their youth and young adulthood and the Brownsville girls' self-definition took place within the limits of its precepts, attitudes, values, and norms. And their lives were also strongly affected by America's middle-class culture.

Brownsville was *insulated,* not *isolated.* During the time in which the women were born, raised, and reached maturity it was, in many respects, like a ghetto. But the outside world came into the community through the media: radio, film, and, after the fifties, television. The newspapers that were carried by the commuters on the New Lots line of the IRT subway were not only the *Jewish Daily Forward* and *Tag* but the *Daily News* and *The Star,* later *The New York Post.* Brownsville men and women worked in "the city," in multi-ethnic Manhattan.

In spite of the different individual experiences of the forties and fifties women, when they were girls they all received and internalized powerful messages regarding women's ideal role in both Jewish and American society. These were essentially the same messages from both sources, and so distinct, unequivocal, and irresistible that all of the women were bound, at least initially, to follow traditional, well-worn paths.

CHAPTER ONE

Missing

Fifty-One Percent of the Stories

> I was just a woman who grew up in Brownsville. I don't have
> a great success story. I didn't do anything special.
>
> —Bea Gable Benjamin

When they talk about their lives today, a half-century after they
came of age in the 1940s and 1950s, the Brownsville women still
call each other "the girls."

In their Brooklyn community these girls were molded into an image
of woman through the mingling of two cultures: not by one exclusive of
the other, and not by either one or the other.[1] The first was dominant:
the eastern European or Ashkenazic orthodox Jewish, immigrant culture
of the community,[2] a community of struggling, poor working-class Jews.
But the other, the middle-class, mainstream culture into which New
York Jews were becoming assimilated, was profoundly influential as
well. During the wartime and postwar decades, Brownsville Jews were
in the process of changing from Jews in America, still deeply rooted in
their ethnicity, to Jewish-Americans; another cultural category in the
endless variety of Americans.

When the girls were teenagers, attitudes about what a woman
should do, should care about, should be, should hope to become, as well
as all of the should-nots, were based on themes that were reiterated in
both cultures. As they were growing into adulthood, the girls were influenced by traditional Jewish cultural norms and attitudes, which were
still strongly enforced by the immigrant generation. And they received

the same message from the broader society, except for the brief time during World War II when women were needed to fill the vacancies in the workforce created by men in service. It became even louder, and stronger, when the war ended and the men came home. The message was, as Lorraine Nelson succinctly puts it: "school, job, marriage, children, housewife."

During the postwar period, the traditional Jewish precepts were joined by a strongly held tenet of middle-class American society: men should be the breadwinners and women the homemakers. "There was that sense always," one of the Brownsville women, Rochelle Feld, said, "that the boys get pushed and the girls do secretarial work until you get married. It was not overt but it was somehow always implied." When working-class poverty was added to the equation—the girls' incomes were needed to help support their families—the options were severely limited.

"Coming of age" is a term that, because of anthropologists such as Margaret Mead, is often associated with exotic cultures; it conjures images of primitive rites of passage. But in fact it simply refers to a process of "becoming": it includes the rituals, formal but more often informal, that contribute to a sense of self, what psychologists call ego, or identity. Adolescence is a time when we experiment with things that are both good and bad for us. It's a time when we try on different attitudes, values, and behaviors, when we internalize those that fit and discard those that do not. Because it is intrinsically connected with how we eventually define ourselves as adults, adolescence is a critical time in our life histories. We begin to formulate our male and female identities from the moment of birth, perhaps before, but it is during adolescence, if we're successful, that our notion of who we are is clarified, as we consolidate our self-image, including our image of who we are as women and men.[3] Through the process of maturation and socialization, however, the two genders become quite different in their attitudes and behavior.

It is precisely because of this difference that Gerald Sorin's book, *The Nurturing Neighborhood*, provoked this study of Brownsville women.[4] As I read it—I knew the neighborhood, I grew up there—I questioned whether the generalizations he derived from his study of the community and its boys could have been valid for the whole of Brownsville, that is, for the girls too. My assumption was that they could not be and were not.

Sorin tells the history of the community through the history of the Brownsville Boys Club, the "BBC," which celebrated its fiftieth anniversary in 1990. The story of the Brownsville boys is a tale of impressive achievement. In explaining the success of the men of the BBC, Sorin noted that it is difficult to "*separate* class culture from ethnic culture" and to "determine precisely the relative influence of class and ethnicity on values and achievement." Gender was not one of the elements taken into account when Sorin concluded that the complex "interaction" between these elements, class and culture, shaped the behavior of the boys and "accounts for the ultimate success of the members of the Boys Club."[5]

In spite of its poverty, the community in which the elements of class culture and ethnicity merged, Sorin said, was a "nurturing neighborhood." It provided the boys with a strong and stable foundation upon which they could build their lives. Sorin's conclusion was that it was the *culture* of the Jewish immigrants in interaction with the American environment, as much as their *class* experience, that accounted for their achievements in both their careers and their personal lives.[6] Again, their gender was not taken into account. It usually isn't, because we are used to thinking of the male experience as the overall norm, and not just the *male* experience.

In 1990, the year that Sorin's book was published, a brief article entitled "Are 51 percent of the stories missing?" appeared in a publication of the Project on the Status and Education of Women. In it, Bonnie Eisenberg (Education Director for the National Women's History Project) wrote: "Since women's activities and contributions have not been well represented in the telling of our nation's history, we have missed out on 51 percent of the great stories."[7] Fifty-one percent of the Brownsville stories *were* missing, not only from Alter Landesman's earlier history of the community but from Sorin's.[8]

When Sorin refers to "the children" and "the people of Brownsville," his strokes are too broadly drawn. As in some Native American societies where the word for "man" is the same as the word for "people," we think of men as people, of women as women. Sorin was writing about the boys and men, *their* history, not about the girls or women. As Carol Gilligan has pointed out, "an hypothesis cannot be tested adequately unless the standards of assessment are derived from studies of women as well as from studies of men. Something may be missed" she warns, "by the practice of leaving out girls and women."[9]

It is not difficult to understand why women's stories are absent from history as well as from the canon of literature. The philosopher, Elizabeth Kamarck Minnich explains that women have traditionally been excluded from both defining and from the definitions of worthwhile knowledge. It was not until many scholars recognized that women *were* worth knowing about that they began to redefine what is worth knowing and to ask questions that included women: What were the women doing? What were their lives like? What do we need to learn from as well as about them?[10]

Since the 1960s and 1970s, more and more scholars have wanted to tell women's stories, to hear women's voices. Women's lives are different from men's, and that difference has "deserved to be visible." A new "consciousness" has developed in literature "about both the facts of women's lives and the many possible ways stories about those lives might be told."[11] At the same time, a similar paradigm shift has taken place in historical research and writing, and today there is at least one, twenty-volume, *History of Women in America*.[12] But it would be a mistake to think that the task of telling the missing fifty-one percent of the stories is done.

Although Brownsville women constitute only a small part of the fifty-one percent missing from American history, their story helps fill the larger and more particular gap created by the fifty-one percent missing from Jewish history. Many agree that Sydney Stahl Weinberg needed to write her "consciously, compensatory history," *World of our Mothers,* because of the omissions in Irving Howe's now-classic *World of Our Fathers*.[13] Because he wrote it more than twenty years ago, it may be understandable that Howe neglected women, but the same offense is still being committed. In her essay entitled "Integrating the study of Jewish women into the study of the 'The Jews'," Shulamit Magnus wrote:

> What the Jewish historical profession needs is massive consciousness training so that we know half a story when we see it and actively seek out the whole . . . if gender is not considered . . . as a category of analysis, it will be a phallocentric study which ignores half of the Jewish population at any given time.[14]

There is good reason for Magnus's concern. One example can be found in a recently published (1992) multivolume history sponsored by the American Jewish Historical Society, *The Jewish People in America*.

In one volume, Henry Feingold discusses major sectarian schisms that occurred in Judaism in the United States during the period between 1920 and 1945.[15] Although the issue of women's full participation in Jewish observance has been controversial throughout modern Jewish history and was raised in debates over the growth of both the Conservative and Reconstructionist movements, it has barely been mentioned by Feingold. In fact, issues raised by women are confined to no more than six or seven pages in the entire book. (Most of these are well beyond the scope of this book; however, some are examined in notes and others discussed in chapter 3.)

In both Feingold's and at least one other volume of the series, that written by Edward Shapiro, it is impossible not to be struck by the lack of references to women's issues and to the well-known and respected women who have written about them (Blu Greenberg, Judith Plaskow, Irene Klepfisz, and others) while the few issues that are dealt with have been either glossed over or summarily dismissed as insignificant. Jewish women have made significant gains within some sects (primarily Reform and Reconstructionist) but not of the scope and magnitude that Edward Shapiro suggested when he wrote that, by the 1980s, "much of the Jewish feminist agenda had been achieved."[16]

It is difficult for traditional scholars to write about women. What has been said about the craft of biography is also true for history: in writing about men it is possible to concentrate on "accomplishments," but "one of the main questions" in writing about women is "what *are* the accomplishments in a woman's life?" Women's lives are "a tightly woven mesh of public and private events," Linda Wagner-Miller wrote, "the primary definition of a woman's selfhood is likely to be this combined public-private identity."[17] The men and women of Brownsville, who came of age in the same neighborhood, belonging to the same social class, at the same historical time, and in the same culture, tell vastly different stories of success, which can only be explained by taking gender socialization into account. The criteria by which we judge success in women's lives are confoundingly elusive and subjective, not least because we cannot use those measures that are most commonly used for men: educational achievement, social mobility, income, professional status or accomplishments in their chosen careers. (Even when careers are included, the women's are generally more modest than the men's.)

The reason I chose to tell the women's story as a collective biography is that "the girls" have much in common *as* girls; together, they confirm and validate each other's experiences and perceptions. They believe that Brownsville nurtured women, like men, for success. Although in many respects I too am one of the girls, I can't fully agree with them.[18] Assuming responsibility for herself, Bea Larkin said, "I don't believe I lived up to my full potential"; I would say (in my role as historian and interpreter of events) that Bea had been socialized, that is, she had internalized values that made her unable to live up to her potential. The culture that permeated the "nurturing" neighborhood had imposed severe limitations upon her full human development.

Another Brownsville woman, Raye Cohen, understood that there were few expectations beyond housekeeping for girls in the traditional Jewish household:

> As long as you did what was required in the house, you were there for *kidish* [the formal blessing over wine or bread], and kept kosher, nothing above and beyond that was required.

Raye was raised to become a homemaker. In the 1940s, few girls, even those from less traditional households, were expected to go to college or to have careers, although teaching was acceptable as a career for women. It was something to do before marriage, something that was compatible with family life once the kids were in school. But teaching meant four years of college and even in the days when the city colleges were free, it meant four more years of being dependent, with, as the women would say, "no money coming into the house."

The fifties girls were somewhat more removed from the immigrant experience (more of their parents were American-born second-generation) and from poverty, as the worst of the Great Depression was already over when they were children. Consequently, more of them were able to enjoy such privileges as higher education and a (limited) choice of professional careers, which, in traditional Jewish culture, had previously been reserved for the boys of the family. But home and family were always their first consideration and responsibility. In the sense that it was so limiting, Brownsville was not a nurturing neighborhood for the women. Their achievements in education and in their careers were not due to, but in spite of, having been raised in Brownsville.

However, while I disagree with the women on the one hand (I say this while imagining my thumbs arcing down in the caricatured manner of the Talmudic student), on the other hand, I do agree that in Brownsville, the women were nurtured to be successful—in their gendered, feminine role, the role of the *baleboste*, the homemaker. They learned to be good Jewish wives and mothers and to transmit a respect for *Yidishkeit* to their children, a concept in American-Jewish life that is not easy to define. Jenna Weisman Joselit, in *The Wonders of America,* described it as

> an inchoate and at times ineptly rendered but consistently heartfelt and deeply intentioned emotional and cultural sensibility. . . . [A] cultural hodgepodge of traditional practices and ideals. . . .[19]

Brownsville also nurtured the women to be successful in another sense. While the girls learned to be good traditional wives and mothers, Brownsville constituted a medium through which the more profound cultural precepts of Judaism were transmitted, those that enabled some of the women to overcome the limitations set by parochial norms. Through their immersion in that thoroughly Jewish community, the girls came to know and internalize the fundamental values of the community's culture. The girls absorbed them and gave them new meaning.

The women who went to college overcame the limitations imposed upon their gender by assuming that deeply held values related to learning and to education applied to them no less than to the boys. They redefined the concept of *takhles*, the expectation for a goal-directed, meaningful life that shunned idleness; the expanded definition encompassed but went beyond homemaking. The concept of *tikn olam*, the repair or improvement of the world, which in modern terms means having a social consciousness, was translated into activism. They expressed *tsedakah*, responsibility for the welfare of the community, through socially redeeming work and through giving, not only in charity but in service.

Like the men's, the women's lives were "deeply informed"[20] by the values of the culture of the old neighborhood. In this sense, the women too were nurtured for success, even if not deliberately. Unlike the men, however, who were propelled by tradition, the women had to struggle against the constraints of values and norms that would have limited them, as one of the girls put it, to "home, marriage, children, family."

What I have learned from and about the Brownsville girls is based on extensive interviews with women who live in the New York area and in Florida. I interviewed forty women face to face and the rest on the phone. I also gathered information from Brownsville women who live all across the country and from other, informal sources.[21]

Although Bea Benjamin called me in response to a notice I published in the Thomas Jefferson High School alumni newsletter (the local high school for Brownsville youth), she was surprised when I phoned back to set up an interview with her: "I was just a woman who grew up in Brownsville," she said later. "I don't have a great success story. I didn't do anything special." Others responded similarly: "There was nothing spectacular about my life," Norma Ellman told me.

I had to convince the women that I wasn't looking for "anything special," or "success stories," or "spectacular achievements"; I was looking for women like them. What I found, however, hidden in their deceptively simple stories, were all of the above; the girls have all come a very long way.

My research questions were straightforward and a direct outgrowth of my musings as I had read about the boys. I had wondered about the women's early experiences in Brownsville, their ambitions, the choices they had made, their successes and their definitions of success. And I had wondered about the images they had developed of women in general, as well as of the women who influenced them as they were clarifying their own self-images. I had wondered about the decisions they had made about their lives as they were coming of age and internalizing notions about women's traditional role.

As I collated what became data, I began to see that the women had a great deal in common but some important differences too. I realized that they settled into two groups, which I sorted into the forties and fifties women. I could have used birth dates as an organizing principle but decided instead to group the women by the decades of their high school graduations to underscore the importance of their adolescent years, when "the girls" were still girls. Because they came from virtually identical backgrounds, I could compare the two groups of women. For the same reason, I could compare the experiences of the women and men.

When I began to organize the information I'd gathered, I saw that I would have to cover some ground that was already familiar to some readers. For instance, it was necessary to include a discussion of historical issues. Although they might seem tangential at first, they are related to the women's life stories because they place their lives in context; they provide a backdrop that helps enhance the focus. And because Brownsville was a community dominated by tradition, it was also important to explore some historical and religious issues related to the history and role of women in Judaism.

One of the things I learned from the Brownsville girls was about boundaries.

Some of the women said that I shouldn't interview them because they weren't "really" from Brownsville. At first, Terry Apter said that she didn't live in Brownsville until she was fifteen. Although she had, in fact, lived in Brownsville most of her life, she meant that she hadn't lived in the heart of Brownsville until then. What some of the women meant, however, was that they lived just beyond Junius Street, the borderline that separated Brownsville from East New York. Brownsville was, literally, on the other side of the tracks, the BMT subway tracks. The bridge they crossed when they were girls, going to and from school, had physically demarcated Brownsville's easternmost boundary for the women.

Brownsville was my neighborhood too; I lived on Legion Street, it's name changed inexplicably from Barrett Street at some point. However, at the BBC dinner-dance I attended, I learned that while Legion Street was, technically, well within Brownsville's borders, it belonged to a different Brownsville. It was in the part of the neighborhood that was considered the "better side of town": the other (western) boundary bordering the neighborhood of East Flatbush.

I hadn't realized that Brownsville itself was made up of such sub-neighborhoods, each with its distinct boundaries. Nor did Alter Landesman appreciate these subdivisions, unless he chose to ignore them when he wrote his history of the community. He wrote that Brownsville, "came to mean more often a state of mind than a geographic area. There is no real natural dividing line between Brownsville, Eastern Parkway, and East Flatbush. . . . So far as the Jewish population is concerned Brownsville, East New York, and New Lots are substantially alike."[22] For the purposes of this study, Landesman's broader, and more encompassing definition is appropriate. Athough some of the women would prefer to retain the distinction, their experiences of Brownsville and East New York *were* "substantially alike."

Because it was an almost completely Jewish community, Brownsville was unique. Its homogeneity made it different, for example, from the Jewish community in Pittsburgh to which my mother's family emigrated early in the century.[23] The area in which Kate Simon grew up and which she writes about in *Bronx Primitive*, a more diverse area, was more common, even in New York City with its large Jewish population.[24]

Although Brownsville was connected to the broader society through the media and the workplace, for a child growing up there it was possible to *think* that almost everybody was Jewish. It was insular—an ethnic pocket in which negative, chauvinistic, and ethnocentric attitudes, sometimes bordering on xenophobia, could be developed. The Jews in Brownsville were not "the others." It was the *goyim*, the gentiles, who were the "others," often to be ridiculed and often feared but usually just avoided.[25] But also, because it was a ghetto, inhabitants were able to develop the sense of "unselfconscious Jewishness" that historian Deborah Dash Moore described, which made it possible for Jews to live comfortably in their neighborhoods even though they were a small minority in the vast city.[26]

Just such an unselfconsciousness was recently illustrated to me by a colleague who grew up, like Kate Simon, in a predominantly Jewish section of the Bronx. Her mother still lives there and it is still a Jewish neighborhood. But, her mother recently told her, the neighborhood is changing: "It's becoming ethnic." Such obliviousness is an amusing contrast to the "mild paranoia" about which we always tease my closest friend, who grew up in predominantly Catholic Worcester, Massachusetts. There the Jewish community still remains very closely knit and guarded, aware that they are the outsiders. Conversations seem, inevitably, to turn to Jewishness and Jewish issues, a fixed point of reference.

Although numerous essays and works of fiction have been written about Brownsville, I draw information on the early history and development of the community primarily from Landesman's book, written in 1971. Landesman was dismayed by the less than favorable image other writers had presented and set out to show "the other side of Brownsville, the warm mutual helpfulness of decent people, and the organized struggle for betterment."[27] Sorin's work, my other principal source, not only brings the history of Brownsville up to date but adds the critical dimension that Landesman's lacks.

Brownsville, the working-class—and working to achieve middle-class—community in which the girls were came of age, was dominated by a culture in which women played a traditional, limited, separate, and, some critics say, unequal role, a role transported from the *shtetlach*, the small towns and villages of eastern Europe.

Most of the mothers or grandmothers of the Brownsville women were immigrants who came to America when they were still in their teens. They were the Jewish mothers who, because of novels such as *Portnoy's Complaint*,[28] have been cast in the negative image of overbearing (if devoted) presences in their children's lives. This image is demeaning to women raised in the European orthodox tradition to be a *baleboste*, which means mistress of the home and carries the connotation of outstanding competence. The negative image is particularly demeaning to those Jewish mothers who often had two jobs in the *shtetlach* and later in the immigrant communities; one in and one outside of the home. These are not women to disparage but, on the contrary, "foremothers to be proud of."[29]

Those who defend the traditionally defined role of Jewish women explain that in Judaism, unlike some other religious traditions, women play a different and complementary but equally important role to that of the men. Jewish feminists, orthodox and secular, disagree. In religious observance as in the secular culture, they claim, men are defined as the norm, women the exception. The concept of woman as "other," they say, was institutionalized thousands of years ago in the Torah, the first five books of the Bible (the Pentateuch), in the Talmud, the commentary that forms the basis of Jewish law, and in *Halakha*, the law itself. *Halakha* is a complex of instructions relating to worship, family relations, sexuality, economic life, proper behavior between Jews and their fellows, behavior between Jews and non-Jews, and even food and clothing. As interpretations were codified in *Halakha*, the rights and responsibilities of men and women were kept "entirely different" and, Jewish feminists claim, women's status as "protected inferiors" was clearly defined.[30]

Because the Bible is such an important document, images of women in the Bible, some distorted by centuries of interpretation, or misinterpretation, have recently become a subject of much interesting scholarship. Since the Bible was written mostly, if not entirely by men during a time when public life was exclusively in the hands of men, and because it focuses on public, rather than private life, it is principally about men. As history, the Bible describes roughly 1,200 years of public life and refers to 1,426 people. Only slightly more than one hundred of them are women. Until the late nineteenth century, when Elizabeth Cady Stanton first challenged the way women were depicted in the Bible, theology was a male-dominated field. Today, the historical role of women in the Bible and in biblical times is being reevaluated by contemporary scholars, many of whom are women.[31]

Women are not only absent from the Bible but from the Yiddish cultural legacy, the *yerushe*. Apart from those few whose names survived in

the Bible, and some rabbis' and bankers' wives, Jewish women have
remained largely nameless (one outstanding exception being the sixteenth century businesswoman, Glueckel of Hamelin, whose diary has
survived). In all of the Jewish historical literature produced since the end
of the eighteenth century, when women are acknowledged at all, it is
only in footnotes. Today, stories of and by women are being told at last
by Irena Klepfisz, Naomi Shepherd, Susan Glenn, and numerous others.

Because they were left out, neither girls growing up in Europe nor
their daughters in American immigrant communities had any nontraditional role models to emulate. They did not know about the many Jewish women in Europe in the late nineteenth century who had longed to
be educated. Nor did they learn about the women who joined socialist
and radical movements or were leaders in the American labor movement.[32] Brownsville girls acquired their images of women from their
mothers, their primary role models, and from other women in the community, all of whom had been raised to play the traditional, supporting,
secondary role as wife and mother. In the middle of the twentieth century, the Brownsville girls were heirs to a persistent ancient culture.

When the middle-class culture of postwar, Cold War America was
added to traditional Jewish culture in promoting the ideal homemaker
image, their combined force was doubly difficult to resist. While "there
were no groups . . . for whom the norms were irrelevant,"[33] the
Brownsville women who came of age in the 1940s and 1950s were particularly responsive to the lure of middle-class security. They had been
born in the 1920s and raised during the Depression, which had mercilessly
battered their poor, working-class community. In order to appreciate how
devastating its impact was on those already living on the margin, we
should remind ourselves that the Depression came at a time before social
welfare legislation was an accepted fact in our society. In the American tradition, which lauds rugged individualism, there has always been resistance
to social welfare programs; only the duration and overwhelming depth of
the Great Depression made these programs, finally, possible.

The girls of Brownsville were poor by any standard, and some
poorer than others. Brownsville was understood by Jews in other neighborhoods to signify poverty. The poet Richard Fein, growing up in the
neighboring community of East Flatbush wrote:

> Eastern Parkway implicitly meant that it wound into the dens
> of Brownsville and toward Jews even poorer than my parents,
> a lower social class my family feared falling back into with-

out so much as saying so, intuitively recognizing those minute class divisions that could be measured by social dividers called avenues. Below Utica Avenue, the Parkway squirmed off in the distance toward the din of Pitkin Avenue, a brassy notch above the hustle of Orchard Street.[34]

Yet, despite the poverty, most of the forties women remember a happy childhood. They were poor, of course, but they were *all* poor. "We were all the same," Shirley Donowitz says. All but a few have good memories of their teen years, at least until the war started and, Bea Siegel says, "the party was cancelled."

Wartime and its increased need for labor provided opportunities for many women but most of these did not extend to the Brownsville girls. For one thing, their parents, struggling to get out of the factories, were not sending their daughters into them; none of these Rosies became riveters! Jewish girls considering their future jobs had to balance their ambitions against a number of factors, including particular cultural restrictions that were placed upon them. When they thought about careers, Brownsville girls had a range of choices even more limited than those available to other women in the 1940s. Consequently, they married within a few years of their high school graduations and began having children before they had even given a thought to the rest of their lives.

Most of the women remained in Brownsville after they married, but the neighborhood began to change, became less safe, more racially and ethnically diverse. When they could afford to leave Brownsville they moved to other Brooklyn neighborhoods: East Flatbush, Flatbush, Canarsie, Mill Basin. Some of the women, such as Lillian Pollack, are still there. Lillian is distressed about changes in Canarsie and the city, about the quality of her life, about not being able "to go out in the streets at night." Sadly, in an eerie replay of her earlier move from Brownsville, Bea Siegel left Canarsie for a "more secure" place in New Jersey, a new phenomenon called a "gated community." Like Bea, others have now drifted ever farther away from Brooklyn: to Queens and Long Island, to "the city," to Riverdale and parts of Westchester such as Bronxville.

"Why *are* you here?" I asked Jean Bleckner when she said that she had never thought she would find herself retired in Florida. "Where was I to go?" she answered with a question. "Everyone was here!"

By "everyone," I understood Jean to mean "the girls"; her friends of fifty years. "Here" was southeastern Florida: Fort Lauderdale, Laud-

erdale Lakes, Delray Beach, Coral Springs. Today, many of the
Brownsville women have reassembled in Florida so that they can live out
their senior years among lifelong friends. Because so many are there, I
was also there, conducting the first of my interviews.

I was sitting in the kitchen of Jean's town house condominium. Over
the previous couple of weeks I'd sat in quite a few Florida kitchens:
modern, bright, and well appointed. They were welcoming; they were
the place where the women and I mutually agreed it would be most comfortable to talk. The refrigerators were decorated with photos of grandchildren, and with valentines and other offerings made in school "For
Grandma and Grandpa." There was always a pot of coffee brewing and
a generous, and sometimes elaborately prepared, snack on the table.
"Do I look as if I need nourishment?" I would ask, falling into cadences
of speech I haven't used for most of my adult life. "So just have a taste,"
they would insist.

As I sat in Jean's kitchen, fiddling with my tape recorder (which had
decided to act up at just the wrong time), her husband, a Brownsville
Boys Club alumnus, came in and tried to help. I had met this couple a
few nights before, at the annual BBC dinner-dance reunion, held in February because so many of the former members winter in Florida. Florida
is host not only to the BBC but to several Brownsville groups. As soon
as Jews move into new areas of settlement, Deborah Dash Moore has
shown, "the visible signs of Jewish ethnic group life" begin to appear.[35]
And, the proliferation of Brownsville organizations in their retirement
communities is reminiscent of the *landsmanshaftn*, organizations of
immigrants from the same regions of Europe, which studded the old
neighborhood in earlier times.

There are hundreds of condo developments in the area between
Palm Beach and Fort Lauderdale. None of them seem to be more than
twenty minutes away from one another, so that many of the women,
friends since elementary school, maintain their relationships without the
formal structure of an organization. Sometimes, when I went to interview one of the women, I would find that another had been invited, or
had just dropped by.

We talked and talked about what their lives had been like when they
were growing up, about Brownsville, about what they learned there
about being a Jew, a Jewish woman, a Jewish-American woman. I asked
them not only to think back over their lives in and since Brownsville, but
to assess their experiences, to define their successes, to articulate their

accomplishments. It proved, at first, to be quite difficult, but in the end it was thoroughly validating—for all of us.

The women who came of age in the fifties are not yet at quite the same point as the forties women, although retirement is fast approaching. Even as they plan for the future, they too are able to reflect back upon their lives. Some have witnessed and gone through cataclysmic changes; all are conscious of the leap they've made in the course of one generation. Comparing themselves with both their mothers and their daughters, almost all of the women unhesitatingly concurred: "We had it the best."

CHAPTER TWO

Brownsville

"The Nurturing Neighborhood"

The whole family was in the neighborhood, your home was always filled with relatives. There was always somebody there, available for you.

—Raye Roder Cohen

P erhaps it could only have happened in that particular time and place: Brownsville in the 1940s.

The Brownsville Boys Club was an organization that was never duplicated either in Brownsville or in similar communities elsewhere, because it resulted from the convergence of a unique set of elements and circumstances, including the cultural values of a Jewish immigrant society, replication of traditional Jewish social institutions in the new world (particularly a reliance upon mutual-aid and fraternal societies), and the almost accidental, suddenly realization of the power of group action. If the club was "an authentic community in microcosm,"[1] Brownsville was, in the 1940s, the authentic community upon which it was modelled, a place that Deborah Dash Moore has called "a world of its own."[2]

As early as the 1920s, Brownsville was a predominantly Jewish, poor, working-class community. It remained basically unchanged through the 1950s, when I, and many of the Brownsville women, were young housewives there. We stayed in the neighborhood after we married; many of our children were born there. As the end of the decade approached I was able to take my newborn daughter home to an apartment on the same street to which I myself had been brought as a newborn, twenty-two years earlier. We lived only two blocks from the apartment building in which I had been a teenager, and where my parents still lived. But by 1960, only a few years later, Brownsville had come to an end as a Jewish community.

Although a broad range of social, political, educational, and religious experience was represented in each of the Jewish communities in New York, each had its own character: Williamsburg was more orthodox than the others, the East Bronx was more radical, Borough Park was more Zionist. The Upper West Side was called the "gilded ghetto"[3] because it was where the more prosperous immigrants, primarily from Germany, had settled during an earlier migration of Jews from Europe.

Brownsville had its character too, "an egalitarianism in tone and manner." Within its boundaries, Moore wrote, it was possible to find the "entire spectrum of Jewish political and cultural associations,"[4] but the religion of Brownsville was orthodox; eastern European Jews were not drawn to the Reform Judaism that had originated in Germany in the nineteenth century, nor to the Jewish Conservative or Reconstructionist movements. The degree of orthodoxy, however, varied greatly from home to home. Jewish-Americans "were given to ignoring, retaining, modifying, adapting, inventing, reappropriating, and reconstructing tradition."[5]

Many in Brownsville were secular Jews who had been influenced by the *Haskalah*, the Jewish cultural renaissance of the late eighteenth and nineteenth centuries and by other movements such as the Jewish labor movement which, unlike the developing American labor movement, had a "socialist orientation."[6] For secularists, being Jewish did not require religious observance. Being Jewish was rooted in the culture and its values, in Yiddish, the language of most European Jews, and in Jewish customs, literature, and shared history.

Brownsville evolved in the early years of the great migration to the United States from eastern and southern Europe, during the latter part of the nineteenth century. The Jewish migration was unlike the migrations from other parts of Europe such as the Mezzogiorno, the Southern region of Italy, which experienced a mass exodus during the same period.[7] Many migrants from those areas deliberately left their families behind, planning to return after earning and saving enough money to improve their living conditions in their homelands. Many Jews also came to America alone, but their intention was to bring over those who had been left behind as soon as they had accumulated enough for passage. To be sure, Jews came to the *Goldene Medine*, the Golden Land, to acquire some of its fabled riches, but in addition, unlike the Southern Italians and others, they were fleeing from religious persecution or, at the very least, from antisemitism. Consequently, the Jewish migration was a movement of families that was intended to be a permanent relocation.

By the end of the century a substantial immigrant community and "a sizeable town called *Brahnzvil* or *Brunzvil* by its Yiddish speaking inhabitants, had taken shape."[8] In his history of the community, Alter Landsman wrote that "for many of the first generation, Brownsville was a completely Jewish world; it came closest to the life of the small town or village, the European *shtetl* most of them had known."[9]

Brownsville began as a rural village. Its streets were not yet paved and it was still without sewers or gaslight when farmers such as Charles Brown (who gave his name to the community) and Gilbert Thatford thought it would be profitable for them to partition their lands for building lots. What made real estate investment attractive was that there were, as early as 1877, steam and elevated railroads that reached into these "new lots" as they were known, and as the township would be called. Along with some others, Brown and Thatford promoted the sale of the lots through brokers on Manhattan's Lower East Side, the area where Jews and other immigrants first settled in New York City.[10]

Ten years later, the first Jewish families made their way to Brownsville. They came despite the fact that its unplanned growth caused areas of it to resemble the very place, the Lower East Side, from which most of them were eagerly escaping. But in 1887, Jacob Cohen later said, there were still "farms, all farms." Cohen, a manufacturer of boys knee-pants, moved to Brownsville hoping his wife's health would improve "in the country." With the help of Isaac Krupitsky, whom Cohen acknowledged as the only Jew who lived in Brownsville before he did, Cohen bought a house on the corner of Blake Avenue and Sackman Streets. It was there that the first *minyan*, Jewish public worship, was held.[11]

Elias Kaplan was rare among Jewish immigrants when he arrived in the United States from Russia in 1847, a time when most Jewish immigration was from Germany and western Europe. In 1887, Kaplan, by then a successful clothing manufacturer, became the true catalyst for the growth of the village. In the same year that Cohen bought his home, Kaplan transferred his shop from the Lower East Side to Brownsville. Only five years later, seventy percent of the inhabitants of the neighborhood were in the needle trades. Kaplan's shop was not the only one to provide employment for the growing population of the community. It may, however, have been the only one that was transformed into a synagogue on the Sabbath.

In the first decade of this century, two bridges were built across the East River, connecting the island borough of Manhattan to Brooklyn, (which had been an independent city until shortly before then but had been incorporated as a borough of New York City). In 1903, the Williamsburg Bridge was built, soon followed by the Manhattan Bridge, in 1909. People were not only forced to move, as many buildings on the Manhattan side were torn down for the construction, but the bridges provided additional access to Brooklyn for Jews living on the Lower East Side. In addition, the subway system, the IRT and BMT lines, was extended to reach into Brownsville. By the early 1900s, Brownsville's population had grown to about twenty-five thousand, and as poor as these immigrants were, Brownsville offered the opportunity for a life that was far better than the one they had left in Europe, not unlike some groups who emigrate to the United States from other parts of the world today.

Ashkenazim, Jews who migrated from eastern Europe—Poland, Russia, Lithuania, Latvia, Bulgaria, Romania, the Austro-Hungarian Empire—were the predominant inhabitants of Brownsville. Yiddish was their common language, the *mame-loshen* or mother tongue. It dominated the streets of the neighborhood at the turn of the century and for many years to come. Many Jews lived in Brownsville for decades without learning to speak English. With Yiddish spoken in the homes, Yiddish daily and weekly newspapers, signs and menus in Yiddish, Jewish shopkeepers, Jewish delicatessens, restaurants and bakeries selling Jewish dishes, there was little need to know English. (The same is true in some immigrant neighborhoods today, such as *El Barrio* in East Harlem, Brooklyn's "Little Odessa" in Brighton Beach, and the relatively new Chinese section of Sunset Park-Bay Ridge.) Some children were like my older brother, Joe Bell, who grew up in Brownsville in the 1920s and spoke Yiddish as a first language. He only began to speak English regularly after he began school. He recently told me that when he entered first grade, using the expression that described *der griner,* the greenhorn, "They thought I just got off the boat!"

"I was an only child," Katie Stavans says, "and my parents spoke Yiddish. I didn't speak English when I was growing up." Some of the women were resentful of their parents' foreignness. Rae Mirsky wouldn't speak Yiddish and her mother, although she understood it, "refused to speak English." They finally came to a compromise: her mother would speak to her in Yiddish; Rae would answer in English.

Yiddish was the first but not the only language of my immigrant parents. (When my parents didn't want us to know what they were saying they spoke Russian;[12] they referred to it as *goyish*, the language of the gentiles.) Like many second generation Brownsville girls, I understood Yiddish and could speak it, if not fluently. It was spoken in our home along with broken English that included what Leo Rosten called "hybrid words": words such as "opstairsikeh," an upstairs neighbor, or "nextdoorikeh," the neighbor next door). Our parents also spoke what Rosten described as "Yinglish," a particular syntax that includes dropping the "of" in "a bowl soup," or adding "go," as in "go see who's at the door."[13]

Even the Brownsville women whose parents were born in America heard Yiddish spoken by their grandparents,[14] or as Irma Greenbaum said, by relatives fortunate enough to have gotten out of Europe in the thirties. They understood at least some of what was being said. A number of the women, like Irma and Rae Mirsky, studied Yiddish in one of the many Brownsville *shules* (schools), which had classes for secular and language studies, rather than for religious studies and instruction in Hebrew (the *loshn- Koydesh* or sacred language).

Many Yiddish words and Yiddishisms became part of New Yorkese.[15] Some, such as *chutzpah*, a word that means a kind of aggressive, nervy daring, or *maven*, the ubiquitous expert, survive as part of the American lexicon. But Yiddish, as a spoken language, can now only be heard in Brooklyn among the orthodox such as the *Hasidim* in such areas as Williamsburg, Crown Heights, and Borough Park. As it has been at other times in its history, Yiddish is endangered today, although in the words of Isaac Bashevis Singer, Yiddish's Nobel prize laureate, "Yiddish has not yet said its last word."[16]

Along with the language, the immigrants also brought the values of the old country to the *naya velt*, the new world. These became deeply embedded in the culture of Brownsville, and included an abiding belief in education, which would bring not only wisdom but *yikhes*, or status; *takhlis*, a belief that one's activities must be goal directed and lead to some positive final result; *tsedakah* and *gemuluth hasadim*, charity and the obligation to help the less fortunate. These values were interwoven with the tradition of social consciousness, based upon the principle of *tikn olam*, the repair or improvement of the world. They were expressed, reinforced, and carried out in *landsmanshaftn*, fraternal and mutual benefit societies, and in other community organizations.

One of the earliest community organizations in Brownsville was the Hebrew Educational Society, located on Hopkinson and Sutter Avenues. It was begun through a fund established by the Jewish philanthropist Baron de Hirsch, in the 1880s, about a decade after the Jews began to settle in Brownsville.[17] As the community grew and the need for them arose, the Brooklyn Hebrew Orphan Asylum and other societies were organized. A society to clothe the naked, the *Malbish Arumim,* was established in 1894. A year later, the *Hesed Shel Emeth* Society was founded. It was a free burial society for indigent poor who had, despite the interventions of yet another organization, the Society for the Aid of the Indigent Sick, succumbed. Finally, an umbrella society, a "Jewish United Fund," the Brownsville Relief Hebrew Charity, was organized to supply coal, pay rents, and render other assistance. Since, in 1900, more than forty percent of the Jewish immigrants arrived with about thirty dollars in their pockets, even then a small sum for families to live on for an indefinite time, these organizations, in many cases, were their life-lines.[18]

Charitable organizations were particularly important to the women, who brought the old world custom of *gehen kleiben*, house-to-house collections, to the neighborhood. It remained a common practice. All of the women recall the *pushkes*, charity collection boxes, which were to be seen in Jewish homes from these early days onward. Although Landesman does not mention them, the "sisterhoods" or women's auxiliaries of these organizations did the tedious legwork; the women were the ones on whom the burden of collection work fell.

Brownsville socialists, anarchists, intellectuals, and others who joined radical and social reform movements included women who advocated women's suffrage as well as other women's rights. Some women thought that access to information about birth control was one of those rights and was being infringed upon by the Comstock Act of 1873, which had classified data about contraception as obscene. Margaret Sanger had recently come to public attention as an authority on the issue due to her articles in *Call*, the Socialist Party publication, and in her own magazine, *The Woman Rebel*.

In 1916, some Brownsville women seeking information about birth control visited Sanger. Each of the women had four children, actually less than the average, which was five; one caller had only recently recovered from a near-fatal abortion. They encouraged Sanger and her colleague, Fania Mindell of Chicago, who were looking for space for a clinic, to consider Brownsville, assuring them that they would find the community hospitable.

Sanger did receive the support of the neighborhood although not of the other local social service agencies. In spite of their lack of encouragement, she established her clinic in Brownsville in October 1916, at 46 Amboy Street. When she and her sister Ethel distributed leaflets announcing the first birth control clinic in America (the only other one in the world was in the Netherlands), she wondered if anyone would come. But when the clinic doors opened they found 150 women who had come from all over New York standing in line, waiting. After only nine days the clinic had been visited by 464 women.

The leaflets did not actually violate the Comstock Act (which prohibited the dissemination of information about contraception through the mail), but the clinic was raided on other grounds. Case histories were confiscated and Mr. Rabinowitz, Sanger's landlord, was forced to sign eviction papers. In spite of an outcry by many, including fifty Brownsville women who attended the trial, Ethel was sentenced to the workhouse for thirty days and Margaret received a thirty-day jail term as a public nuisance. The beleaguered clinic never reopened in Brownsville, but a Brownsville woman, Dr. Lena Levine, carried on its work through her practice as a psychiatrist, gynecologist, and marriage counselor. She was a pioneer in the Planned Parenthood Movement and later became an associate director of the Margaret Sanger Research Bureau of New York.[19]

In the 1930s, in the midst of a "sprawling, indifferent, and impoverished urban society, Brownsville was a place that shouldn't have been,"[20] but still was, a neighborhood. Only two years earlier. "the community of Brownsville took to the streets to celebrate its Golden Jubilee." Pitkin Avenue, a thoroughfare lined with shops, Brownsville's "Main Street," was decorated for the event in a "bewildering display" of colored lights. Marching bands drummed their way down the avenue, "five cantors entertained passersby with a medley of Jewish tunes" and "a parade of twelve hundred baby carriages proceeded grandly down Pitkin Avenue." Some of the Brownsville women might have been in those baby carriages or among the babies chosen by a team of doctors as "100 percent specimens."[21]

There was a sense of cohesion in the community that had a good deal to do with "ethnic homogeneity."[22] Brownsville was a *kehillah*, a

Hebrew word meaning "the community where each is responsible for all and all are responsible for each."[23] Each street seemed like a mini-community, a neighborhood in itself, "like a little city," Katie Stavans remembers, "because of the big apartment buildings." Each street had its grocer, its candy store, its pharmacist who took care of little bruises and scrapes and got things out of children's eyes. In spite of being so densely populated, Brownsville typified what sociologists call a *gemeinschaft*, a closely knit and intimate community.

Everyone's address was fixed by identifying cross streets. As Shirley Donowitz explains: "Everybody said two streets, no one just said where they lived. The avenue was very long, so you always said the corner." They named three streets if they were asked, "Where are you *between*?": Powell Street between Blake and Dumont Avenues, Rockaway Avenue between Sutter and Pitkin, Saratoga between Livonia and Riverdale.

Among the immigrant neighborhoods in New York today, "Little Odessa" in Brooklyn's Brighton Beach, where the Russian emigrés have settled, is reminiscent of Brownsville before the war. Although "Little Odessa" is much more multicultural than Brownsville was, the language of the immigrants, in this case Russian, is widely spoken. Brighton Beach Avenue, in the shadow of the elevated D-train, reminds me of Livonia Avenue where the entire length of the street tunnels under the IRT El. Like the Yiddish or Hebrew signs in the shop windows of Brownsville, signs in Russian advertise ethnic food (including imported and domestic varieties of caviar, sausages, the dozens of kinds of smoked fish that used to be found in Jewish appetizing stores in Brownsville—not just white fish, carp, sable, and lox but other fish that are all but extinct in New York today, such as *tchabak* and *kuptchunka*). *Pelmeni*, similar to the potato *knishes* that were sold by vendors on the streets of Brownsville, are sold from carts and kiosks. Clothing and discount shops reflect the flamboyant taste and preferences of the immigrant population. There are dairy restaurants, restaurants with selections of typically Russian dishes, bakeries selling Russian pumpernickel and corn bread; not the corn bread of the American south but a sour, corned rye. There are social organizations, social clubs, signs announcing cultural events.

Obvious displays of community such as these in "Little Odessa" tend to conceal the darker side of poverty. In the same way that poor communities suffer them today, Brownsville had higher health risks, higher rates of infant and maternal mortality, higher rates of sexually transmitted diseases, more tuberculosis and diphtheria.[24] The neighborhood also had its fair share of delinquents, street criminals, alcoholics, gamblers, prostitutes and pimps. And Brownsville shared one more feature with "Little Odessa." As Brighton Beach is said to be home to the "Russian Mafia," it was commonly known that a nondescript corner candy store on Saratoga and Livonia Avenues, Midnight Rose's, harbored one of the major crime syndicates of the Depression and wartime eras: Murder, Inc.

The candy store was on a busy corner, a stop on the IRT El. I remember this corner; just above the candy store was a Chinese restaurant advertising "High Class Chinese Food." Next door to the candy store was the best sour pickle store in the neighborhood; diagonally across was a cafeteria (where my father and "the boys," pronounced "boyess," met in the early morning for "a cup coffee" before they boarded the El-train to their jobs in Manhattan). One of the local movie houses called the Blue Bird, later sensibly renamed simply The Cinema, was across the street. On this seemingly tranquil urban corner, and unknown to the more naïve residents of Brownsville, Louis "Lepke" Buchalter conducted his notorious business.

Just as today's anti-heroes, drug dealers and criminals, become heroes and role models for children in New York ghettos, in Brownsville there was concern, among those who were aware of the notorious celebrity of Lepke, Abe Reles, "Bugsy" Goldstein, and others, about the effect the gang might have on the neighborhood children. Crime figures *were* increasing but, in fact, the rates of Jewish crime, including juvenile delinquency in Brownsville, were, and remained, disproportionately low.[25]

The people of Brownsville "felt at home on the streets of their own neighborhood,"[26] for in spite of Murder, Inc. and despite the local crime, Brownsville was a relatively safe place. The boys and girls growing up in the crowded community of the 1930s and 1940s—by this time Brownsville had grown to a quarter of a million people—were generally safe from muggings, stabbings, shootings, rape, the face-to-face crimes so common today. They were made to feel even safer by the sense of community. Minette Cutler worked as a hatcheck girl. "I used to walk home alone at night with my pocket full of quarters," she says, "I never thought about it." In striking contrast, a young man was recently interviewed for a *New York Times* article about teen rape on the very streets where, as children, many of the women had played. "Nobody feels safe living in the neighborhood," he said.[27]

Another reason that the women remember feeling secure when they were children in Brownsville was that, for most of the women, there was always a caretaker nearby—a grandmother, an aunt, an older sister. Raye Cohen recalls:

> My father had a very large family, five brothers, and everyone lived within a radius of two blocks. My parents were busy in the butcher shop. In the morning my mother would say, "When you come home from school go to *tante* this-one, or that one: go to Grandma." There was always somebody there, available for you; the family was always involved.

"There were no latch-key children," Lorraine Nelson says. If, by some chance, there was no one of the extended family about, a neighbor was just as apt to tell you to go in if it was getting late, to make sure you had an after-school snack, or, in the absence of a working parent, to scold you if you were misbehaving. "We had to behave ourselves," Bea Larkin says, "people were watching." Because everyone shared the values, everyone could be involved; and more important, everyone had permission to be involved.

My father told a story of someone who stopped him in the street when he was a young man to chastise him for smoking on *shabes* (the Sabbath). He didn't know the man's name, he referred to him as *feter*, a Yiddish word that literally means uncle but was used as a term of respect for any older man. My father didn't know him except as someone from the neighborhood, nor did he remember seeing him after that, but he never questioned the man's authority (and never again smoked on *shabes*).

Although New York Jews tended to cluster in neighborhoods that were predominantly (at least seventy percent) Jewish, "none, including the Lower East Side, were more Jewish than Brownsville."[28] It was no longer ninety-five percent Jewish as it had been in the mid-1920s, but in the 1940s when the BBC was founded and the women of this study were coming of age, eighty percent of the population was still Jewish. Brownsville youth developed, and have retained, a strong sense of Jewish identity. Growing up in Brownsville, boys and girls were enveloped in *Yiddishkeit*, in "Jewishness" and a way of life that reflected cultural attitudes and norms.

Shopkeepers still spoke Yiddish. It was possible to find kosher products in every grocery store (if nonkosher items, such as bacon, were sold, they were not visible). There were still fresh carp swimming in tanks, for *gefilte* fish. The aromas of the *shabes* meal still permeated the air on Friday nights. Most people knew enough Yiddish to translate for an elderly person who might not have absorbed any English at all.

Throughout the 1940s and 1950s Jewish cultural programs, mostly in Yiddish, could be heard over the radio in many homes. They were broadcast by WEVD (which still serves foreign language populations and whose call letters, it was rumored, were the initials of Eugene V. Debs). Programs ranged from Seymour Rechzeit, Moishe Oysher, and the Barry sisters singing folk and popular tunes to Art Raymond's Sunday morning Jewish news, to the popular, if somber, "*Tsores bei layte*" (People's troubles).

Even the schoolteachers in Brownsville public schools were predominantly Jewish. There had been a growing presence of Jewish teachers in the city schools since the early part of the century. In 1916, aided by their understanding of the labor movement, Jewish teachers helped create the first teachers' union in the city, which later became Local 5 of the American Federation of Teachers. Some among this group of six hundred teachers were socialists, some were pacifists, and others, joining the crusade that would culminate only a few years later in women's suffrage, were supporters of women's rights. By 1924 a Jewish teachers' organization, the Jewish Education Association was formed.[29] By the 1940s, twelve thousand Jewish teachers had been placed in schools in Jewish neighborhoods as, with its reductionist thinking, the Board of Education "saw them as more effective in socializing" Jewish children.[30] In looking over the names of the teachers who signed my autograph album in 1946 when I graduated from sixth grade, I found three names that I couldn't identify as Jewish (one was the school nurse, Cecile Bates). The teachers who signed my book were: Florence Barth, M. C. Kalkstein, Ida Esakov, S. C. Fox, D. W. Levitt, R. Braverman, S. Schwartz, F. G. Ruderman, Dorothy Sacks, Mildred Becker, and the Principal of P.S. 156, Mr. Goldfarb.

If, by the 1950s, Brownsville had lost it's *shtetl* quality, there was still much that lingered of the Jewish community and its small town character. The women confirm that Brownsville was not only a place where people felt physically safe but within what Moore called the "sheltering neighborhood,"[31] they were able to acquire the "psychological attitude of a majority."[32]

In urban neighborhoods that were more multicultural or in Jewish communities in other, smaller cities such as Pittsburgh, or even on the

Lower East Side with its mix of Jews, Italians, Irish, and other ethnic groups, it was impossible not to be conscious of your ethnicity. But the women and men confirm that when they were growing up in Brownsville they were oblivious to their cultural difference, their Jewishness. It was something they didn't think about very much because, as Minette Cutler explains: "Brownsville was a Jewish ghetto, we were all the same." They didn't think of themselves as "other," it was the rest of America that was made up of *der anderers,* "the others."

While Brownsville continued to follow the orthodox tradition, Moore wrote,

> it reflected a pattern of Jewish religious behavior characteristic of New York Jews. Its synagogues regularly attracted a mere 8 percent of the neighborhood's adult Jewish males. Most Brownsville Jews did not follow Jewish religious practices and ignored the synagogue and its activities.[33]

Only five of the women in this study were raised in observant homes—Raye Cohen, Minette Cutler, Sarah Lieberman, Lorraine Nelson, and Lila Perlmutter. Although all of the women who participated in the study developed and have retained a strong sense of Jewish identity, only Lorraine, Sarah, and Lila are strict observers today. "There are six hundred and thirteen *mitzvoth* [required religious obligations] in all," Lorraine explains, "the more of them you observe, the more religious you are." Of the twenty-three families who lived in her building, Lorraine said, only two were observant. In these families the men prayed each morning in their ritual garb: the *t'filin,* the phylacteries (two small leather cases holding Hebrew texts), held in place by leather thongs wound around their arms and across their foreheads; the *yarmulke,* the skull cap, on their heads; the *talis,* a prayer shawl, wrapped around their shoulders. They prayed again at sundown. Some attended the synagogue to say their prayers, others performed the obligation at home. *Succoth* and *Purim* were celebrated primarily by the orthodox along with other, lesser, holidays ignored by the rest of the neighborhood. The men and women observed the traditional *shabes,* Sabbath, prescriptions which forbade work. The women prepared meals for the Sabbath in advance, since it was forbidden to shop, or cook, or even to turn on lights or the radio. Lorraine again explains, "These restrictions were to ensure that the Sabbath would be peaceful and kept for contemplation, meditation, and prayer."

The girls whose families were orthodox were not allowed to go the movies with their friends, which was the thing to do on Friday nights, or to travel on Saturdays. "There were a lot of things I couldn't do because of my religious background," Minette Cutler says but as they entered their teen years some of the girls began to defy the Sabbath restrictions. Raye Cohen, although she was strictly forbidden to do so (and didn't openly challenge the rules,) remembers "going riding" with her friends. At fifteen, she made a conscious decision to abandon religious observance and, in typical adolescent fashion, became more secular than friends from the least observant households. She was the first of her friends to confront a sirloin steak: strictly *not*-kosher.[34]

At home, many families did not strictly observe *kashruth,* the dietary laws. But many who did and would never bring *treyf,* nonkosher food, into their homes did eat it away from home, sometimes at the neighborhood Chinese restaurants.[35] Some who ate nonkosher food, however, would draw the line at eating pork, ham, bacon, or shellfish. By far, the most popular eateries were the kosher delicatessens, a Jewish-American invention. There was a deli on every block, "because a hot dog and a pastrami sandwich and a *knish* was a way of life," said the manager of Grabstein's, a Brooklyn deli, in a recent interview. With their "salami sandwiches and pickles wrapped in coarse white paper," the delis were "the culinary hearts, if not the heartburn, of working-class and immigrant Jewish neighborhoods . . . dining at the delicatessen constituted a big night out."[36] In spite of the fact that the vast majority were no longer observant, in the 1930s and 1940s there was still a synagogue on almost every Brownsville street. On "*Kol Nidre* night," Landesman wrote about the beginning of the most solemn holy day of the year, *Yom Kippur,* "Pitkin's stores were all dark."[37] When the shops and schools were closed for the high holy days, almost the entire population filled the synagogues. While the Passover *seder* became more like a Jewish equivalent of the Thanksgiving Day feast, an opportunity for a family gathering rather than a solemn commemoration of the story of the Exodus, it was celebrated in most households. *Chanukah* was not yet elevated, to compete with Christmas, from its relatively insignificant status;[38] it was celebrated, but modestly. I remember receiving *Chanukah gelt,* usually fifty cents but sometimes a silver dollar, from my father. "Here's a *shekl,*" he would say (long before the state of Israel reappropriated the biblical term for their currency).

Fifty cents was enough for admission to Loew's grand movie palace on Pitkin Avenue, a special treat. But mostly, as Minette Cutler says, "we made our own times." Most of the women remember their childhood in Brownsville as carefree. "We lived in the streets," Fayge Lubin says. The girls came home from school, did their homework (on the roof if it was warm), and, with their skate keys on a soiled string around their necks, went out to play. They roller skated, played with jacks, jumped rope singly or in groups—some turning the ropes, which almost always were shortened clothesline. If they were very skilled they played "Double Dutch," in which two ropes were turned simultaneously, alternately and rhythmically hitting the ground as the girls jumped from side to side. They played other, typically "girls" street games such as "potsy," which, I didn't learn until I was an adult, was a sidewalk version of the ubiquitous hop-scotch. Sometimes they ran around the block playing "ringalevio" with the boys. They had few playthings but found active ways to amuse themselves. "We had to, we didn't have TV to entertain us," Minette Cutler says.

Over and over again, as with their Jewish "unconsciousness," the women echoed the same perception, that they were poor but so was everyone else. "You didn't know you were supposed to have things," Sarah Lieberman says, somewhat wistfully. "I knew there was no money but I wasn't upset about it because all my friends had nothing; we had one rope, one ball, we shared a pair of skates," Shirley Donowitz remembers, but adds, "After the crash, when I was about eleven or twelve, World War II started and my father started to make a living. He was an operator in furs." (Operator, an innocent term that has acquired a very different contemporary meaning, meant that Shirley's father "operated" a sewing machine.)

Many of the girls' fathers were employed in some aspect of the garment trade, which always suffered from unemployment, and even in the best of times from seasonal unemployment. Dolores Plaxen's father was also "in furs." My father, like many others, was in "cloaks." (He pronounced it "clucks.") His shop made "reefers," another innocent term in those days: a short, fingertip-length coat. Zena Bloom's father was "a cutter for women's hats." In the needle trades, cutting the fabric was considered a very highly skilled and high-status job since the cutter was responsible for ensuring that there was little waste. Sally Forman's father was a sample maker, another job in the higher ranks of the industry.

Some fathers were in other skilled trades: Norma Ellman's was a jewelry designer, and Eleanor Chernick's father was a jeweler. Jean

Bleckner's and Lorraine Nelson's fathers were printers, Roslyn Bowers's father was a carpenter; another was a house painter, another a roofer. But even the fathers who were not in the skilled trades "made a living," as Sydelle Schlossberg says. Her father, like Lillian Pollack's, was a conductor on the BMT subway line. Rhoda Nemerofsky's father was a milkman. Bea Benjamin's father had an unusual occupation for a Jew: he was a Merchant Marine. During the Depression Sylvia Zinn's father, who was a plumber, found work driving a taxi. Others struggled to maintain their small shops. Harriet Portnoy's father ran a newsstand outside of Macy's department store. The fathers of some of the women were even more marginally employed, and Rochelle Feld's father couldn't find work; he was blacklisted in the thirties as a union organizer!

In contrast with many of the women, Irma Greenbaum and Fayge Lubin were well aware that they were poor. A few years older than the others, they had a clearer understanding of the family's plight, but in addition, as Fayge says, "We were even poorer than most." For most of the girls, however, the consciousness of being poor didn't come until later, when they finally were old enough to venture out of the community to other, "better" neighborhoods or to "the city," as Manhattan is still called by New Yorkers who live in the other boroughs.

It was in this cultural milieu, in the early days of World War II, just before the conflict spanned the Atlantic to envelop the United States, that the unique phenomenon of the Brownsville Boys Club was conceived by a group of teenagers. Before long, the founding members had their clubhouse and had built a self-governing, mutual-aid and self-help organization on their own, that is, without the intervention of adults. It continues today in the form of the BBC Alumni Association, but also continues informally through friendships that were established more than fifty years ago.

By the 1950s, the BBC had become a fixture in the community. Their clubhouse had grown into a million-dollar community center and was taken over by the city's Department of Parks and renamed the Brownsville Recreation Center. By this time, however, both Brownsville and Brooklyn had changed dramatically. Between 1950 and 1957 (the year that the Dodgers left for the West Coast and broke it's heart), Brooklyn lost more than a quarter of a million inhabitants, many of them Brownsville Jews. At the same time that the Jewish population dropped, the black population rose. The trend continued until the end of the decade, by which time the white population had declined by almost 20 percent and the black population increased by 150 percent. The other growing minority group in the borough were Puerto Ricans, who had grown from a "negligible, less than half of one percent of the population" in 1950 to more than twelve percent toward the end of the decade.[39]

Jews dreamt about leaving Brownsville even as they were moving into the neighborhood. Dolores Plaxen says, "My mother never wanted to fix up the apartment because we always had one foot out the door." Brownsville represented working-class poverty, "the dust of the earth," Kazin wrote in 1951. It was "notoriously a place that measured all success by our skill in getting away from it,"[40] a situation that is unique neither to Brownsville nor just to poor neighborhoods.

American society is characterized by its mobility, physical as well as social. Jews are no exceptions. In her oral history of three generations of Pittsburgh women, Corrine Azen Krause reported that, for Jews, "to move East was to move up." Deborah Dash Moore wrote that for East Bronxers, moving up meant going west, at least to the West Bronx.[41] When they married, the first move made by the women in getting away from Brownsville often was also to the west. It was only a short move west to the neighboring community of East Flatbush but the beginning of a continuous flow of movement to "better" neighborhoods. From East Flatbush they went to Canarsie, later to Queens, to Long Island, and to the suburbs. In the decade between 1950 and 1960, as many of the women joined the almost half-million who left Brownsville, the neighborhood became more heterogeneous, and then the sadly different place that it is today—for along with the influx of people of color came the complexity of their particular problems, exacerbated further by problems related to inner city life.[42]

In his examination of "white flight" from Brownsville, Sorin found it difficult to separate race and class as causes. Whites left Brownsville because many reached middle-class status before the arrival of many blacks and Hispanics, which "suggests that class and economic status played a primary role." However, he adds:

> white flight significantly intensified as the numbers of immigrating nonwhites increased sharply. . . . Race fear on the part of the whites was not necessarily the primary motive for leaving Brownsville; but when added to a variety of other critical factors, race fear made leaving easier.[43]

Recently, Elaine Cohen recalled being frightened of walking near her home on Herzl Street because the block between Sutter and Pitkin, she said, "was all black." Her mother had an almost paranoid fear of blacks which Elaine internalized to the point that, she says, she was "almost a bigot."[44]

More than 175,000 Jews lived in Brownsville in the 1930s and 1940s. In the late 1960s, after a "wholesale exodus," fewer than five thousand were still there, mostly the elderly who found it difficult to break their ties with the community.[45] In 1968, after having been in Brownsville for nearly a century, the Hebrew Educational Society moved to Canarsie. By this time Jews from Brownsville had resettled there in substantial numbers. The former H.E.S. building on Hopkinson Avenue was purchased by the Catholic Diocese of Brooklyn. The Ladies Day Nursery was taken over by the Bethany Gospel Chapel. The last synagogue, on Stone Avenue, between Pitkin and Belmont, closed in 1972. On a recent drive through Brownsville I noticed that the once-glamorous Loew's Pitkin movie theater and the Eastern Parkway Roller Rink are now Pentecostal churches.

Alfred Kazin began his much-quoted memoir, *A Walker in the City*, "Every time I go back to Brownsville it is as if I had never been away." Kazin was writing in 1951. If he were alive today and stepped down from the train on Rockaway Avenue he would step into the culture shock of another world, the world described in *The Ville*.[46] "The ville," Brownsville in the 1990s, is a place of "unrelenting misery and danger."[47]

Returning to Brownsville today imparts a surreal feeling. It has the quality of some dreams: you see yourself in a familiar place but at the same time it's not quite that place. Streets have been renamed, quite appropriately, for the folk heroes of the present residents. There are newer, different buildings, and many others are gone, not where they should be. It was never possible to see much sky when you walked the densely packed Brownsville streets in the forties and fifties. Now the vistas are strangely expansive because so many building have been torn down leaving empty, debris-strewn lots in their place.

Some of the women marvelled that others—Martha Optiz as a social worker, and Bea Larkin who had been executive secretary to the principal of her own *alma mater*, Thomas Jefferson High School—would venture back into the old neighborhood. Indeed, you can't enter Thomas Jefferson High School, where a student was killed in 1994, without passing through a metal detector.

Brownsville youth of today will leave the neighborhood with incomparably different memories from the ones that are carried by the girls and boys who came of age there in the forties and fifties. "You *went* there?" the women would ask me, incredulous that I would drive on Eastern Parkway to the Interboro Parkway, enroute to my interviews with them in Canarsie, Queens and Long Island.

Although they moved away, those men and women affiliated with the BBC have retained their strong sense of affiliation, along with the belief that growing up in the "nurturing neighborhood" provided a foundation for their future success. Their success is impressive.

Ninety-two percent of the BBC members graduated from high school in the forties, compared with less than 50 percent throughout the city as a whole. Only 20 percent of New York City graduates came from the homes of manual laborers; almost all of the Brownsville graduates were raised in working-class homes.[48] There is no comparable organization from which to derive percentages for the women, although all of the women in this study graduated from high school.[49]

Subsequent achievements of the men are even more impressive: 56 percent entered college and 48 percent completed their studies, a rate that is four times higher than the rate for New York City as a whole. Almost one-quarter of them became professionals: social workers, doctors, lawyers, dentists, engineers, college professors, and accountants; others became businessmen and entrepreneurs, and still others went into education or civil service. Sorin wrote: "The boys rarely rose from rags to riches but they did move, at least, from rags to respectability."[50] Because a number of the women in this study are wives of BBC alumni, they rose along with the men—but the women also achieved in their own right.

Sorin wrote that "the relative influence of class and ethnicity on values and achievement" is difficult to determine precisely.[51] Nevertheless, he does show that, in the case of Brownsville, ethnic culture was an important variable: that Brownsville was a nurturing neighborhood— for the men. In order to determine whether Brownsville constituted the same nourishing medium for the women, "gender" must be added to the already complex amalgam of class and ethnicity.

Assessing the achievements of the women involves not only a different organization of criteria but also different criteria from those of the men. Without, at this point, elaborating upon why it is so, it is an observable reality that women live in what might be described as a separate culture (I sometimes think a separate dimension) from men, even from men who share their ethnicity, social class, historical time, community—and in some cases their beds and intimate lives. In the period of this study, and in the neighborhood of Brownsville, the reality of gender difference in innumerable areas such as upbringing, relationships, aspirations, possibilities, sensibilities—ingredients that have made women's lives profoundly different from those of men—renders simple comparisons meaningless.

The Brownsville women share their deep fondness for the old neighborhood when they meet at children's weddings and grandchildren's *Bat* and *Bar Mitzvahs*, or for special events such as the *Bat Mitzvah* of Ruth Berman, one of "the girls." Some have periodic or annual gatherings of friends clubs. I was invited to one on Long Island and another in San Francisco.

Some meet more formally, at reunions of the alumni associations of their junior and senior high schools or of the BBC. There, like the men, they "tell and retell the stories . . . share, and share again, the memories of their childhood and teenage years."[52]

But as the women tell their stories, they construct a much different picture from that of the men—and it often begins with the stories of their own mothers.

CHAPTER THREE

Jewish Women

Mothers

As I get older I see more of my mother in me; I open my mouth and my mother comes out.

—Florence Bain Grosswirth

M y mother decided that she had waited long enough.
It was 1910. Five years earlier, my mother's parents had left her, the oldest child, with her maternal grandparents and with a promise: they would send for her as soon as they had the money for her passage. The younger children, her parents told her, could travel "on *their* tickets" but my mother, twelve at the time, needed one of her own. She waited a very long time, it seemed to her, for it to arrive. Finally she left the *shtetl* for the city of Kiev, found work there, saved most of her wages and paid for the voyage herself. She journeyed across Europe from the Ukraine, the Pale of Settlement, to Bremerhaven. She was seventeen—and alone.[1]

My mother disembarked at the port of Baltimore, and somehow, without a word of English, made her way to her family in Pittsburgh. (Why they settled there is a detail long lost to our family history.) She did not remain there with her family for too long; she soon left for New York where she became a "boarder" and pursued a brief but not very notable career on the Yiddish stage before she took a job in the garment trade. Around the outbreak of World War I she married the son of the family she boarded with—but only after she had ended a forbidden infatuation with a "*Talyener*," an "Italian boy," she said when she told me about him.

My mother's story is not unusual as immigrant stories go. Many of the mothers of the Brownsville women emigrated to America around the turn of the century and in the years before the war began. Each one had a story to tell. Many were very young. Katie Stavans's mother travelled to America from Austria with a cousin; both were fourteen! Flo Grosswirth's mother arrived in America at the age of fifteen and found her father living with a "girlfriend." She felt she was "in the way" and left. She found a way to support herself and, as my mother did, boarded until she married.

Much of the personal history of our mothers is now lost. I wonder now, but when I had the chance I rarely asked my mother for more of her stories, more details of her youth and of that time of her life. How could she have been brave enough to travel so far on her own? Did she realize the dangers? Many of the women who emigrated to America around the turn of the century, or in its early years, did know of the dangers, of highwaymen, of swindlers waiting to prey on innocents. They heard stories of young Jewish women abducted into prostitution by the white-slave traders, many of whom were Jews themselves.[2] But the women, nevertheless, headed for *der goldene medine*, the golden land. It strains my sensibilities to try to imagine what my mother, what the mothers of other Brownsville women, must have been thinking and feeling.

One reason I didn't ask my mother more questions about her youth is that, as the columnist Russell Baker pointed out, we don't think of our parents as people who had lives before they were parents; or sometimes, as in my case, not until it's too late. But there is another reason. Although I knew a good deal about the history of Jewish immigration, I was ignorant of the history of Jewish immigrant women. Therefore, I wasn't impressed by my mother's participation in that history. I didn't take her experiences seriously and didn't appreciate how important they were to understanding my own cultural and personal history. And because I didn't know the history, I also didn't know what questions to ask. I was not alone in my ignorance, however. One Yiddish writer, Irena Klepfisz, called it an "injustice and a misrepresentation of Eastern European Jewish history," an "absurdity," that "generations of men and women inherited a Yiddish *yerushe* [legacy] devoid of women."[3]

It is only since Charlotte Baum, Paula Hyman, and Sonya Michel's groundbreaking study, *The Jewish Woman in America*, that women have been able to acquire any sense of their importance in Jewish history. Since then (the 1970s), feminists and other scholars have given us the true gift of our mothers' personal histories, entwined with the stories they uncovered. The women they write about are not distant, disembodied historical figures.

It is as a result of recent scholarship that we are able to appreciate nineteenth- and early-twentieth-century women, such as those in Naomi Shepherd's collective biography, who formed women's organizations, founded coeducational schools, and encouraged higher and even religious education for women, some of whom claimed the right to remain single and independent. In the nineteenth century there were women, fighting against enormous social pressures, who were seeking an education and profession. In doing so, they were challenging the traditional role of women in public arenas. A unifying theme that emerges from the stories of many of the women about whom Klepfisz, Shepherd, Sorin, and others write, is their rejection of paternalism and of women's archetypical role in Judaism. For the first time these historians have given us nontraditional models, many of whom emigrated to the United States alongside some of the mothers of the Brownsville women.

But the history of Jewish women, and of our mothers, does not begin with immigrant women, or even with the role they played in the life of the European *shtetl*. It begins even farther back with women's role in Judaism itself. Blu Greenberg believes that the role of women in Jewish life hinges upon *halakha* which, she says, was not, and is not today, just a collection of laws, but represents a way of life, "or more correctly, a way of living."[4] In Brownsville, Judaism *was* a way of living. "We got dressed up on Saturday. We didn't realize we were observing the Sabbath," Katie Stavans says, "it was part of our lives."

Although most of their families were not observant, orthodox Jews, Brownsville girls lived amidst the orthodox culture and religious tradition. Our mothers kept kosher homes. Our fathers went to *shul* on occasional Saturdays, or to say *kadish* (the mourners' prayer that is said on the anniversary of the death of a relative), and for other, particular occasions. They always went to *shul* on the high holy days and, like the others, when I was a girl in Brownville, I used to visit my parents there. Ours was the Congregation *Ezrath Achim,* on Newport Avenue and Bristol Street.

Our *shul* had three stories; my father's customary seat was on the ground floor, which housed the more modest part of the *shul* and had a small square corner of the room set aside for the women.[5] When I was very little I was still allowed to find my father, who always sat in the same place, and sit with him for a while. As I got older I was told not to "bother him," to remain with the women behind the *mehitzah* (the formal partition that separated the women's from the men's section). It was from there that I observed my father in his well-worn *talis* and new *yarmulke*, usually a souvenir from the most recent *Bar Mitzvah* or wedding. He could participate in all of the important rituals and honors: carrying the Torah, being called to the dais "for an *aliye*" (reading from the Torah), opening the ark. The women were "excused" from these practices as they were excused from the *minyan* (the quorum of ten required for communal prayer.) The women sat behind the *mehitzah* and prayed there. They were dressed in their holiday finery, but didn't wear special garments; they were in ordinary street clothes, they wore ordinary hats.

Although it was a long walk from our apartment and there were many other orthodox synagogues along the way, we went to the Congregation *Ezrath Achim* because it was our family synagogue; the entire *mishpokhe*, our extended family, could be found there on the holidays. I was told that Chaya Sore, my father's mother after whom I was named, had worshipped there and, when she died, was honored in a way that was rare for women: her funeral procession passed in front of the *shul* and stopped there for a moment, long enough for the doors to be opened. It was a token of respect for this charitable woman who epitomized the Jewish guiding principle of *tsedakah* or righteousness. She was the *eyshit chayil,* the "woman of valor," revered because she "stretcheth her hand out to the poor."

As girls in Brownsville, our early religious experiences were full of messages that, while unspoken, were clearly articulated nevertheless. Women didn't wear those special garments, they were not part of the prayer group, they were sometimes (often!) scolded for being too noisy, they were not leaders in the synagogue—and they were kept apart from the men who were taking care of the important business of the religion. If women were honored at all, it was for playing a supporting role, for having lived a life full of caretaking and giving to others. All of us who grew up in Brownsville learned the lessons in the silent messages. It was clear that we were not only different but (like the "negroes" who had to sit in the back of the bus or who were segregated in schools) we were not equal.

I was vividly reminded of this when I recently saw a documentary film, *A Life Apart*,[6] about *Hasidim* in Brooklyn today. In *shul*, the girls and women hang over the balconies. The women watch, the little girls watch. Below, the men and boys engage in all of the rituals, touch the Torah with the fringes of their prayer shawls, sing and dance. And at other important ceremonies, the girls simply . . . watch.

It is not difficult to see how women raised in the orthodox tradition came to accept a subordinate and supporting role in religious life: traditionally their piety was in helping their husbands and sons to study, in being facilitators. Nor is it difficult to see that Jewish women also could come to believe they should play the supporting role in their personal, secular lives. As Susannah Heschel wrote, in Jewish culture, women's role and their identity both became "entangled with the theological positions that legitimate them."[7]

Jewish women have historically been raised in a tradition whose commandments and teachings are based upon the first five books of the Bible, the Torah; upon extensive commentary and interpretation, the Talmud; and upon the elaborate codification of Jewish law known as *Halakha*. Those unfamiliar with the orthodox tradition may not know, as the Brownsville girls did (although without comprehending the ramifications), that women are excluded from the study of Talmud. And if women do not study, they cannot understand the law; if they do not understand the law, they are not able to participate in the all-important interpretive decisions.[8] With regard to issues that directly affect their lives, they are effectively disfranchised.

Women, like children, slaves, and "sexually impaired men," (an oblique reference to homosexuals?) have fewer prayer responsibilities and are exempt from the *mitzvoth*, the religious obligations, that must be performed within a given time frame such as morning, afternoon, or evening prayers.[9] Lorraine Nelson, one of only three participants in this study who is orthodox and observant, offered the historical explanation that women are not meant to be excluded but rather are exempt from duties that would interfere with familial responsibilities. Another Brownsville woman, Dolores Plaxen's, interpretation of the exemption has an interesting twist. "Men need to have obligations," she says, "Women don't need to have obligations to do what they're supposed to do." Like Lorraine, Dolores believes that "the Jewish woman has very important place in Judaism"; she doesn't take it as a "putdown" that women are excluded from particular obligations.

But at the very least, Adrienne Baker, a lecturer at London University, sees an inconsistency in these apologetics: in Orthodox communities men perform all of the liturgical roles, including those women *are* permitted to perform, such as the blessings over wine. Women are not allowed to wear ritual garb. In orthodox practice, she continues, there are no birth or life cycle rituals for girls (in spite of sporadic efforts to institute them) equivalent in meaning to those for boys: the *Brith*, the ritual circumcision that takes place on the eighth day after birth, the *Pidyon Habeyn*, the celebration (literally the redemption) of the firstborn son which occurs one month later, or the most important coming of age ceremony, the *Bar Mitzvah*. Because these practices have nothing to do with time constraints, Baker raises the "vexed issue of where in religious practice exemptions become exclusions."[10]

There is a phrase in the morning prayer that men recite: "Thank You God, that You have not made me a woman." The orthodox deny that there is any degradation implied in the blessing. They claim that it is simply an expression of gratitude that a man is called upon to serve God more completely, fully, directly. (What, then, is the converse?) And even if there is no degradation, there is privilege implied; surely, there is not the submissiveness of the "parallel prayer" in which a women says thank you to God, "for having made me according to Your will."[11] Students of semantics know that the uses of language are significant. An example is the Hebrew word *ba'al*, which carries considerable symbolic meaning; it means both husband and master.

The Brownsville girls may not have been aware, but the messages were being received nevertheless. It was not simply in the distant past that Jewish fathers "were sometimes pitied and consoled on the birth of a daughter . . . more an occasion for sadness than of celebration."[12] Sylvia Zinn's father never forgave her for being a girl. Even toward the end of his life, when she was caring for him in his illness, she felt the need to convince him that she could "do the things a guy can do."

As Rachel Adler wrote, "Judaism's implicit view of women . . . not just teachings, but images which convey messages unconsciously—persist although their origin is in classical sources."[13] In Jewish lore, the images of women are contradictory. In contrast with positive and complimentary images, such as the *eishit chayil*, are images of the seductresses, Eve and Lilith (who is characterized as a demon in one of the moral tales of the *Midrash*.)[14] Other seductive and demonic images—at their worst, women are depicted as witches—must inevitably have given rise to the variety of rules for women, both prescribed and proscribed behaviors[15] including their physical separation from the men by the *mehitzah*. Through this device, distracting images are obscured and the seductress is disabled—but at great cost: a severe limitation on women's full participation in Jewish life.

Defenders of the orthodox tradition reject these interpretations; they claim that women are held in high regard in Judaism, that they are "respected in a way that women in the nonreligious world rarely are."[16] Orthodox women agree that their roles are different from the men's but they vigorously deny any inequality. They reject the claim of feminists that "different" necessarily implies inferior, and on the face of it, it certainly does not; this position is also held by those who defend the notion of cultural pluralism. They see their roles as a natural consequence of inherent differences between the sexes but believe that men and women's roles are equally important and complementary. Based upon the Biblical injunction, "and you shall teach your children," women are entrusted with raising their children as Jews; they are honored as the carriers of tradition. Sarah Lieberman, one of the orthodox Brownsville women asked, "What could be more important than family, than raising your children, passing on *Yidishkeit*?"

While they do not participate in formal religious study, orthodox women do not accept the negative judgment that their own, more limited education results in superficial knowledge or compromises their educational responsibilities. They make a distinction between "socialization" and "education" and they believe that transmitting a love for the Yiddish tradition does not require the kind of technical understanding and knowledge of the law that can only be acquired through Talmudic study.

Transmitting *Yidishkeit* to their children was but one aspect of the role of the Jewish woman in the European *shtetlach* from which the mothers and grandmothers of the Brownsville women came. In the *shtetl*, the role of the Jewish wife and mother had, of necessity, great latitude. As it was performed, more often than not, it was far from the ideal devoted solely to domesticity. A girl was raised to be a good wife— a hardworking helpmeet to her husband, a *baleboste*, from the Hebrew, *ba'alat habayit*, meaning mistress of the home—but was also expected to do more than keep house and tend the chidren. (Even rich women who had servants were expected to work, at the very least to spin their own wool, since "leisure" they were told, "leads to idiocy.")[17] The *baleboste* who "became a legendary figure "because she could make a meal from a potato"[18] was doing a great deal more to sustain her household than planning clever, albeit humble, spreads. *Shtetl* women made significant contributions to the economic survival of their families.

Women earned a living at a variety of enterprises in the *shtetl*, and through which they also acquired exposure to the outside community. Jewish working-class women may have made up a full one-quarter of the work force; they owned shops where they sold food, staples, linens, piece goods, crockery, china, glassware, and "fancy goods." They managed inns and taverns. They peddled their wares in the marketplaces or, going house to house, baskets over their arms, they sold rolls and bagels that they had baked, butter that they had churned, or tea, beans, and other foodstuffs. They raised chicken and geese and sold eggs, and when they slaughtered the fowl they made feather pillows, quilts, and *perenes* (featherbeds). Some women bought small lots of manufactured articles in the cities to barter for the produce peasants brought to the markets.

Young girls too, even preadolescents, were expected to work; some were apprenticed to skilled craftsmen or craftswomen. They rarely attended school; generally they had a minimal education, if any. They might have been taught to read and write Yiddish, "the women's language," by the *melamed's* (the elementary school teacher's) wife. They may also have learned enough letter writing and enough of the local language—Russian, Polish, Lithuanian—to negotiate in the marketplace. Some taught themselves to read and write. My cousin Shifka, the ninety-two-year-old elder of our family, taught herself both Yiddish and Russian. When I asked her how she did it, she said, "How did I do it? I just figured it out, the same way I figured it out later, how to read and write English."[19]

Jews idealized the scholar, but the scholar was never a woman; the highest position a woman could aspire to was to become the wife of a scholar (remember, her piety was in helping her husband and sons to study). Religious education was not considered necessary for the girls, and this tradition was carried to the New World and was brought forward in Brownsville through the middle of the twentieth century.[20] Girls might have been taught to recite some prayers in Hebrew but not to translate. For a girl in the *shtetl*, as for the uneducated male, the *am ha'aretz*, the primary text for religious instruction, was in Yiddish: the *T'sena Ure'ena*.[21] Although it was the single most important publication for young Jewish women, it was unlike the Talmud, the commentary that was written on every aspect of the Torah, every word of which is studied and examined by men. The *T'sena Ure'ena*, which was their education and identified their role in Jewish tradition, was not merely a "patronizing but good-humored version of the *Torah* for women and ignorant men," it contained "no real dialectic of the kind that exercises men's minds."[22]

While they may not have been reading the *T'sena Urena* in Brownsville in the 1930s and 1940s, the underlying messages still prevailed. As Raye Cohen, who was brought up in an orthodox family, says:

> My family didn't think it necessary for girls to go to *kheyder*; they didn't need religious instruction. And it was a natural thing to accept. Girls were not taught to question. Boys learned to question and it was expected of them to question.

Fayge Lubin gave another, related, reason that education for women was discouraged when she said, "My father didn't approve of religious training for women; he wanted the girls to be at home." In the *shtetl* there was the fear that education would open a Pandora's box, that girls would be less satisfactory as wives in the traditional manner, that knowledge might make girls less satisfied to remain at home. And secular education posed an even greater threat: it was feared that girls would want too much, that they would get romantic notions about love that conflicted with customs—such as arranged marriages—that allowed the families to retain control over their lives.

Such fears were not unwarranted. Many stories have now been uncovered about educated women who were encouraged to rebel against both traditional proscriptions and expectations, at least in part, as a result of their secular learning. Many were politicized and radicalized, and they became activists and reformers. Some, in seeking change, rejected Judaism itself.

In America, many Jewish immigrant women expressed their commitment to change through their involvement in the labor movement, particularly through their activism in unionizing the garment trades. By the 1920s the women of the ILGWU, a large number of whom were Jews, formed one-quarter of all the women in America's unions, but there was a large decline in Jewish membership in the next decade.[23] A dramatic change in women's participation in the paid work force was brought about by the onset of the Great Depression, but even before this cataclysm occurred, Jewish women left the factories as soon as they were able. They were enjoined to stay home by the combined force of the middle-class aspirations of both American and Jewish society. Middle-class status required women to remain at home to perform their traditional roles but also (perhaps more importantly), by remaining at home they proved that they had moved into the middle class.

Radicals and activists notwithstanding, many Jewish women were predisposed to being homemakers. As early as 1915, just when my mother and the mothers of some of the girls were setting up housekeeping, the Council of Jewish Women opened a "Home Making Center and Model Flat" in the heart of Brownsville. "Within six months, over 1,500 Brooklyn women and young girls had visited the Center, attending its lectures on interior decor and 'sanitation' and absorbing American 'domestic methods.' Joselit shows that in America, as religious observance declined, the Jewish home and family life came to represent Jewishness itself.²⁴

The role of homemaker was sanctioned by Jewish tradition. Although the women in the *shtetlach* and in immigrant American communities did not model the role in its ideal version, the ideal remained the goal. Jewish women, including mothers of some Brownsville girls, were assisted in their quest to become the ideal *baleboste* by guidebooks and manuals, by Jewish social reformers, by courses in domestic science, home economics, and "home engineering,"²⁵ and by American commercialism which, in the 1920s, had discovered in the Jewish housewife a new market.

Companies with products such as Maxwell House coffee, Mazola oil, Borden's evaporated milk, Lifebuoy soap, Bon Ami cleanser, Gold Medal and Pillsbury flour, and many others targeted the Jewish housewife for their promotional campaigns. Ads were run in all of the popular Yiddish publications, in Yiddish with illustrations that made it plain that the good American (and Americanized) wife stayed home and— baked donuts, "*der Amerikanish begelech* (American bagels)—cleaned the tub, "*a fargenign*" (a pleasure), with the right cleanser—sanitized to kill germs and disease because "*di mame iz di doktor*" (the mother is the doctor)—and, since "*ir milkt nit di ku an rayst nit di grinzen*" (you don't milk the cow and don't pick the vegetables), as you did in the old country, why not buy cookies?, kosher, ready made and already in the box. After all, the ads claimed, that's what the modern American housewife and the *baleboste* did. *In der "gute" alte tsaytn*, in the "good" (read with sarcasm) old times, *zeyde* (grandfather) may have had to go without dinner while *bobe* (grandmother) finished washing the clothes on a stone in the river, but that was no longer necessary. After fifty years of progress in America, the *yidisher froy* (the Jewish woman) could send her children off to school in the morning with a couple of slices of pumpernickel, *di beser broit far skul-kinder* (the better bread for school-children), and then relax at home and enjoy her cup of brewed coffee which was *"gut bizn letsten dropl"* (good to the last drop).[26]

Many of the girls' mothers, reading these ads in the Yiddish press in the 1920s and 1930s, certainly were influenced by the image of the ideal Jewish homemaker, modified to conform to the image of the modern, middle-class American housewife. Many were convinced of the superiority of American ways and ready to discard the old ways; they hated being thought of as "greenhorns."[27] But they were poor, working-class women and even if they called themselves "homemakers" it was understood that their homes were often ones to which shops were attached or in which adequate space was made for "home-work."

Like women in the *shtetl,* many mothers in the Jewish immigrant community of Brownsville had two jobs: they were "working" mothers, precisely as their mothers and grandmothers had been before them. They ran the grocery stores and the greengrocers, were the milliners, worked part time in the local factories, took in sewing and mending—and boarders. They worked to augment the marginal incomes of their also hard-working husbands. Only three of the mothers of the Brownsville women in this study, all American-born, had office jobs. Although Isabel Cohen's mother had a college degree, she worked as a secretary for her attorney husband; Martha Optiz's mother worked as a secretary at the East New York YMHA (Young Men's Hebrew Association); and Ruth Kesslin's mother was a legal stenographer who supported her scholar husband. "It was the *shtetl* model," Ruth says.

Rochelle Feld's mother, who quit school to go to work at the age of thirteen, tended the family candy store. Terry Apter's mother turned their candy store into a general store during the war and also did home sewing. Harriet Portnoy's mother and father ran their family newsstand. Raye Cohen's mother worked in the family butcher shop. Claire Moses's mother tended their grocery store. Lois Rusakow's mother worked in her mother's, that is, Lois's grandmother's, grocery. Sarah Lieberman's mother had a "dry goods" store. Katie Stavans's mother had a knitting store. These small family shops or local businesses rarely demanded less than a twelve-hour work day. Minette Cutler's mother had a grocery store on Dumont Avenue and Watkins Street. "It was the women's business," Minette says:

I went from high school to my job after school, then to the grocery. I let my mother go home to prepare dinner and I closed the store. My father never set one foot in the business, or my brothers.

Other mothers, like Sylvia Zinn's, did tedious "home-work" or repetitious and physically demanding work in local factories or, as my mother did, worked long hours in the local garment factories during the height of the season. Some of the work was not quite respectable: one of the mothers was a bootlegger during the Depression!

Fayge Lubin, Bea Siegel, and Norma Ellman tell heroic stories about their mothers, young women in their twenties and thirties, immigrants without language or other skills, who were widowed in the midst of the Depression. They credit their mothers with the survival of the family. "My mother was the kind of woman you can't find today," Fayge Lubin says.

Fayge was eight years old when her father died of a heart attack, with only a fifty cent coin in his pocket, a family keepsake for many years that has now been lost. They were living in Harlem, where there were still many Jewish families. Her uncles urged their sister to put the children into a home but it was completely unthinkable to her. Instead, to be near Fayge's grandmother, her mother rented a tiny apartment on Powell Street in Brownsville for eleven dollars a month and kept the family together by bartering her cooking and housekeeping skills for meals for her children and by doing odd jobs such as plucking chickens—10 cents a bird. She did this until "home relief" was finally instituted for widows with children. Even by Depression standards, her family was poor, but even so, the dole was difficult to accept; it was a *shande*, a deeply felt shame and humiliation.

Fayge's mother coped, as others did, but many were worn down by the relentless pressure of rearing large families and maintaining their households in the days before labor-saving devices. "My mother was old before her time," Terry Apter says. They didn't realize it when they were girls but now they appreciate how hard their mothers worked. "At this age, my age," Shirley Donowitz says, "my mother was like an old woman." The women also can understand why, in contrast to the stereotyped image of the Jewish mother-martyr, their mothers never became resigned to their lot but rather, as Rochelle Feld said about her mother, became embittered.

For most of their lives their mothers had few, if any, of the familiar conveniences that the women have learned to take for granted. There were no phones in many Brownsville homes until the late forties or early fifties. Lorraine Nelson says, "People got phone calls at the candy store." Today, unless the electricity fails, the women don't think about their toasters, coffee makers, can openers, juicers, food processors, refrigerators, washing machines, sewing machines, clothing and hair dryers, vacuum cleaners, dishwashers, microwave ovens, garbage disposals—the familiar list can go on, it seems, endlessly. (Although I don't think of myself as being susceptible to every new gadget that comes along, this particular list is of appliances I've acquired. I'm sure there are a few more stored away somewhere that I've forgotten, as I forgot the computer I was using when I first wrote this.) Their mothers could not have conceived of readily available services such as takeout food, nowadays from gourmet shops as well as the neighborhood Chinese restaurants and pizzerias. Bringing appetizing or deli home was a special treat. Their mothers rarely "went out" to a movie or a show, or "ate out" at a restaurant. It was only on special occasions that their mothers had today's common and easy dual luxury of not having to prepare a meal for their families *and* of having someone serve them. Getting ready for the holidays, particularly Passover, meant weeks of cleaning and preparation. When the women compare their lives with their mothers', it seems obvious that their lives have been much easier, and not only easier but better in other respects. Many of the women believe they have better personal relationships with their husbands, their children, and their friends than their mothers had. They believe they have more loving and compatible relationships with their husbands than their mothers had with their fathers. Some of their mothers, if not in arranged marriages, were in marriages of convenience. One, albeit atypical example, was Rae Mirsky's mother; she didn't want to marry and resisted until she was thirty-three, a relatively mature age even in the 1990s, when women are marrying later than ever. Around the turn of the century she was highly unusual. However, Rae says, she got "tired of being a boarder, being a single woman moving from room to room." Rae's mother "gave in to the pressure" and married because she was "tired of making her own way."

Although most of the Brownsville women are glad that, when they faced the inevitable marital crises, divorce was not an easy alternative for them, they recognize that divorce was far less of an option for their mothers; their mothers faced even greater cultural pressure to work things out or, if they couldn't, to "stick things out." Joselit relates the story of a woman who was divorced in the 1930s whose "family kept her hidden."[28] For their mothers, divorce was an alternative only in the most extreme and most severe cases of neglect, philandering, and physical or other abuse. Divorce was such a *shande* that even Lila Perlmutter's father, who left his family on the day she was born, was never sued for divorce; there were no divorces among the parents of the Brownsville women in this study. Divorce, as it often does today in female-head-of-family households, would have exacerbated their already serious financial problems, sinking them deeper into poverty. Their mothers had little recourse if the marriages turned out to be unhappy ones. It was one of the reasons, some of the women said, that their mothers became bitter.

Many of the Brownsville women believe that their marital relationships are "more equal." Their immigrant parents, reared in rigidly patriarchal homes, duplicated those patterns in their own homes. Jean Bleckner's father "always came first." Minette Cutler remembers her mother saying, "When poppa finishes eating, then you'll talk to him." Shirley Donowitz's mother married at sixteen and a half. "My father never allowed her to work," Shirley says. "She was a typical housewife." Claire Moses describes her father:

> He was the boss. One time when we were at a country resort
> in the Catskills my mother told me she wouldn't go to play
> Bingo, although she loved it. "Your father said I shouldn't
> go"—and she didn't go.

Roslyn Bowers's father made all of the decisions, he was the "Czar of the house," she says, the mythology of the domineering Jewish wife and mother notwithstanding.

At home, the women never saw their fathers "pick up a dish to wash" or cook or help with the household chores. (My own father did; I suppose he was unusual in this way.) The women conjured up vivid childhood memories of holidays, such as Passover: the women scurrying around to prepare and serve the ritual *seder* meal, sometimes not even sitting down to eat, and then scurrying around again to do all of the cleaning up. After the meal, the men never even "got up to take a plate off the table." (They admitted, however, that this hasn't changed very much. Scenes similar to the ones they remember still take place after holiday meals at their own homes today. While their husbands can be prevailed upon, they "always" have to be reminded and urged to "help out.")

Most of the women claim that they have closer relationships with their children than they had with their mothers. "Our kids have more rapport with us," Katie Stavans says. Their mothers, who were tending the shops or busy with their other work, had no time or weren't able to "take them places" and "do things together." Few of the women worked at second jobs while their children were in primary school; they were able to chaperon school trips, to work for the PTA. Elaine Cohen says, "I was involved with my daughter; I was part of her life."

It is clear that for many in Brownsville, as in the European *shtetlach*, reality directly contradicted the revered and idealized conception of the definitive homemaker, the *baleboste* and the ever-nurturing Jewish mother. Nevertheless, in characterizing their mothers, the women said: "My mother always came last, the children were first"—"My mother was always there for me"—"I could smell the food cooking when I came home"—"My mother's life was her children"—"Children were the center of her world." These descriptions are all the more interesting when juxtaposed with the images of mothers who were otherwise described as embittered, frustrated, angry, resentful, critical, jealous, and even hostile to their daughters. Despite evidence to the contrary in the testimony of the women themselves, the common and romantic perception of the ever-patient, loving, nurturing, welcoming Jewish mother endures. Their memories may be, as Paula Hyman once said, "sanitized by nostalgia" but the image is deeply rooted in Jewish culture and is the overpowering ideal.

Women raised in the orthodox tradition, according to at least one critic, become "peripheral Jews."[29] Jewish law puts women in a secondary role in Judaism and, consequently, in Jewish life. Because they can neither study nor participate fully in religious observance there is no role for them but to be facilitators and caretakers; and they come to believe that they should play a peripheral, supporting role in their secular lives as well. As Susan Weidman Schneider wrote: "The membrane between religious Judaism and secular Jewish institutions and cultural patterns is highly permeable."[30] Patterns established and institutionalized through religious law and tradition are reflected and reinforced in the secular culture. The secular culture, in its turn, sustains these Jewish laws and traditions; the dynamic is cyclical and thus the patterns are self-sustaining. In this sense the Bible, the Torah, the Talmud, the *T'sena Urena*, *Halakha*—all of these, which created and sustain Jewish women's traditional role—had an impact on the lives of the mothers and consequently of the girls growing up in the orthodox tradition in which Brownsville was steeped.

The Brownsville girls saw themselves growing into an important role, rooted in tradition. They had internalized not the reality but their mothers' "culturally-defined self-image."[31] Like their mothers before them, they did not see that they had a choice, that they could do more than limit themselves to a supporting role—enabling their husbands to study and work, transmitting *Yiddishkeit* to their children, helping their children go forward in the world and rise to an even higher station in life than they expected to achieve. Because women are praised, even honored, for performing the traditional, secondary, supporting role well, the girls made decisions that ensured that they would continue the tradition: a self-fulfilling prophecy. And, of course, the problem is not in doing these important jobs well, but in "the exclusion of all else."[32]

The girls' image of what a Jewish woman should be was shaped by Jewish history, which, until recently, did not provide alternatives to the traditional model. The image was reinforced by Jewish culture and tradition. It was affirmed, even if not modelled, by their own mothers and by external, but also powerful, social forces. The girls who came of age in Brownsville in the 1940s and 1950s, therefore, had a limited perception of the possible. It limited their freedom of choice and set them on well-trodden paths.

CHAPTER FOUR

Coming of Age in the Forties

Choices

Choices! Who had choices? We had no choices!

—Bea Siegel

"This is a bad question!" Bea Siegel said.

I had just asked her about some of the critical, consequential choices she had made: those regarding school, career, marriage, children. "Choices! Who had choices? We had no choices!" Bea's sharp and intense reaction told me that I had, in fact, asked a very good question.

I was interviewing Bea on a snowy day in January. We were in the kitchen of her home in Canarsie—first of the many kitchens I would sit in during my talks with the Brownsville women. It was the home she moved to when she left Brownsville many years before and which she would leave before the writing of this book was completed. It was immediately easy to talk with her. Bea exuded a warmth and positive energy that put me at ease and made me feel she was a woman I had always known; she could have been my sister. Because it was my first interview, I was especially interested in Bea's responses to my questions.

Like other Brownsville women of her generation, Bea was born in the 1920s, raised during the Depression, completed high school in the 1940s, and was married soon after (to one of the original Brownsville boys). She held an office job until her first pregnancy, when she settled down to become a housewife. Bea remained at home until her children were "old enough." It was a typical pattern for the forties women. She was the "transitional" woman Blu Greenberg described: a woman who, having internalized traditional values, was "generally content" to play the role set for her. As Sydelle Schlossberg says, "The girls expected to be like their mothers." But later they would also, tentatively, begin to step outside of that role.[1]

If Bea was generally content it was, at least in part, because she couldn't perceive alternatives to traditional patterns; she didn't see herself in other possible roles. There was a lack of opportunity for women in the forties and fifties but it was more than that: values and attitudes that prevailed in the Jewish culture were reinforced by beliefs about the appropriate role for women—"*deeply entrenched ideologies*"—that were also embedded in middle-class American culture.[2] Together, both cultures acted as powerful inhibitors. The Brownsville women's sense of limitation, rather than choice, was one of its more obvious effects; it explains Bea's response.

Flo Grosswith's response was very similar to Bea's. "Choice? What was modelled?" she asked, and then answered her own question: "How you were supposed to be!" Flo put it so clearly:

> I did what was expected of me. I was raised to be a good helper, not to complain, to do the best I could. . . . I never heard my mother complain, not at the worst times. She did what she had to do.

The women of Brownsville would try, and most would succeed, with varying degrees of emotional expenditure, in becoming models of the good Jewish wife.

Since early in this century there have been "dozens of guides and manuals on modern Jewish living."[3] Although the girls would not have read *The Guide for the Jewish Homemaker* (it was not published until the late 1950s), they might have read one very much like it. It described the role of the Jewish wife perfectly. Offering both information and injunction, *The Guide* made an effort (in a most condescending tone, however unintentional it may have been) to persuade its readers to look at the "business of being a housewife" not as a "series of chores—cooking, baking, cleaning, washing, shopping, getting the children off to school, keeping a husband well fed and comfortable." It was, rather, to be seen "as a vocation of the highest significance," requiring the development of a many-sided character: "wife, nurse, mother, cook, confidante, teacher, diplomat, economist, companion, interior decorator, hostess."[4]

The *Guide* was a what-every-Jewish-girl-needs-to-know-in-order-to-make-the-home-a-"*mikdash-me'at*" (a miniature sanctuary) book. Some of the chapter headings give a sense of its scope: Occupation: housewife; From cradle to canopy; The Sabbath; The yearly round: Holy days and holidays; Family fun; Making the most of your money; Basic recipes. It concluded with suggested inspirational readings, books that gave "direct, authoritative answers to many questions on matters of daily living in the Jewish home."[5] (As you can well imagine, the listing did not include a book that had made quite a splash when it was published just one year before the *Guide*. Its title was *The Feminine Mystique*.)

Although the *Guide* was written with a particularly Jewish *tam* (flavor), it was similar to others, filled with homilies, that had been written many times before. It was especially reminiscent of *Things Girls Like to Do*,[6] which had been written for a general audience in 1917, during a time when homemaking was first being awarded the more lofty titles of "home economics," "domestic science," and even "home engineering." The things it assumed that girls liked to do in 1917 were eerily similar to what women were told, in the *Guide*, they should be liking and doing a half-century later. Its chapters paralleled those in the *Guide*. They included: Housekeeping; The Business Side (this was a 1917 version of the chapter in the *Guide* entitled "Making the most of your money"); The Kitchen; Menus and Marketing; Cooking (here are the recipes); and so on.

Like its predecessors, the *Guide* sent a clear message. Tucked in between the recipes—for chopped liver, potato *latkes*, and *tsimes*[7]—and amid the household hints—was more insidious fare. Alongside an effort to bolster the self-image of the Jewish homemaker and to help her "raise her status in her own eyes" to that of "an important executive,"[8] was a message that served to obscure the issue of choice by establishing the "career" of homemaker as the taken-for-granted norm against which any other choice would have to be justified.

The women did take it for granted that their lives would revolve around their husbands and raising a family, although they had some vague sense that they might want to do "something" once the children were grown. They might become widowed, but they were young—mortality was not something they thought about, let alone planned for. Nor did they consider the possibility of divorce and that they might have to support themselves. Divorce is permitted in Judaism because, in spite of its importance, marriage is not a sacrament. But the *ketubah*, the marriage contract, has always been "imbued with holiness," a "contract blessed by God."[9] Divorce happened, but it was so rare, so remote from their experience, that it seemed to be something that happened to the rich—or in Hollywood.[10]

And there were many marriages. Unlike Bea Siegel, who resisted the pressure to marry before her boyfriend went into the service, many married in Brownsville, as elsewhere, because of the heightened romanticism and urgency created by wartime separation. The Census Bureau estimated that more than a million more marriages took place between 1940 and 1943 than would have occurred during normal times. But there were also other, more pragmatic, reasons for early marriage, such as the modest economic support provided for dependents by the government. "And there were a lot of bad marriages because of the war," Bea says.[11]

How could they not have taken it for granted that they would marry? In Judaism, marriage is not only considered essential for the preservation of the religion and of Jewish society but also for the individual. A tenet of the Jewish religion, unlike some others, such as Catholicism, is that a person cannot be fulfilled until he or she is married." Marriage is not only sanctioned in Judaism, there is no "approved role for celibacy."[12] As recently as the 1980s "an East Coast rabbi said 125,000 single Jews in New York City was 'disgusting.'"[13]

If choosing to be a single woman is not completely accepted even now, at the end of the 1990s, it isn't difficult to see why, in the 1940s and 1950s, women rarely considered the possibility of remaining single, or at least not by choice. Katie Stavans was one of the exceptions. She says:

> I wanted to do a lot of things. I didn't want to get married because I minded my sister's children; I was sick of kids. I had aspirations of being somebody. I wanted to be an airline stewardess, airplanes were glamorous; or a nurse, to join the WACS. I wanted to do a lot of crazy things but my mother had visions of me just getting married and just being a proper girl. My mother said: "Don't be silly, those things are not for Jewish girls."

Katie didn't get married until she was twenty-four. Today it seems very young but "at this time, twenty-four wasn't such a youngster," comments her friend, Shirley Donowitz.

Women who did remain single in the 1940s were never believed to have freely chosen such an option. They were either pitied as spinsters or dismissed as neurotics; "psychologists insisted that women could enjoy mental health only through dependence on a man."[14] And even "worse" than being thought of as neurotic, single women might have been suspected of being "perverts": lesbians. In high contrast with the visible and outspoken presence of Jewish lesbians today (one of the Brownsville women in this study is among this outspoken group), in a Jewish community in the 1940s such a "shameful" possibility would have been whispered about or, even more likely, would have remained unspoken.[15]

Such concerns were far from the minds of naïve Brownsville girls as they were growing up in the Depression years. Their struggles with shame had to do with poverty, the "shame and humiliation," Fagye Lubin says, of being on "home relief"; of having to go "pick up scraps" with her brothers at the lumberyard on Junius Street. Both Fayge's and Irma Greenbaum's family had to "go on home relief" when their fathers died in the midst of the Depression. Irma's memory is fragmented—she learned about her father's death from a neighbor's child and remembered the social worker saying, "No, it is not in the budget," when her mother asked the social worker if Irma could have a penny. But Irma remembers clearly that her mother had to take in "boarders." And she remembers that, by the age of ten, she already felt "degraded."

Most of the women don't have such wrenching memories. Their recollections are more like Lorraine Nelson's. "Yes, we were poor," she says, "but we never felt deprived. The holidays came, we got shoes, maybe a new dress." For most of the girls the consciousness of being poor didn't come until, like Eleanor Chernick's, their worlds reached beyond the neighborhood. Eleanor made friends outside of Brownsville, and some from Flatbush "were much more well off," she says.

Generally, the girls were not conscious of their social class or their ethnicity. They were unaware of being poor, they were unaware of being "different" because they were Jews. Of course, they knew the often repeated tales of their families' histories, they had heard stories of discrimination in Europe and of much worse: Terry Apter's mother had lost her family in a *pogrom*; Irma Greenbaum's relatives had barely made it out of Poland in the thirties. Raye Cohen's family emigrated from Poland when she was only four, and so her memory is very limited. But one picture does stand out:

> I remember walking with my father, bouncing a ball. It rolled away and I started to chase after it but my father stopped me because a Polish child had picked it up. My father said, "We can't take it back from a Polish child."

But this was America!

It wasn't until later, when they were no longer insulated within the neighborhood, that the girls would learn that they were discriminated against in America, too; that there were quotas for admission to some colleges; that there were not only places that were restricted, but entire professions.[16] Discrimination and ostracism were the primary reasons that my family moved back to Brownsville from Jeffersonville, a community in upstate New York where my mother ran a small boarding house. I had some horrendous antisemitic experiences when I was in kindergarten and grammar school in the early years of the war. The older children wouldn't allow me to sit on the school bus (how could the driver have permitted that, I wonder?). I still dream about being pushed down a flight of stairs at the elementary school; one of my front teeth was broken. Claire Moses's family also moved to Brownsville from Westchester, where she had suffered name calling and exclusion. "I was told I couldn't come to a party because I was Jewish," she says. But most Brownsville girls were not conscious of themselves as part of a denigrated minority; they were unaware that people came from other parts of Brooklyn into their community to shop on Pitkin and Belmont Avenues—"Jewtown"—and hone their bargaining skills with the shopkeepers, to practice what they cynically called "Jewing them down."

It wasn't until later that they made meaning of discussions they had heard at home about how "they"—the *goyim,* the gentiles—were not like *undz,* like us. Then the full recognition of their difference intruded upon them; they began to notice that their parents spoke with accents, or with inflections that sounded foreign. Flo Grosswith says, with sarcasm, that her mother didn't exactly fit the "movie" image and admits, painfully, that she was ashamed because her mother wasn't "American." Others admitted these feeling as well; their deep shame now is that they were ashamed of their parents then.

But it wasn't until later that these understandings came to them. When they were teenagers, the women say, they were comfortable and secure in the neighborhood where whole families might live within the radius of a few blocks.

"We socialized on our block," Fayge Lubin says. Occasionally the girls sat on the porches of the few private (usually two-family) homes, but you were more likely to find them sitting on the front "stoops" of their apartment buildings (a New York word taken from the Dutch, meaning steps). It was long before portable radios boomed from groups of teens and, in any case, radios were for the evenings. "We didn't go out at night on weekdays," Sydelle Schlossberg says.

It wasn't uncommon for snacks to be sent down to a youngster in the street from an upstairs window, via a paper bag tied to a length of string. This was also a favorite way to send change down for a quick trip to the corner grocery. The grocery was one of the meeting places. "We would sit on the milk boxes," Rae Mirsky says. Sometimes, in the afternoons, the girls went for malteds, for walks to look in the bridal shop windows (where Terry Apter worked after school), and, if they could afford to, stopped at a deli where they could get a hot dog, fries, and a Coke, each for a nickel. "Everything took place in groups," Minette Cutler recalls, "groups of girls, groups of boys. We were always together and hanging around a candy store." For Sydelle Schlossberg, "Nanny Goat park was the central point; right after school we ran to the park." Few of the girls participated in organized after-school activities.

Freed from school on weekends, Raye Cohen says, they might "hang around" Lincoln Terrace Park and sometimes, from there, dare to cross the boundary of the neighborhood into Crown Heights to skate at the Eastern Parkway Roller Rink or to walk almost the entire length of Eastern Parkway to the Botanical Gardens, the Brooklyn Museum, or the huge Brooklyn Public Library on Grand Army Plaza.

Susan Schneider wrote "Jewish girls have been discouraged from moving their bodies." She described a woman's childhood experience at an orthodox summer camp where "the boys played basketball and the girls sat on the sidelines, cheering and crocheting *yarmulkes*."[17] Even among the less religious, girls generally sat on the sidelines, but surprisingly, a good number of the forties girls were athletic. They played stoopball (throwing a rubber ball against the stoop and catching it) or handball or basketball; occasionally they played with the boys, joining in their street games.[18] When they could, Rae Mirsky says, "two or three girls would chip in to rent a bike for an hour."

Girls in Brownsville had their own clubs, parallel to the streetcorner clubs of the boys (which had coalesced into the Brownsville Boys Club), although the girls' clubs were not generally organized around athletics. Sydelle Schlossberg belonged to a club that was an exception:

> The Comettes was an athletic club. They played basketball and baseball. The instructors who worked for the Parks Department were exceptional. The Parks Department organized competitions all over the city.

But most of the girls' clubs were primarily a way of advertising a collective identity. They were called "social clubs." Members were part of a group, spent most of their time together, and often dressed alike—parading through the streets like a chorus line, in costume. They were invited to, or held parties in their homes as a group so that the less "popular" girls were included with the others. And, while within each of them there was a definite pecking order, and often cliques, clubs gave the girls the security of "belonging," which filled an important adolescent need: they never felt isolated. "As kids, our club meetings were very therapeutic," Shirley Donowitz says. "We didn't realize what we were doing, we were having support groups. We really talked, we were never afraid to tell each other our inner feelings." Girls' clubs were a phenomenon that persisted through the 1950s.

During a joint interview with Shirley and Katie Stavans, they quickly reeled off all the names of their friends in Club Emeralds: "Shirley B., Ida, Bunny, Bella, Sydelle, Honey, Laura, and Lillian." Without any particular prompting the women were able to repeat the names, along with their identifying "colors." The scenario was repeated time and again as the forties women remembered: "We belonged to the Comettes, Vixens, Emanons (which spells "noname" in reverse, because they couldn't think of a name they liked), Amies, Amarrodz (an anagram using the first letter of the girls' names), Doucettes, Diablos, Juleps." "Our club sweaters (the boys had club jackets, but they were rare for the girls) were . . . blue and gray . . . green and yellow . . . chartreuse and gray . . . orange and black." Sydelle Schlossberg had already joined the Comettes when she also joined the Emeralds. She admits, somewhat sheepishly, that she wanted the Comettes' sweater, "but the Emeralds were saving for a jacket."

Girls who had an affinity for sports were not helped by the public schools, because they had no girls' teams. Most Brownsville youth attended Thomas Jefferson High School on Pennsylvania Avenue. A few of the girls attended high schools in "the city": Central (Girls) Commercial and Central Needletrades, which later became the Fashion Institute of Technology. Some went to the newer Samuel J. Tilden High (which I attended), one of several schools built throughout the city as WPA projects during the Depression. Tilden was in the more middle-class neighborhood of East Flatbush but took students from those fringes of Brownsville that were adjacent to its cachement area. The two schools enjoyed an intense local rivalry, which climaxed, as everyone remembers, in the Tilden-Jeff Thanksgiving Day football match. For most girls, not simply those in the orthodox summer camp, cheering their school team on was the extent of their participation in sports.

Instead of playing sports some of the girls, like Raye Cohen and Norma Ellman, took singing, dance, or music lessons; Eleanor Chernick took piano lessons "now and then, when there was money." Lorraine Nelson longed to take piano lessons but says, "There was no money for frills like that." Although most were, like Lorraine, too poor for private lessons, some of the girls did take lessons at the Hebrew Educational Society. The H.E.S. was housed in its own building on Hopkinson Avenue. It provided music lessons along with a variety of other cultural services. It also offered Hebrew language instruction. My own foray into learning Hebrew took place there when I was still in grammar school, and ended abruptly after only two lessons when I found myself in the wrong, advanced, class. I pretended that I was reading the Hebrew script but actually read the transliteration. I felt so humiliated by my deceit and was so fearful of being found out that I never returned nor did I seek other alternatives (much to my regret now).

If I had, I might have found one of a variety of Hebrew schools or other organizations at which to study: the *shule* (school) on Stone Avenue; the Workman's Circle, the *Arbeteringschule* which held classes in Yiddish language and Jewish, secular rather than religious, instruction; a *kindershule* (for younger children) on Bristol and Newport Streets; and the Young Israel of New Lots, which Lorraine Nelson attended. A number of the girls did learn Hebrew; Jean Bleckner graduated from Hebrew school at her grandfather's insistence. But that was not common; in an orthodox community, "beginning in elementary school, the girls studied Israeli folk dancing while the boys studied *Talmud*."[19]

My parents never insisted that I return to Hebrew school. If I'd been a boy there is little question that I would have had to go to *kheyder*, a school for religious as well as Hebrew education. I would have studied for my *Bar Mitzvah*, the ritual that symbolizes that a boy has reached his religious majority and is expected to obey the commandments. Although they may have found their studies boring and unappealing, very few boys did not attend Hebrew school, although some went to *kheyder*, as Raye Cohen's brother did, with a baseball glove hanging out of his back pocket, ready to join the game immediately afterward. ("What kind of *goy* is he?" Raye's father would ask, in despair.)

In the forties, girls did not study to become *Bat Mitzvah*, as has become the custom today, in a ritual similar but not equivalent to the *Bar Mitzvah*. It evolved in America to provide girls with recognition of their coming of age but it was not, and still is not, part of the orthodox tradition; none of the forties girls were *Bat Mitzvah*.

With very few exceptions, the women have fond memories of these years. Their recollections have surely become romanticized over time, masking their feelings of deprivation and genuine poverty, and obscuring unpleasant images of life in crowded tenement-like apartments. If I brought it up in our conversations they remembered the cockroaches scrambling away when we turned on the bathroom light at night. I can remember my father cursing under his breath because, despite all of my parents efforts, they couldn't rid the apartment of them.

Few women recall the *sturm und drang* we associate with adolescence; they've forgotten the "conflicts" and the "ambivalences," as Stephanie Coontz noted in *The Way We Never Were*.[20] "We were never bored," Fayge Lubin says. It's difficult to imagine a time before the existence of teen boredom but in the hot Brooklyn inner city summer days the girls swam in the public pool at Betsy Head Park, or sunbathed on the roofs—the "tar beaches." They went to dances organized by the Parks Department in the evenings. Often they went to the movies. Once in a while, "we pooled our money to go to shows at the Paramount," Bea Siegel says, but there were many small motion picture houses dotting the neighhorhood. There was also one of the grand and elaborate movie palaces that had been built in the thirties (not much more than ten years earlier) for the "talkies": the Loew's (pronounced Low-eeze) Pitkin. Boys and girls would climb to the balcony which had little fairy lights overhead that sparkled and twinkled through openings in the deep blue velvet ceiling. One of the girls thought it must have been what the sky really looked like in "the mountains," which everyone knew meant the resort towns and hamlets dotting the countryside of Sullivan County in the Catskills, "the borscht belt."

Some of the girls were fortunate enough to actually get away to "the mountains" in the summertime. They joined the long trek from the city along "the derma road," as Route 17 came to be known.[21] Those families who could afford it might spend a week in the country at a hotel, or they might stay at a boarding house, a step below a modest hotel, such as the one my mother ran, where she called herself, "chief cook and bottle-washer." (Today it would be advertised as an "old country inn.")

Raye Cohen, whose father worked as a *shoykhet* (a ritual slaughterer) in Swan Lake during the summer season, spent her vacation in a *kokhaleyn* (literally meaning to cook for oneself, but referring to summer cottages or bungalows where vacationers did their own housekeeping).

It was during their teen years that many lifelong relationships developed among the girls, among many of the girls and boys who later married each other, and among couples. Some friends, still not bored—or bored with each other after more than fifty years—still spend several weeks together in the country, in the mountains—the Catskills—in the summertime.

The women reconstructed an oddly peaceful scenario of their teenage years, set, as they were, in the midst of wartime. The war was unreal to them—and they were naïve. Shirley Donowitz reminded me of a favorite pastime, the Ouija board. "That was the big game, we even believed it." The Ouija board, they convinced themselves, was able to tell them where a loved one was and, even more important, if he (almost never she) was safe. When my brother went overseas I gave him a cigarette case which he told me he would keep in his breast pocket, over his heart, at all times. I convinced myself that it was a talisman that would protect him.

Although the realities of war were sanitized and glamorized in films, from which most of the girls got their images of combat, some of the women who had friends and relatives in the armed forces remember anxiously awaiting "v-mail," letters that looked like aerograms. They recall having nightmares in which bullets pinged by and bombs fell, exploding around them. "World War II made me cry many times," Shirley Donowitz says, "my friend's oldest brother was killed in action, and an aunt's brother got killed. I was very frightened after that." Claire Moses remembers "being totally absorbed by the war." Her idols were the war correspondents because their lives seemed so exotic. "We couldn't travel," she says. "Far away places were only in books, they weren't real."

If the harsher memories were particularly repressed, if the women have vague memories of the war itself, their memories of how it affected their social lives stands out in high relief. For the older adolescents this was an even greater crisis than the war itself. Shirley Donowitz says:

> We were deprived of dates, all the fun. I read books, and girls
> have dates and meet guys and have choices—you like this

one, that one. There were very few guys around. I remember
walking around the park and just crying and crying. When I
had my Prom I was really upset, my boyfriend was in the
navy, I had to ask my brother's friend.

Claire Moses's clearest memory of the war is of the boys leaving the
neighborhood. "All the young men were coming to say goodbye," she
says sadly. Bea Siegel sounds angry:

> The party was cancelled. The older boys were gone, when
> this time should have been the most memorable social time
> of my life, a time for many boyfriends and experimentation
> with relationships.

The women said: "We never learned how to socialize"—"We felt
cheated"—"Our social lives had collapsed"—"Our teen years were
interrupted, we couldn't make plans"—"The war limited our choices"—
"We were shortchanged . . ."

While they were referring to their social lives, the girls growing up
in the forties were not only shortchanged in opportunities for social
development and in their choice of available males, they were cheated in
other ways as well. Although they were not consciously aware of it then,
it is apparent to them today that their life choices were narrowly limited.
They had accepted as a simple fact that whatever they were going to
do—or to be—would be temporary and subordinate to being wives and
mothers. "That was what was expected," Flo Grosswirth says, "and
what we expected." As it turned out, they were right; almost all were
married and had children within a few years of their high school graduations. Raye Cohen says:

> As a girl, I couldn't go beyond being exactly as my parents
> expected me to be which was to marry Jewish, teach my chil-
> dren to carry on the traditions, and conduct myself in a rea-
> sonably Jewish manner. It's as if there was no other way. You
> never pondered about it, you never questioned why or
> thought any differently than the way they expected of you.

In fact, Raye Cohen, like Eleanor Chernick and Irma Greenbaum,
was among those who "held out," that is, did not marry right away.
Irma actually moved away from home before she married, a *shande*, a
disgrace for the family in those days. She held a variety of jobs, beginning an interesting pattern that would persist throughout her life; dur-

ing the war, she delivered messages for Western Union. Raye tried to get into the WACs but was rejected because she was too thin. She laughs at this because she was trim, but far from the anorexic look that has become the ideal today. And Eleanor Chernick actually joined the navy. She became one of the few Jewish girls from Brownsville who joined the 400,000 women who served in the armed forces during the war.[22]

Eleanor graduated from high school in June 1941, just six months before the United States entered the war. Because she couldn't afford to attend college as a full-time student, she took a course offered by Sperry-Rand in the use of a bookkeeping machine, the comptometer. No one in Eleanor's family was eligible to serve in the war because the men were married and had children, and it wasn't until later in the war that married men were drafted. All the neighborhood boys she knew "were being called up, and I felt," she says, "that just because I was born without a penis I wasn't being called into the service. I felt that wasn't fair."

What finally convinced Eleanor to enlist was the GI Bill, which was passed when she was about nineteen. Eleanor served as a WAVE for more than a year and a half. She was trained as a nurse's aide at the Bethesda Naval Hospital, worked in a hospital at the Brooklyn Navy Yard and was later transferred to a ten thousand-bed hospital for war injured in San Diego. Although she'd had an interest in nursing during high school, her notion of the career was romantic; she found this experience overwhelming and "disillusioning." Hoping to transfer, she applied and was accepted for training back at Bethesda, in laboratory technology. She remained there for the duration of her enlistment (and, incidentally, took blood from Secretary of State Cordell Hull). Eventually Eleanor did indeed make very good use of her veterans benefits under the GI Bill.

Like Eleanor, few of these Brownsville women who graduated from high school during the forties, even those who had taken the academic college preparatory course, actually began college right after high school, and all who did dropped out. They were bright; many of the girls had been in the "R.A."—the Rapid Advance track, homogeneously grouped classes for high academic achievers. They completed the eighth grade in one term and graduated from junior high school half a year early. In spite of this, however, most were discouraged, by their parents among others, from enrolling in the college-bound course of study. Eleanor Chernick was so determined to take the academic course, she says, that she "fought" bitterly with her mother over it, but in the end lost the argument. Bea Siegel remembers her mother asking, "What do you have to go to college for, to learn to wash diapers?" Bea says, a bit wistfully, "College was not in my future."

It was not only their parents but school counselors who "guided" girls away from the academic track; that is, if the girls were not, as Irma Greenbaum was, simply neglected by them. She loved music, wanted to go to Juilliard, but, "I didn't think I was college material and had no one to direct me." This unfortunate but common phenomenon was not limited to Brownsville schools nor did it originate in the forties. Around the turn of the century women who wanted to go to college were told, sarcastically, that proper schooling for women should be in "motherhood"; what they needed were "Ma" degrees.[23]

Bea Larkin thinks that if she had gone to college she would have become a social worker. She was bright, but had no confidence in her ability. Her math and science teachers discouraged her from pursuing an academic course, another experience that was all too common. (Almost ten years later Lila Perlmutter had a similar encounter with her science teacher. He told her to "forget about it" when she said that she wanted to become an astronomer. He said, "No man would let a woman, and certainly not a Jew, into *that* club.") Minette Cutler could be speaking for the others when she says, "There was always something that pushed me away from getting an education . . . I lost out."

Like Minette, Claire Moses regrets not being able to attend college, but most of the women thought of careers (the ultimate reason for attending college) as something that would be only "for the duration," that is, only until they married or, if they were willing to acknowledge it, "just in case. . . ." Few thought of jobs as careers or professions. Claire Moses briefly considered becoming an army nurse (a recruiter had offered her free tuition) but she would have had to join the army for at least two years. "My parents would have been hysterical," she says. In both Eleanor Chernick's 1941 Jefferson High School graduating class, and the class of 1950, almost a decade later, a small number of the women said that they wanted to become teachers. Teaching and nursing were the only professions mentioned by the forties group of women,[24] professions that were, and still are, compatible with family obligations.

In contrast with many working women today, the Brownsville women who came of age in the 1940s did not have conflicting career and domestic expectations. Unlike many of their own mothers and other women of the working poor, or married women today who work and raise their children simultaneously, they expected their pattern of employment to be serial; work and family roles would be held sequentially.[25] While we believe today that this pattern has serious implications for career success and achievement, it simply wasn't an issue for them.

Feminist historians have written about the accomplishments of many exceptional women who went into nontraditional fields in the first half of this century, but they were quite rare among working-class Jewish women. Generally, the exceptional women were from more privileged backgrounds where their life chances were greatly enhanced by having been born into middle or upper-class families, or into professional families with traditions of higher education. I wonder whether any, among the sprinkling of women in that 1941 graduating class who aspired to become scientists or doctors, actually achieved their goals? (I can't help hoping that, somehow, they did.)

The Brownsville girls' ambitions were modest and, it seems today, their career plans were most reasonable. But if the plans involved college or professions, they soon found that they were fantasies—impossible to realize. The women weren't challenging the social order or trying to open tightly closed doors, but their aspirations were thwarted by a number of determining factors. The most compelling were poverty and propriety.

Of these hurdles, poverty was cited most often as the reason the women didn't pursue professional careers: the need to help support the family or to put a brother through college. In Minette Cutler's case, it was three brothers. Minette says:

> I wanted to go to college but I didn't because of my three brothers. My parents felt I was going to be a secretary and my brothers would go to college. My ambition for college ended with a commercial course.

Shirley Donowitz tells an almost identical story:

> My brothers went to college. My mother did not motivate me to go to college; my mother felt that the man makes a living, he's the one to worry about his future. I loved children. Teaching was in the back of my head because when we played school I was always the teacher. But I decided to definitely be a secretary. If you worked, you gave some money into the house.

Although Terry Apter's family received allotment checks, they weren't enough to make ends meet and Terry got her after-school job in the bridal shop. Not surprisingly, doing her homework after such a long and exhausting day had an effect on Terry's grades; she didn't even consider college. And there were other stories of hardship.

Norma Ellman's father died when she was only three. Although she graduated from Tilden High School with an academic diploma, it was impossible for her not to work. Florence Kusnetz attended a two-week orientation to the dietician's program at Pratt Institute. At the end of the two weeks, when the tuition had to be paid, she decided that she couldn't continue. "I felt it wasn't fair. There were three other children in the family," Florence says. "It was guilt, I needed to bring money home." The women echo each other repeatedly—they simply *had* to work (although Florence says that she isn't sure whether she actually had to or *felt* she had to). Both Norma and Florence subsequently took business courses.

Another obstacle that prevented the Brownsville girls from even thinking about career possibilities had to do with the question of "propriety." That Katie Stavans was a risk taker was evident by her choice of careers; she wanted to be an airline stewardess when it was still, in the early 1940s, a comparatively new field. Her mother "wouldn't hear of it," Katie says: not because it was dangerous, but because it wasn't considered "suitable." Norma Ellman wanted to be an actress. Even the long tradition of excellent Yiddish theater in New York didn't make the profession acceptable to her mother.

In spite of the important role nurses played in the war, even nursing was strongly discouraged at that time, if not prohibited. Flo Grosswirth's parents said "it was out of the question." They were appalled that if she became a nurse she would have to carry bedpans and look at naked men. The idea was not only a total offense to their pride, and not only beneath the aspiring "middle-classness" of the Jewish culture, it was also a violation of the principle of *tzni'ut*, a "concept that embraces privacy, modesty, restraint, decency and chasteness."[26] This attitude would change, but it was still the case in 1950 when Lillian Pollack graduated from high school. Only six women in her graduating class of 420 listed nursing as their chosen profession, less than two percent. "In those days," Flo says, "Irish girls became nurses."

Almost everything, it seemed, was "out of the question." Two of the women wanted to become fashion designers. Fayge Lubin went to the Central High School of Needle Trades with this goal in mind, but became a milliner since at that time (when women wore hats) it seemed a more practical occupation. Bea Siegel's parents forbade her to enter the garment industry as anything but a clerical worker. They feared she would get "stuck" in the factory. It isn't difficult to understand that they wanted her to avoid the harsh factory conditions and have the more genteel occupation of secretary. Although the most "spectacular"[27] occupational gains for women during the war years were in factory work, Jews were still struggling to get *out* of the factories and sweatshops. Factory work was acceptable only if there were no other options. In fact, contrary to the image of "Rosie the Riveter"—which by now has become so much a part of the folk culture that a children's book was recently written about the women who "worked in shipyards, aircraft plants and munitions factories, as police officers, taxicab drivers, welders, electricians and boilermakers"[28]—among the Brownsville girls, only Fayge Lubin and Jean Bleckner (who took a summer job) worked in factories during the war.

In addition to poverty and propriety, there was a final, significant, limitation placed upon the aspirations of the Brownsville women: the possibilities for women were still extremely limited. Women continued to have few career options. Whatever changes that took place were understood to be "for the duration," for the family, an extension of the "role of nurturing wife and mother,"[29] to bring the men home more quickly. However, one permanent change affected the Brownsville women directly. More women became clerical workers as that field expanded and became increasingly feminized. By 1950, more than one in four women were clerical workers, a fact that was reflected in the commercial course of study pursued by almost all of the forties women.

In Jefferson High School's 1941 graduating class, 239 of the 477 young women whose career goals were noted in the yearbook aspired to some variation of office work: secretary, stenographer, bookkeeper: more than fifty percent. In 1950 the numbers were about the same and, indeed, at some time in their lives all of the forties women, without exception and regardless of the course they had followed in high school, worked at office-related jobs.[30] Rae Mirsky says: "Not me. I loved to work in an office, but the people who really wanted choices felt bad."

Brownsville girls faced extensive prohibitions that originated in their culture and social class and were exacerbated by the sexism of American society. If there were few career options for women, these Brownsville girls, Jewish and poor, growing up in a culture dominated by the orthodox tradition, had fewer still. A "nice Jewish girl" could go "to business," that is, be a secretary or clerk, or she could go into one acceptable profession—teaching.

The result was that most of the forties girls took the commercial course and began working in offices when they were still in high school. After school they took the El to Downtown Brooklyn or Manhattan, to their part-time jobs, and returned home early in the evening to do their homework. When they graduated, all of "the girls" worked as clerks, secretaries, bookkeepers, stenographers, typists, office managers, comptometer operators.

"But so what?" Blu Greenberg asked. They were "waiting for Mr. Right to come along and take over where parental support left off."[31] And he did. The war ended, they left their jobs and set up housekeeping—for the Brownsville girls, as elsewhere, there soon was a "return to normalcy."

Roslyn Bowers (seated) and friends

Claire Spielman Moses (left),
and Bea Meiseles Siegel (right), with Nancy

Bea Meiseles Siegel in Nanny Goat Park

Twirlers Linda Gralla Brasco (left), and Valerie Gordon Greenberg (right)

Roslyn Wohl Bowers (left), and friend at high school graduation

Florence Moglinsky Kusnetz (left),
and friend Selma Siskind at 556 Dumont Avenue

Terry Apter

Roslyn Wohl Bowers in front of egg store next to entry to her apartment

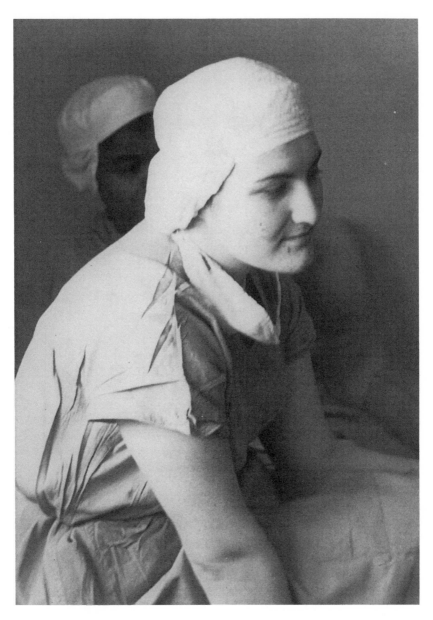

Rhoda Bratkowsky Nemerofsky, Beth El Hospital, Brooklyn, 1959

Linda Gralla Brasco (left), and Arlene Gralla Feldman (right) at Arlene's Sweet Sixteen party

Carole Bell Ford, Elaine Epstein Cohen, and friend Judy (left to right)

Carole Bell Ford (seated fourth from left) with Club Jills and friends, 1952

"Beatty" Bea Finkelstein Larkin (left) and friends (from left to right), Edith Dreizer Harris, Doris Find Elias, Alice Asher Pinkas, and Mary Machulum Levine

CHAPTER FIVE

The Cult of Domesticity

Coming of Age in the Fifties

The message from everywhere was: "Learn to make a good
meat loaf."

—Linda Gralla Brasco

Linda Brasco's mother was gentile but Linda was, she says, brought
up "without religion."

Linda's mother was Russian Orthodox; her father was a Jew.
Because these circumstances were so unusual at the time her parents
married, it is tempting to think of Linda as atypical for this study. However, Linda and her sister Arlene Feldman were raised in what was still
a predominantly Jewish, if changing, Brownsville. In the 1950s, when
the girls were coming of age, the community was still dominated by the
powerful Jewish culture. All of their friends, most of their schoolmates,
and most of their teachers were Jewish.[1] Arlene, in fact, eventually converted to Judaism when she married.

If Linda and Arlene developed attitudes and values that were significantly different from their one hundred percent Jewish contemporaries,
I have not been able to identify them. Like the other Brownsville girls,
both sisters were raised with the understanding that women, as well as
men, would become engaged in worthwhile pursuits and would lead
meaningful lives. For the women, this meant family; their goals were to
facilitate their husbands' efforts to achieve material and/or intellectual
success, and to nurture their children. "When a woman gets married she
doesn't work. The husband earns a living for you," Elaine Cohen's

mother told her. "The idea," Rochelle Feld explains, "was that you would have the babies and he would do the hard work."

What does make Linda Brasco unique in this study of the Brownsville women is that she, perhaps more than any of the other women, came to epitomize the "feminine mystique": the image, conceptualized by Betty Freidan, of the homemaker busily and hummingly going about her daily routine; the image, Freidan said, to which American women tried to conform. The problem was that the image did not fit the reality of women's lives as homemakers, which was often accompanied by an odd, generalized malaise.[2] Linda is also unique among the Brownsville women who participated in this study because of her ability to articulate the frustrations of a woman who had perfected her attributes in all of the categories—body, hair, clothes, voice, skin, movement, emotion, ambition—that Susan Brownmiller has catalogued in *Femininity*.[3]

Linda Brasco struggled with the same strange lack of self-esteem that some beautiful women, like Marilyn Monroe, are said to have. They question their self-worth because, it seems to them, that their value is related to something that was not achieved, but is accidental to their biology. "You are what you think you are," Linda says. "We were never affirmed, so I haven't gotten out of those conflicts; I'm still stuck in the fifties."

Linda, as adolescents do, spent much of her teen years in trying to form and consolidate her self-image, trying to answer the question, "who am I?" Linda's self-image, her identity—that part of ourselves that becomes our frame of reference for what is "me" and what is "not-me"[4]—was reinforced within the high school, analogous as it was to the broader society. If her biology was, in fact, not her inevitable destiny, by the time she graduated from Thomas Jefferson High School in 1958, she was convinced that it was and she had become, in her words, the "all-American dream girl."

An examination of the *Aurora*, the Thomas Jefferson High School Yearbook for June 1958, clearly reveals the issues on the minds of Americans less than one year after the launching of Sputnik. The overall graphic theme of the issue was "Space"; the front cover has an imprint of a satellite; the frontispiece shows lunar landscapes. A letter to the graduates reads:

> Due to Russian achievements in the scientific field, many people
> have expressed doubts as to the adequacy of our educational
> system. They advocate that we emulate the Russians by empha-
> sizing the science courses to the exclusion of the humanities.[5]

The title page shows a scientist holding a test tube; nearby a rocket is taking flight; and a diagram of charged energy particles surrounds the scene. The scientist is, of course, male. There was probably little or no thought given to representing a scientist as female, or showing both, a male and a female. It was the end of the 1950s. The sexes were considered to be opposites, and if they were not officially segregated in their academic courses, most were tracked into different streams and differentiated in the high school in many other ways as well. The first photo you see as you turn the yearbook pages is of the Principal, Mr. Irving Cohen, "ready to take charge of our galaxy," the caption reads. He is shown with his Secretary, Mrs. Kramer, pad in hand.

Linda was co-captain of the "Twirlers," more skilled than the cheerleaders because of their proficiency with the baton. She was also active in other clubs and popular in school. The "Twirlers" (which, incidentally, had a male teacher as advisor) was only one among a number of gender-differentiated clubs. There were also Boosters and Cheer Leaders: female. There was "Kagathos," the honor society of the Health Education Department: female. The "Hostess Club": female, of course. The "Amplifier Squad": of course, male. There was a "Mixed Chorus" and a "Girls' Chorus," but no "Boys' Chorus." Although the orchestra had a large number of girls, mostly playing strings, the concert band had only a sprinkling, in woodwinds. Happily, girls did better in governance and service committees, and there were four girls in the math club.

Six pages are devoted to "athletics" in the Yearbook. On the first of these is the picture of a "Twirler." The following pages, which show sports activities, include only males (the basketball team was, by this time, predominantly and disproportionately black). In the high school, there were no teams for the girls. Those girls interested in athletics, such as Lois Rusakow and Harriet Portnoy, were thought of, and thought of themselves, as tomboys. The final two pages of the sports section, entitled "Just Gym Dandy," show the girls—finally. But they are not involved in sports activities. The girls assume cute or balletic poses and there are the cheerleaders again, holding their megaphones aloft. The hidden message, what is not stated overtly but is implied, is eloquent and articulate. As my friend Myra Sorin, whose yearbook this was, says, it was, "Look pretty, stay in the background, root for your man."[6]

Linda Brasco's life history, like that of the other Brownsville women who came of age in the fifties, was shaped by such messages and images both from inside and outside the school. It was shaped by all of the socializing agencies of society, formal and informal, in concert: family, church, community, government, schools, media. Linda had become the epitome of the "good girl." She was promised that she "would be taken care of" if she became "the perfect wife and mother, if she learned to make a good meat loaf," and if, she adds, using the romantic phraseology of the period, "I hitched my wagon to a star."

The women who were reaching adulthood in the 1950s entered a frustrating time; I know, I was one of them.

"A World Well Lost," is the title of Elayne Rapping's review of an oral history of the 1950s. When I saw her title I thought, "I wish I'd said that." It seemed to express exactly my own view of the decade, redeemed in retrospect only by the birth of my two children. I understood completely why she hadn't been interested at first in reading a book about "dull years and even duller lives."[7] However, when she viewed the decade in the context of major changes that were to take place, she found the story an important one with interesting incongruities.

We experienced astonishing contradictions during the fifties, a decade that accommodated both Senator Joseph McCarthy's neofascistic purges and the historic and groundbreaking liberal rulings of the Warren Court; the entry of rock and roll into pop culture and *The Sound of Music*, Rogers and Hammerstein's homage to traditional family values prevailing against totalitarianism; the Korean War and the "Domino theory," alongside the growth of the antinuclear and peace movements represented by SANE, (The National Committee for a Sane Nuclear Policy) and the Women's Strike for Peace. These were not historical abstractions to us. We watched McCarthy on TV, we celebrated the Warren Court, we were not sure about how we felt about rock and roll, we loved the Trapp Family, we waited for our boyfriends and husbands to get home from Korea, and then we marched on picket lines protesting the nuclear fallout that was getting into our babies' milk bottles.

The "fifties" probably began when the World War II ended and, most agree, concluded with the counterculture movement of the sixties. It began with a tone of hysterical urgency in celebration of the "return to normalcy" with the "traditional" family at its center, although data show that the "traditional" family of the 1950s was a new phenomenon, a historical anomaly. It was qualitatively different from any other period in American history because "all the trends characterizing the rest of the twentieth century suddenly reversed themselves."[8]

Images of the ideal domestic environment and the ideal family were created, defined, and relentlessly promoted in the 1950s with the obsessive quality of a cult. These images, with which the girls were bombarded, declared and at the same time advanced the predominant ideology, or rather the "cult of domesticity,"[9] which became a transcending creed, linked intensely as it was to the perceived need for stability during the Cold War. In fact, as Elaine Tyler May explains, "the cold war ideology and the domestic revival" were "two sides of the same coin."[10]

The "family values" upon which the "cult of domesticity" was being constructed were congruent with the values of the traditional Jewish culture of Brownsville and both were joined, even more firmly than in the previous decade, with energy provided by the Cold War. They forged a strong chemical bond, as "the family seemed to offer a psychological fortress," a protection against the dangers of communism. Nothing else, May wrote, "on the surface of postwar America explains the rush of young Americans into marriage, parenthood and traditional gender roles," except the relationship that developed between "political and familial values."[11] And there were no groups in America that were exempt from pressures of the domestic revival, and certainly not Jews who were still reeling from the decimating effects of the Holocaust.[12]

Neither the Brownsville girls who came of age in the forties nor those of the fifties had been prepared to have choices. Like the women of the previous decade, but with even more certainty, those who approached adulthood in the postwar period were told to prepare themselves for domestic bliss. They were told that there was no need to prepare themselves for a career, that they could "find *everything* in marriage."[13] They learned, as Lila Perlmutter did, what was expected of them—and what was not. "They had no expectations for me, because I was a girl—beyond marriage, of course." Zena Bloom's aspiration was the domestic American dream: to have a house in the country and two children. She had even decided on their names and their genders, one of each. "I was molded into a pattern," Zena says, "I didn't deviate too much, I never thought I had a choice." Lois Rusakow says, with the same quality of passivity: "I just fell into my life."

Domesticity, idealized, was promoted by all of the popular media: women's magazines, movies, and the greatest, newest persuader, television. As TV became a boom industry it also became a potent tool for socialization.[14] We might not be able to prove that television leads directly to specific behaviors but we know that it teaches, and we know how it teaches: television can motivate interest, it can present models, it can reinforce lessons through repetition and through visual images. These are the very strategies that teachers use in the classroom.

In the fifties, as we were enjoying television parties, we were also learning the dogma of the cult. I can remember when the first of our friends in Club Jills got a TV set, complete with magnifier. We all gathered at Marlene Litsky's house to watch the shows of the fifties that are considered kitsch today: *Ozzie and Harriet, Father Knows Best, The Donna Reed Show*. We didn't know it, but we were being taught. We were receiving lessons about what women looked like, what they did, what they thought. And we were also getting lessons in consumerism. We learned all of the things we needed to *buy* and to *have* in the ideal household in order to act out our domestic roles. The Brownsville girls who lived in families that were desperately aspiring to middle-classness were vulnerable to these gender stereotypes. At their best, the TV mothers depicted caring, competent women—to the Brownsville girls they were Americanized (no accents) and secularized *balebostes*—who were always at home and rarely made a mistake in their job as ideal wife and mother. It was these women that the girls were watching as TV sets made their way into Brownsville homes in the 1950s. It was shows like these on which the fiction of the "typical American family" relied and which gave Zena Bloom her romantic vision of a picture-perfect house in the country. It was a TV picture.

Hollywood, even more powerful then, before television's preeminence, promoted these images as well. Films of the fifties did depict a few career or professional women. Fewer, however, than previously. And the weekly movies the Brownsville girls ritualistically attended set the standard for beauty—for Ruth Berman who was "chubby"; for Rhoda Nemerofsky who was "always on a diet"; for Lillian Wellen who was "too tall." Martha Opitz worried about whether she would "attract a man." The movies, she says, had a major impact upon her. She became "very romantic and spent a lot of time fantasizing."

Like Martha, I was a movie addict. I remember the strong and capable women—played by Myrna Loy, Rosalind Russell, Katherine Hepburn—but roles that portrayed such women were rare. More common were the women-as-sex-symbols—Marilyn Monroe and her imitators—or women who were sexy and pretty—Elizabeth Taylor—or women who were stunningly sexy—Ava Gardner. Sexy women were desirable, but it was the wholesome girl next door—Jeanne Crain, Debbie Reynolds, or

Jane Powell (my idol, she could really sing)—who was mentally healthy: emotional, submissive, and dependent upon men.[15] In contrast, one of the girls described a friend, a "tomboy" who must have had "psychological" problems because she didn't conform to people's expectations:

> Even though she was feminine and liked to dress and was very curvy, she was very scholastic. And she was always debating, twenty-four hours a day. She was confrontational. She was athletic too, she used to be able to climb a fence. And she was intimidating because she was tough and independent.

As it still does today, the print media reinforced stereotypes not only through articles but in advertising. And, at the same time, it turned the pervasive ideology of the fifties into revenue.[16] There was a heightened commercialization, a media blitz, in fact, of marriage and family life. Recently, a reviewer described an exhibit tracing women's image in advertising. He wrote that it vividly demonstrated the growing feminization of consumption over a one-hundred-year period as women were placed in the "center ring of the cacophonous circus known as the American consumerist society."[17] In the 1950s, the homemaker image, promoted by advertisers and commercial interests, found a lucrative market in selling the domestic ideal to the ideal domestic.[18] Who can forget Betty Furness and the modern kitchen with its appliances and a pantry full of products that the housewife couldn't do without?

Throughout this century, advertising had been increasingly directed at women and in the fifties, since women were marrying at younger and younger ages, the newly discovered teen market became the target. Exploitation of the teen/women's market began with the commercialization of the wedding celebration itself, but no aspect of the process, from courtship to setting up home, was overlooked.[19] *Seventeen* magazine became more and more important in the marriage trade in promoting the "hope chest." "Educational" films by home furnishing companies were shown in Home Economics classes.[20] The formal "modern white wedding" had existed before, but after World War II a full scale wedding industry was put in place. Bridal registries and showers became the norm, *Brides* magazine was published, Emily Post prepared a new guide, and films such as *Father of the Bride* gave the girls a concrete image to emulate. Elaborate weddings, "affairs" as they were called, were in keeping with a tradition that began in Jewish communities early in the century, making it "hard to resist . . . America's bridal culture."[21] By the

1950s, Brownsville weddings, along with the rest of the country's, were stereotypically grand occasions and had become one of the symbols of middle-class status.[22] Forty-year-old posed photos are proudly displayed in the homes of the Brownsville women today, pictures of themselves, many still teenagers or just barely out of their teens, and their brand new husbands. The brides appear to rise up amidst a cascade of white satin, which falls in carefully arranged folds from the trains of their wedding gowns to rest in a carefully draped pool around their feet.

Many of the Brownsville girls reaching adulthood in the fifties had lived through two major upheavals: the Depression and World War II. Even if they were young children at the time and did not directly experience these alarming events, their families experienced lasting and sobering effects. And the world of the 1950s appeared more perilous than it had ever been before. The girls remembered the A-bomb drills, which had replaced air raid drills in the schools. Other dangers, the girls were told, lurked everywhere—from the real and immense dangers of fallout, radiation, or even a third world war, to the trivial and microscopic dangers of germs and body odors—bad breath, underarm and vaginal odors.[23] The decade was fraught with an excitement, a tension, that was heightened because so much was forbidden.

Few warnings were as ominous to the Brownsville girls in their teens as warnings about sex. Those who took the ultimate risk, as many did, could become pregnant; I remember my mother saying about a neighbor's daughter, with all of the solemnity the situation deserved, that "she got caught." In one girl's club it was kept a grave secret that a member had become pregnant.[24] Her life might have been ruined had it been known, because she would surely have been labelled a tramp. At the very least, a girl known to be too "easy" would get a "reputation" and might no longer be eligible, marriageable. At a time when marriage was everything, a tarnished reputation was not trivial; it was calamitous.

Beneath the idealized and romanticized version of marriage was yet another view, a cynical "marketplace view of sexuality," in which, in its crudest form, sex was a commodity purchased by marriage.[25] (I remember my sister actually saying to me: "Why buy the cow when the milk is free?") The Brownsville girls were trapped in the familiar but intensified dilemma raised by a double standard and contradictory messages. Boys were encouraged to "play the field," they didn't understand any part of "no." They were told, in fact, and were convinced, that no *didn't* mean no, that, rather, a nice girl "wanted to" but couldn't "give in" too easily. She was supposed to be seductive and demure at the same time. She had to be coaxed, or a boy would think of her as "loose." But she was in a double bind: if she was seductive and "gave in," she was loose; if she didn't, she was a tease.

Sexuality, like everything else that was directed toward women, led to the same point: safety was in marriage and family; safety for the individual, safety for society.[26] Marriage and family, it was insisted, were the bedrock of our society, the foundation of capitalism. The "fifties family" became an icon, for the danger from communist subversion, from "pinko commies," the McCarthyites told us, was all around us. The Cold War and domesticity were blatantly joined in a *Life* magazine cover story which showed a young just-married couple; snug in their very own bomb shelter, secure because they had each other, a supply of water, canned goods and a battery-powered generator.[27] The family was the only thing that could truly stem the tide of what commonly came to be known as the "red menace."

One comedian, Milt Kamen, had a difficult time taking the image of a "red menace" seriously, and constructed a routine about a "giant tomato" that was threatening the world. But for many Brownsville families it was no laughing matter, because they were victims of the surveillance, wiretaps, loyalty oaths, and purges. Those Brownsville women who were politically aware, some whose families were socialist or leftist-leaning, were particularly sensitive to the neofascistic threat that sat just below a veneer of normalcy. Martha Opitz's parents and others, including some friends and members of my family, found their civil liberties seriously jeopardized. Their phones were tapped, they were "visited" periodically, or followed by the FBI. The ordeal of my cousins, the parents of Carl Bernstein of Watergate fame, is recounted in his book, *Loyalties*.[28] It left Carl and other "red diaper" babies such as Martha Opitz, who "rebelled against politics," with permanent scars.

Some of the girls were particularly and profoundly affected by the plight of Julius and Ethel Rosenberg, who were executed as spies, albeit in different ways: Dolores Plaxen was embarrassed that they were Jews and "wouldn't sign a petition"; Doris Levinson identified with them and others who were "persecuted in the witch hunt." I wanted to view them in their twin coffins, at the I. J. Morris Funeral Home on Rockaway Parkway and Church Avenue. (In sympathy, surely. But with morbid interest, too? Probably.) I dragged my boyfriend along and we stood on a very long line which extended almost the full length of Rockaway

Parkway, a very long block. Later, his brother was furious; he was in law school and was afraid that our having been there would, somehow, have negative repercussions for him. This was not an unreasonable concern at the time. The FBI, as we now know, was taking photographs so that they could identify anyone who had attended the viewing or the funeral.

The Civil Rights movement also caught the attention and generated the participation of many Brownsville Jews. It was completely in keeping with their history and value system: with their disposition toward social justice, toward communal responsibility, and toward the principal of *tikn olam*, the repair and improvement of the world.[29] For Brownsville youth there were numerous progressive organizations, such as the Young Progressives of America, the Labor Youth League, and the "Joe York Club," that took up the cause of the Negro, "idealized," Martha Opitz thinks, as "noble and wronged." Roslyn Bowers and Sylvia Zinn became Civil Rights activists in their teens. Sylvia had been radicalized by her boyfriend's brother, Howard Zinn, today a well-known historian. "Howard made me aware," Sylvia says. "He made me start thinking." The resurgence of feminism, characterized as women's liberation, had also begun, however feebly, in the wake of the Civil Rights Movement.[30] Violations against other groups who faced discrimination, such as women, became more evident as it became apparent that civil rights was but one aspect of the broader category of human rights.

"Women's Lib," however, did not penetrate Brownsville's protective borders. "Be like your mother!" Arlene Feldman says. This was the persistent message in the 1950s. Doris Levinson adds, "You just accepted that this is what you do." And the Brownsville girls had a firmly fixed image of their mothers. "She was always cooking, cleaning, shopping. She was the typical Jewish mother, always in her apron," Elaine Cohen says.[31] With respect to gender differentiation, Brownsville hadn't budged; it was in the same place that it had been in the forties and before the war.

Brownsville was the same in other ways, as well. In the 1950s, although in the midst of irreversible change from the community it had been earlier in its history, it was still mostly Jewish and still had its small-town character. Isabel Cohen says:

> Brownsville was provincial. Everything was in a small
> nucleus. I was taught in Brownsville, met a boy from
> Brownsville. When I got married and my husband was

offered a fellowship at Duke University, how could I leave my
mother? I couldn't have a baby without my mother nearby,
couldn't go off to a far place like Duke.

Although families had begun to disperse in what Jonathan Rosen,
an editor of *The Forward*, termed "the re-diasporization of American
Jews,"[32] the girls were still able to visit with aunts, uncles, cousins, who
lived only a short walk away (many still did not have telephones in their
homes). Ruth Kesslin's grandparents lived "upstairs": it was still common for more than one generation to share a two-family home. Zena
Bloom's family all lived in the same apartment building.

Like the forties women, Roslyn Bowers says:

> We spent our time out in the street. We went into the yard,
> calling up to our friends. We didn't have a phone, we didn't
> have to be formal. It was a more open, accessible environment.

When they were teenagers, Doris Levinson recalls, "our friends
did everything together." Sometimes they didn't even part for meals;
"A bag came down on a string from the fire escape," Harriet Portnoy
says, "and we ate on the stoop." Doris continues: "We walked to
school, studied, went to school dances, club meetings, house parties."
Like the forties girls, they went to the park together, to Betsy Head
Pool, to Brighton Beach. Elaine Cohen, my friend from Club Jills days
asked me:

> Don't you remember, we hung out in the little park on Hop-
> kinson Avenue with the boys on Friday nights? My father
> wanted me to stay home but when he went out to play cards
> my mother would send me out so I could be with my friends.
> On Saturdays we went to the movies at the Ambassador.

I did not remember the park but one thing I did remember, vividly,
was trying to learn to ride a bicycle. I never did learn, not properly. It
was too late: I was already thirteen and frightened to death when my
friends finally let go and I went careening down the street. Rochelle
Feld never even tried: "Girls don't ride bikes," she was told. Nor did
Isabel Cohen: "My father wouldn't permit us to have a bicycle. They
were too dangerous!"

Zena Bloom and her friends went to Ebbetts Field for Dodgers
games, and some of the girls actually played ball with the boys. Harriet
Portnoy says:

> I was always athletic but by high school most girls became
> girls; they gave up sports. They became spectators. They
> would sit on the bench rather than run around with the boys.

The girls who remained in Brownsville throughout the fifties were
still part of an authentic, living Jewish culture: of Yiddish speakers and
Yidishkeit. Many of their families were non-observant, or "partially
observant," as Roslyn Bowers said, but their identity as Jews was not
dependent for its existence solely upon the blood bond created by the
Holocaust or loyalty to the State of Israel. Every house had its *mezuz-
zahs* in the doorways and its *pushke*, its collection box, in the kitchen,
often for the Jewish National Fund or the United Jewish Appeal with its
blue Star of David. Many of their mothers "kept kosher"; if not, a
friend's mother did, and all the girls knew the rules. Everyone celebrated
the holidays. They got dressed up, even the girls from nonobservant
homes; they "played 'nuts'" on the street during Passover," Lois
Rusakow recalls. The girls wandered about with their friends during
Yom Kippur when it was forbidden to ride, to play music, to eat. They
stopped at the *shul*, Dolores Plaxen said, to see a parent or grandparent
who was ensconced there for the entire day. They visited the women in
the balconies, or sitting behind the *mehitzah*. My aunt, *Tante* Hudel,
examined my tongue on *Yom Kippur* for a white coating, to check
whether I was fasting. What the girls absorbed while engaging in these
and many other simple acts was a deep, visceral, internal realization of
their Jewishness, and their Jewish woman-ness.

Some of the girls went to neighborhood *schules* to study Yiddish
and Jewish culture; some studied Hebrew. Rhoda Nemerofsky refused to
go back to Hebrew school after "a falling out" with her Hebrew teacher.
He had a singularly narrow-minded reaction to a visit she made to a
church for a non-Jewish friend's confirmation. Rhoda says:

> I was never in a church before. I was excited about it so I told
> my Hebrew teacher. He said my parents were irresponsible
> that I should be allowed to go to a church. My parents didn't
> make me go back.

Hebrew was not a required course for girls and none of the girls
were studying to become *Bat Mitzvah*. Instead, their great rite of passage
was the "Sweet Sixteen" party which, for the more affluent, took on the
grandeur of a formal celebration. Some were held in hired halls, some in
restaurants or even in night clubs.

As they were coming of age, many aspects of their physical environment and culture were very much the same for the Brownsville girls of the forties and fifties since, in the fifties, some of the old ways lingered in the neighborhood. But there *were* differences, some subtle, some not so.[33]

The girls who came of age in the forties were closer to the immigrant generation. They had more direct experience of the Depression and the war. They were older when the horrors of the Holocaust were revealed. They were adults before the postwar/Cold War came to dominate American culture. In contrast with the forties women, more of the fifties women had parents who, if they were immigrants, were somewhat more acculturated and Americanized. And more were American born, better educated and more secular; Jews in America becoming Jewish-Americans.

As a group, the girls had higher educational expectations than the forties women, but their choice of careers was still extremely limited. It was precisely because there were two choices for Jewish girls—teaching or nursing—that Lillian Pollack didn't go to college. "I didn't know what I wanted to do but I knew I didn't want to do that," Lillian says. "I did not really care to do either one." But, in the fifties, a steadily increasing number of the girls did expect to go to college and did want to become teachers and nurses. They had learned to value education and also to assume that they had the rights that, in the Jewish culture, had previously been reserved for men.

This is not to say that education in the 1950s was as valued for Brownsville women as for men. Arlene Feldman's mother didn't expect her to go on to college. Her mother said, rather harshly, "I don't expect A's, you're no genius. Just graduate." A high school diploma would have been a major accomplishment a decade earlier; many of the forties women were the first women in their families to graduate from high school. In the fifties, however, many of the Brownsville women were the first women to earn college degrees.

Arlene Feldman did graduate from high school but, living down to her mother's expectations for her, did not go on to college, not then. Although more Brownsville women were going to college in the fifties, the proportion of women among American college students, which had risen in the early part of the century and would rise again, had declined. Of those who enrolled, about two-thirds dropped out,[34] and the fifties Brownsville women dropped out in just about the same proportion. In addition, the percentage of women who received professional degrees was lower in the fifties than at any time since before World War I. It was no secret that medical and law schools had very low quotas for women: five percent. The three Jewish girls who indicated these professional choices in the 1954 Yearbook, and the three in 1958, had an even slimmer chance of being accepted.[35] If things hadn't been that way, Rochelle Feld says, "I could have become a doctor or something outrageously different."

Rhoda Nemerofsky's mother did not want her to go to college. Rhoda says:

> In order to do it, in the environment that I grew up in, you
> had to have very strong self-determination because there was
> no encouragement. It was not an expectation by any stretch
> of the imagination.

Even in families that supported the notion of higher education for their girls, the boys were still favored—and the girls were still aware of it. Rochelle Feld says:

> My mother thought she's got to educate my brother because
> he'll have to support a wife. I would manage somehow . . .
> like saying, you can have what's left over.

Rochelle wanted to go to nursing school and, while her parents didn't object to nursing as a career, they couldn't afford to send both Rochelle and her brother to school. Although Rochelle had been born with a cleft palate and had a slight facial deformity, her parents were not overly concerned about whether she would marry or would be able to support herself. In fact, she did both.

For many of the Brownsville families, however, improved economic circumstances meant they no longer had to choose between educating either a son or a daughter, and higher education was becoming more acceptable for Jewish women. Some of the girls, Roslyn Bowers, Isabel Cohen, Ruth Berman, Doris Levinson, Martha Opitz, and others, were encouraged to go to college, although a few think that their friends, as much as their families, had a great deal to do with their decision. Lila Perlmutter says that all of her friends took a commercial course but "other groups of girls went to college. They all became teachers. I was amazed that all it took was a different group of friends."

The Brownsville girls who were coming of age in the 1950s experienced their rites of passage—makeup, high heeled shoes, sweet sixteens, cigarettes, high school graduations, first sexual encounters—in a different Brownsville than the girls of the earlier decade. While they agree, as Dolores Plaxen says, that Brownsville was "a safe place for a young girl," or as Elaine Cohen says, "a pretty good place to grow up," their individual memories tend to be less romanticized. Arlene Feldman's teen years were, she says, "a disaster." Ruth Kesslin's were "difficult." Sylvia Zinn had a "terrible homelife." She had a tyrannical, abusive father, who was "proud that he had a girl who looked like a *shiksa*, but he didn't want a girl." When he became angry with his wife or with Sylvia he would withhold money, capriciously, so that her mother had to take in "home work"; Sylvia helped her mother put hairpins on cards, or babysit, and took a part-time, after-school job, because her father wouldn't pay for the rental of her cap and gown for graduation. Neither does Dolores Plaxen remember happy teen years. "I thought that I wasn't entitled to my feelings. I was being a bad girl if I was complaining." But she resented living in the family's "railroad flat," an apartment where Dolly, as she was called, had no privacy.

In the 1950s Brownsville was still a poor community and, with the influx of disadvantaged minorities, was becoming poorer. But, Dolores's impressions notwithstanding, the Jewish population was not. Doris Levinson's recollections are more typical:

> I had no perception of poverty. There was always food, the
> fridge was stuffed. I always had clothes. We went to Radio
> City and to the Roxy, to the museums and planetarium. And
> we ate at Horn and Hardart's.

While the median annual income in the United States was $4,500 in the mid-fifties, in Brownsville it was less than $3,900. But compared to the marginal existence that many Jewish families had suffered there during the Depression (and in contrast with Brownsville's growing black population in the 1950s, whose median income was only $2,600[36]) the Jewish community was enjoying the relative prosperity of postwar expansion. Their families were generally more "comfortable," a common euphemism. As a group, the women who came of age in the fifties were not only less poor and further removed from the hardships of the Depression than the women of the earlier group, but many of the girls experienced the rising expectations that accompanied a rising standard of living. Doris Levinson's father had a car, a 1941 Plymouth. Roslyn Bowers's too: "My father had a car, I went to H.E.S. camp, we took a

bungalow in South Fallsburg. I thought we were rich." (Note that neither woman said, "Our *family* had a car.")

Unlike the forties women, many of the fifties women were highly
conscious of class and ethnic differences, their own and others', as they
saw Brownsville change from the insular Jewish community it had been
earlier. By the 1950s, it was already ethnically and racially heterogeneous.
A number of the women recall black families living nearby or on their
blocks. But judging from a sampling of representative Thomas Jefferson
High School yearbooks, there were also other ethnic groups moving into
the once-Jewish neighborhood. The black population of Brownsville
doubled between 1940 and 1950, and the data show that the Puerto
Rican population was also growing.[37] The percentage of blacks in the
Thomas Jefferson yearbooks reflects that trend, although the actual number of black graduates was tiny: there were only eight of a total of 799
graduates in 1941, and still only fifty blacks out of 561, predominantly
Jewish, graduates in 1958. (These figures are of high school *graduates*,
not blacks in the population of the school or in the community as a
whole.[38]) The number of black graduates in the years 1941 and 1950
were about the same, about one percent. By 1954 the number of black
graduates rose to three percent and to nine percent by 1958.

High school graduation remains an important rite of passage, even
today when so many go on to college. In the fifties, it was momentous,
a time of expectation that perhaps accounts for some of what, to me, is
the otherwise unaccountable nostalgia for the period; the girls were in
the midst of launching their adult lives. Some were having a taste of
independence through their first earned incomes and others were testing
out new freedoms, albeit very timidly by today's standards.

A number of the Brownsville girls were taking courses, tuition free,
at Brooklyn College. They knew very few people who went to out of
town schools. Isabel Cohen says:

> When my daughters started to go to college my mother said:
> "How come they're going away?' Why can't they go to
> Brooklyn College?" I said, "Ma, there's a world out there." I
> never knew about going away to sleep-away college.

Roslyn Bowers did know "someone who went to Cortland," a State
University college in upstate New York but decided that travelling all the
way from Brownsville to Hunter College on Manhattan's Upper East
Side, was getting far enough "away from the neighborhood."

Roslyn Bowers did not marry right out of school; she wanted to "spread her wings," she says. She knew she would marry; there was no hurry. Roslyn didn't actually move away from home until she was twenty-four, but in Brownsville, because it was still a *shande* for a woman to live alone, her parents "never told anyone." Bea Benjamin, too, got her own apartment. Both women were unusual. Elaine Cohen, on the other hand, was engaged before she graduated from high school, which was more common. Elaine failed a regents examination and would graduate with a general diploma unless she took the exam over again and passed. She didn't bother. She says, "I was getting married soon anyway; it didn't seem to matter."

Elaine was right. As early as the beginning of the decade, only marriage mattered. The media promoted the current psychological and sociological theories that held that any woman who did not fully embrace the ideal of home and family as her true vocation was not normal.[39] In the Cold War era, the image of the "normal" woman—Donna Reed, Harriet Nelson—was promoted by television, film, and the print media not only because it was profitable but because it was politically correct. It enforced a "striking conformity."[40] Betty Freidan concluded that, by the 1950s, the feminine mystique of the perfect and content woman-wife-mother-homemaker, had been elevated into a scientific religion.[41]

Because women's choices became more and more limited as the fifties progressed, the Brownsville girls found it difficult to believe that there could be an alternative to marriage. Tracking in the schools, guidance counselors and teachers reinforced their perception. "There were so many 'supposed-tos'," Ruth Berman says, that she was one of those who conformed to a life that was wrong for her. "I was born too soon."

The girls were convinced that they could not combine marriage and a serious career. If they tried, they were told, they would have to sacrifice the quality of one or the other. They would have "a token career or a token family"—or perhaps both.[42] If it was to be a choice, there was no choice. Whether they read *Seventeen* or books such as the *Guide for the Jewish Homemaker*, Brownsville girls were getting the same message. From an article in *Seventeen* titled "How to Be a Woman": "There is no office, lab, or stage that offers so many creative avenues or executive opportunities as that everyday place, the home"; from the *Guide*, a description of the challenges of the homemaker's "many sided" role: "She must be wife, nurse, mother, cook, confidante, teacher, diplomat, economist, companion, interior decorator, hostess." But she was not to worry, since there was a "whole shelf of books on the modern arts and sciences of homemaking available to her."[43]

The Brownsville girls did not need to be told that a well-functioning family relied on the woman who was exclusively committed to its health and survival. They did not have to be convinced that America needed them to teach the values of a free, democratic society to their children. They had been raised on variations of these themes. They already believed that the family depended upon the mother's dedication, they already knew that the survival of the culture rested with the woman. Brownsville girls could hardly resist the tide—no, the tidal wave—that carried them into domesticity. "Our image," Doris Levinson says, "was house, children, do some kind of charity work."

Arlene Feldman believes that "life was decided at the age of twelve"; she exaggerates by only two or three years. Certainly by the time they chose, or rather settled into their high school courses of study (since choice assumes freely selected preferences among alternatives), their lives were decided for some time to come. In eighth grade, Arlene worked for the guidance counselor, who was placing students in high schools. Arlene remembers that all of the boys were put in the academic track, while the girls, except for a few, were tracked into the commercial course.

"None of my friends," Lila Perlmutter says, "none of us, were expected to go to college. We were expected to take a commercial course." In 1941 more than half (fifty-three percent) of the female graduates of Thomas Jefferson High School who indicated chosen careers in the yearbook had cited business studies or clerical work: secretary, stenographer, clerk, bookkeeper. By 1950 the percentage had fallen (to forty-seven percent). The difference was primarily due to an increased interest in teaching. However, by the mid-fifties, as even interest in teaching as a professional career was suppressed, interest in clerical professions rose again and climbed still higher: this time to a full fifty-eight percent, a figure that was duplicated in 1958. Teaching, consistently cited earlier by about fifteen percent, had dropped back correspondingly. Social work appealed to very few. Besides secretarial work or bookkeeping, followed by teaching, the girls showed only a sprinkling of interest in other areas. The only other occupation that had some appeal was accounting, which was more an expression of self-esteem than a realistic goal since it was a totally male dominated profession.

Few girls planned to become nurses. Oddly, the highest percentage of interest in this area was in 1941 when, as was discussed earlier, nursing was not an acceptable occupation for Jewish girls. But even at its height it was only six percent. Interest later dropped to two percent and remained constant at that figure. Rhoda Nemerofsky was one of the few in her 1956 graduating class to choose a career in nursing despite her mother's objections that nursing was "for blacks," as it had, in an earlier period, been for Irish girls. Rhoda says:

> It never came up, why don't you go to medical school instead? That wasn't a girl thing. You wanted to go into medicine? Become a doctor! That wasn't an option. Jewish girls became teachers."

By contrast, the boys' choices did not cluster heavily in so few areas.[44] What is most striking, however, in comparing the choices of the boys and girls of Thomas Jefferson High School, is not that the boys made different choices from the girls, but that the boys cited twice as many occupations, and that most would be considered true or high-status professions, as opposed to teaching and nursing. Still, something was afoot, since the number of different occupations cited by the girls, although still limited, actually increased somewhat over the decade.

With all of the media and all of American popular culture repeatedly enumerating the satisfactions of family and home life, and Jewish culture fully supporting this ideal, it's remarkable that any of the girls gave thought to anything but marriage. They were, in fact, the "most marrying generation on record."[45] Yet several factors that had interceded for the fifties women supported educational and even some career planning. Because there was less strain on the family budget, education no longer had to be reserved exclusively for the males. To be learned, *gelernt*, although not an obligation for women, was revered in Jewish society. In the curious amalgam of Jewish and American culture in Brownsville at mid-century, this value spilled over onto the girls. In addition, education, even for girls, was in keeping with the middle-class aspirations of many Brownsville families. And there was also the issue of "just in case . . ."

Their parents understood "just in case." They understood it far better than the girls, who thought, as adolescents will, that they were invulnerable. Their parents knew that even if they married there was always the possibility of widowhood, divorce, or abandonment. This consideration added weight to the other reasons that parents allowed and even encouraged some of the girls to go on to college. Consequently, while most of the girls did not go to college, but married shortly after high school graduation, more of the Brownsville girls who graduated in the fifties than in the forties did. One-fourth of the fifties women completed their bachelors degrees at Brooklyn and Hunter Colleges; all were in teaching.[46] However, afraid that being "scholastic" would compromise their feminine image, some of the girls, like Martha Opitz, went through college "in stiletto heels."

In spite of the total lack of encouragement for women's self-development, there were many "women's firsts" in the 1950s. One of the Brownsville girls, Lila Perlmutter, had been dissuaded by her science teacher from pursuing an intense interest in astronomy. It would have meant a great deal to her to learn that in 1956, after twenty years in the astronomy department at Harvard, a woman became a full professor.[47]

But the stunning accomplishments of such women were not publicized in the media. Instead, the lives of the Brownsville women who came of age in the fifties were shaped by messages and images of home and family that forced women to make the choice "between a family and meaningful work" that men "never have to make."[48] As their counterparts had in the previous decade, they married, many dropping out of college to do so; they quit their jobs when they became pregnant. Sylvia Zinn was "dismissed" from her job when she "started showing." Then they settled down with their first babies.

Before the decade ended, all of the Brownsville women, dominated by the conservative philosophy that was reinforced everywhere—in the schools, in the media, in advertising, in psychology, in sociology—would attempt to pattern their lives after the TV image of Donna Reed: the perfect woman, the perfect housewife, the perfect mom. This image, superimposed upon the image of the *baleboste*, was a perfect fit—for a while—until the next decade, when the fifties girls, along with their older sisters, would finish their unfinished business.

Brownsville girls came of age in the 1950s with "traditional expectations and limited opportunities," but when they reached their thirties, their opportunities and options expanded. Although many complexities and conflicts intruded into their lives as the women faced what Myra Dinnerstein has described as the "bifurcated experience" of "being split between two worlds,"[49] the women successfully evolved from traditional wives and mothers to women who combined careers with family life.

Changes that occurred, beginning in the 1960s, provided the Brownsville women with even more than opportunities, they provided them with what Ruth Kesslin calls "possibility thinking": a changed consciousness of possibilities, in which they could see that opportunities were emerging and could take advantage of them.

CHAPTER SIX

Unfinished Business

Becoming Your Own Person

I was convinced that my brain had atrophied.

—Florence Moglinsky Kusnetz

It was unnatural, unwomanly, unhealthy, for a woman to make a serious commitment to any career other than homemaking. It was also unacceptably, unthinkably un-Jewish.

This message was reiterated by all of the socializing forces of American and Jewish-American culture in the 1940s and 1950s. It was the message that the girls who were coming of age in Brownsville received and internalized. Fortunately, however, we continue to develop throughout our adult lives and most of the girls changed and developed as they confronted and adapted to changing circumstances and needs.

In the 1950s and early 1960s the media always showed young mothers with small children at home, never at work anywhere else. Yet young mothers were entering the work force in ever-increasing numbers, and at the very same time that the "cult of domesticity" was at its height.[1] Although most of the Brownsville women waited, unlike many others, for their children to complete elementary school, by the end of the 1960s almost eighty-five percent had returned to work. They not only joined but exceeded the clear trend that has continued steadily until the present time.[2]

World War II had permanently altered the face of the work force by breaking down barriers to the employment of wives and older women. During the war, married women working outside the home had become an accepted fact;[3] by the beginning of the 1960s, twenty-three million women, more than one-third of all women over the age of sixteen, were in the workforce and half of these women had school aged children. By the end of the 1960s, a majority of working-age women held paid jobs.

The initial rise in the number of working mothers after the war came with the growth of fields that were becoming feminized, such as clerical work.[4] The women of Brownsville who reached adulthood in the 1940s, and who married and started their families soon after they graduated from high school, were at exactly the right point in their lives to join this workforce. By the mid- to late fifties their children were in school and all of the women had been trained for clerical work. Even those like Norma Ellman, Eleanor Chernick, and Florence Kusnetz, who had taken the academic course in high school and found that they didn't have marketable, that is, clerical, skills, enrolled in business schools.

All of the forties women engaged in some kind of clerical work before they married. Many, like Shirley Donowitz, had jobs while they were still in high school. Lorraine Nelson's mother used to meet her at the high school every day to carry her school books home so that Lorraine could walk to her job in nearby East New York. Rae Mirsky took the El at Livonia Avenue to her daily three-hour job in the city. Bea Siegel hurried home to change from her school clothes before she boarded the subway. "In those days," Bea says, "if you worked in the city, you had to wear stockings and heels."

All the women continued to work after they married but they all expected to become full-time homemakers once their children were born. There was no question of this; it was part of almost every girl's plan. Bea Siegel says, "You got married, you worked for a year, then you started a family."

Being a young mother in the late forties and early fifties was, for most of these women who had been friends since childhood, an extension of other shared experiences. Rae Mirsky recalls that "everyone was moving to Canarsie in those days; people joked about it because they thought of it as farmland, the boondocks." In moving to the boondocks, en masse, the women were continuing an earlier pattern begun by New York Jews; they gravitated to neighborhoods where they would be with friends and relatives.[5]

Through the fact of their community the women had formed, spontaneously, what would later have to be fabricated through "support groups." They were all young, newly married (most to upwardly mobile men), and starting their families. "We all did it together," Terry Apter says. The women kept busy. They were establishing their homes, raising their young children, taking care of the daily chores, and doing all of their own housekeeping. In spite of all of the new and so-called labor saving devices, "housewifery," Freidan wrote, expanded "to fill the time available."[6] Homemaking and mothering was meant to be a full-time job. Her husband "always came home to a hot cooked meal," Bea Siegel says, proudly. "I was home all day; why shouldn't I do this?"

Unlike many of their own mothers, who had been busy with "home work" or tending the shops when the girls were in school, they became actively involved with the PTA as their children got older; some were class mothers, some went along on school trips, some volunteered for other activities. After school or on weekends the women took their children to the library and the museum. They took them to the doctor and dentist, often taking the subway or several buses from the remote areas of Canarsie or Queens that had attracted Brownsville families. None of the women had learned to drive yet; some, in fact, were "not allowed" to drive, Bea Siegel says. Their husbands wouldn't "permit" them to learn. But at least one of the women found a way. She says:

> My husband didn't want me to learn how to drive; he wanted to be a male chauvinist. Then my brother gave me a car he wasn't going to use. I managed to scrape together, from my food allowance, money for driving lessons.

Bea Siegel, with her characteristic feistiness, was the first among the women to get her license and quickly informed the others that "they better learn," because she was not going "to be their chauffeur." As it was for Bea, learning to drive became an important moment in the lives of a number of the women, an adult rite of passage. Norma Ellman says, disdainfully, "Someone always had to take you somewhere." Bea says almost the same thing. Before getting her license she had to depend upon her husband to go shopping and elsewhere; afterward, that "responsibility" was hers. Driving gave the women greater control over their own lives and they felt more in control. "I was Miss Independence," Bea says, "and I had wheels!"[7] Learning to drive was one of the things that Irma Greenbaum also did, when she was "home with the kids."

Irma was one of those girls who (this was repeated by many) didn't think she was smart enough to go to college. Irma says:

> Nobody spoke to me and I felt, I guess, defeated. I thought,
> what kind of college material am I? And nobody ever said to
> me, "Why don't you try?"

Irma loved music and actually wanted to go to Juilliard to study voice but, inevitably, she took the commercial course and worked as a clerk and a receptionist until she was well into her first pregnancy.

Irma, always a maverick, says, "My lack of commitment to a career left me free to do other things." She began to explore a wide variety of interests, each one more interesting than the last. She joined the Earl Robinson Chorus; she took classes in cooking and car repair; she learned to drive; she joined the Brooklyn Heights Players (a semiprofessional community theater that performed at the Brooklyn Academy of Music) as props mistress. She not only learned enamelling and batik but became expert enough to teach these skills as a volunteer to senior citizens and in an alcohol and drug rehabilitation program, and, finally, she travelled all over the world as a courier. She's made more than twenty trips to such places as the Netherlands, England, Germany, Israel, Hong Kong, Australia, and Argentina, often at a moment's notice.

In this group of forties women, in addition to Irma, only Lorraine Nelson and Sarah Lieberman never returned to paid work. Lorraine and Sarah also are, perhaps coincidentally two of the three Brownsville women who are orthodox and observant. Lorraine said that she didn't know "anyone" who worked; perhaps "working women" were less common in the orthodox subculture of the neighborhood. Perhaps she and Sarah were a bit more strongly pressured than those from less observant families to remain exclusively in the role idealized for both Jewish and middle-class women. But neither regrets having remained a housewife: quite the contrary. And this is true not only for Lorraine and Sarah; few women questioned, or question still, the importance of a mother's being home with, and for, the children. "We grew up believing that a woman's place is in the home," Lorraine says.

For the Brownsville women, the image of the aproned Jewish mother—waiting at the door for the children to return home from school, in her "housedress," a *nosh* (snack) on the table—endures despite the large number of their own mothers who did work in their homes, shops, and local factories. None of the women, including those who eventually did return to the workforce, question that they made the right decision by not working during their child-rearing years. "Home, children, family, are primary," Claire Moses says, "Everything else is 'in addition to'; that's good for everyone."

None of the women regret the years they spent at home. "I was a young housewife; I was home, happy and content to be with my baby," Norma Ellman says. We "thoroughly enjoyed being housewives and mothers," says Sydelle Schlossberg. The day she gave birth to her first son, Bea Siegel says, was "the most important day of my life, even more important than the day I was married." Bea attained a major goal, accomplished something that meant more to her than "anything before or since," because "I accomplished something a man can't do." She adds, "Maybe I was a women's libber and didn't know it?"

Bea resisted the pressure to return to work until she felt the time was right. "I'm not going to lose this part of my life," she told a friend. "Why miss it?" When the women did return to paid work after their children were in school, they returned to the work they knew and for which they were qualified. Some, like Bea Larkin, Terry Apter, and Jean Bleckner, sought jobs as school secretaries because, as Bea says, in the school system "secretaries had teacher schedules." Jean was eventually drawn into working as a teacher's aide. Like a number of others, she says that she regrets not having gone to college to become a teacher. Sydelle Schlossberg found part-time work as a school librarian. Others, like Rae Mirsky and Bea Siegel, worked as secretaries, bookkeepers, office managers, and in other capacities in their family businesses. Norma Ellman worked for one of the municipal unions, but briefly. "When I saw the organizers reading the *Daily Worker*, I got out fast. I didn't want anything to do with communism." Shirley Donowitz worked at Brookdale (formerly Beth-El) Hospital for eighteen years.

Some of the women who wanted the flexibility of part-time work, so that they could be home when their children returned from school, came up with creative solutions: Fayge Lubin (who, out of necessity, had worked until the eighth month of her first pregnancy and then didn't return to work until her children went off to college) found a job in which she alternated, weekly, with another woman.

It isn't surprising that they returned to the workforce; there were many underlying causes. Working outside the home was modelled by many of their own mothers, or by other women whom they identified as role models: a friend's mother, an aunt. There is a powerful censure in the Jewish cultural tradition against idleness and the lack of goal-directed activities; influences such as this surely provided a kind of "cultural" motivation. But the Brownsville women also returned to the workforce for a number of overt and pragmatic reasons.

A few returned to paid work because, like their mothers before them, they simply needed the income. Some, in fact, went back quite reluctantly, when their children were, they thought, still a bit too young. But in the tradition of the real, rather than the fictionalized, Jewish mother, they helped support their families by earning needed income; their work meant survival for the family no less than their husbands' work did. Of course, maintaining another tradition, they continued to assume full responsibility for the household as well. For these women, particularly, the following selection from the *Guide for the Jewish Homemaker* is bitterly ironic:

> Since you are likely to have more leisure time than your husband, show consideration for him. Don't crowd your social calendar to such an extent that he isn't free to go to meetings of the synagogue, the men's club, the Zionist organization or other service groups.[8]

Most of the women of the forties generation, however, were considerably more "comfortable," than their mothers had been (the euphemism means that they had some financial security). Although their families didn't need their income, their earnings were for "bettering the family" or for those "extras" that might add to their quality of life. They wouldn't have to squirrel money away for a show or to eat out, for a vacation, a trip, or a second car. Some used their supplementary earnings to help pay for a more lavish *Bar Mitzvah* than they otherwise could afford. It enabled them to send their children off to summer camp, or to college with a bit of a financial cushion. Their children wouldn't have to work their way through school, as many of their husbands had done, and could concentrate on their studies.

Jean Bleckner loved her independent earnings when she worked, as a youngster, at her uncle's deli on Ralph Avenue and Park Place. When she went back to work as a school aide, she loved saving and having money for extras but, as many school aides report, they often do much more teaching than they are credited with (or, technically, are supposed to do). Jean worked with the teacher she was "assisting," in developing an individualized reading program, but for eight years she was the unacknowledged teacher, the one who "did it."

Because of her work, and as she made her financial contribution to the family, Jean began to regard herself with more esteem. She returned to business school for retraining and when she went back to full-time work it was at the City University's Graduate Center for Clinical Psychologists, as executive secretary to the president, a job she held until she retired to care for her mother.

By the time their children were in school, some of the women wanted something more challenging to do than domestic chores. Like Sally Forman, they were bored and restless. Although work outside the home was not an economic necessity for them, it soon became important for other reasons: it gave them their own income and made them feel grown up. They (not all, but most of the women) could make independent decisions about their own money. Norma Ellman says:

> I started to become financially independent and I enjoyed my money. I set it aside and did whatever I wanted to do with it. I didn't have to say, can we afford it? I didn't have to ask anybody, it was my decision. It gave me a good feeling, a wonderful feeling. Then I got involved in a lot of other things I wanted to do.

Above all, paid work gave the women a feeling of accomplishment in something other than their homemaker roles. In describing that feeling, several of the women used exactly the same expression: "You became your own person."

Like the secretary in their high school yearbook who sat patiently with pad in hand, waiting for instructions, the women were supposed to have been socialized to follow, not to be leaders. But the presence in their lives of women who were strong, if traditional, models, coupled with their own innate abilities, made it possible for some of the women to have successful careers as supervisors and administrators.

"I run the New York office," Minette Cutler told me over a cup of *Swee Touch Nee* tea. She started after high school and, over the almost-fifty years that she has been with the same insurance firm, has worked for "three generations: the grandfather, father, and the son," owners of a small family business. Although she never attempted to get her broker's or sales license, she administers and manages the business. "Even though I didn't go to college, that didn't keep me from getting where I am," Minette Cutler says.

Claire Moses was different from her friends when she was a girl because she did aspire to a professional career. But like them, she married at nineteen, shortly after the war, and worked as a homemaker for fifteen years before she returned to paid work. Claire says:

> I was lucky to have the husband I had because he didn't stop
> me. He realized I needed this. He helped me, he was there for
> the children.

In 1963, Claire passed a Civil Service exam and went to work for the New York State Teachers Retirement System. She took in-service courses in management, supervision, and in the intricacies of pension systems and, in 1979, became Deputy Director of Administration, the first and only woman in top-level management in her department at that time. "One of the reasons I got the job is they needed a woman," Claire says. "But they knew I could handle it." When she first started she was told never to pour coffee, but "just sit there!" Still, there was a double standard. "If I come in, I've interrupted, " Claire says. "If 'X' comes in, it's okay."

Claire spent the next ten years, until her retirement in 1989, as an accepted outsider in what she describes as an "old boys network." She dealt with condescending male colleagues,

> especially older guys. They tell you how pretty you are and
> other things, totally unrelated nonsense. You have to listen to
> all kinds of language, everyone turns around and looks at you.

Not only the men, Claire said, but some of the women, trying to negotiate new ground, were often defensive and difficult to work with. "They become a male counterpart; they can't seem to keep their feminine values and attitudes."

Claire became the career woman she aspired to be as a young girl and was recognized for her work when she received an award for outstanding accomplishment from the Academy of Women Achievers. Claire says, "I always felt if I went back to school I would have been a teacher." But she feels good about herself. "I believe I did very well. Although my career took another direction, I had a dynamic, interesting career. I ended up doing what I wanted."

Not all of the women believe that they have done what they wanted. Throughout their child-rearing days and unintended careers, some of the forties women carried old longings, frustrations, and ambitions: not

having become a nurse, not having become a designer, not having pursued a love and talent for art. Their aspirations had been thwarted for
the variety of reasons discussed previously: there was no money for their
schooling or training, or "it would have been a waste" since they were
expected to work only until they married; the work was not appropriate
for a Jewish girl; what interested them was not appropriate for any girl;
in any case, it was not a job or career that a girl, Jewish or otherwise,
could hope to have in the forties or fifties. As I spoke with the women,
however, it became clear to me that for some of them, embedded in their
homemaking or other unintended careers, were aspects of the careers
they had originally chosen.

Although she had never thought of it in those terms, throughout her
adult life Fayge Lubin has been the fashion designer she wanted to be.
At first, friends brought things for her to mend, or to alter, but then her
work expanded. For many years, Fayge, following a tradition for Jewish women that goes back to the *shtetl*, had a successful sewing business
that she conducted out of her home. She made her own patterns and
constructed custom-made clothing; she even designed and constructed
her daughter's wedding dress.

When she was in school, Bea Larkin wanted to be "something in the
helping profession. Social work would have given me the most satisfaction." But in spite of the fact that she was in the "rapids," the accelerated
track, she was discouraged from taking the academic course by her science teacher, who told her she "probably wouldn't ever get more than in
the seventies"; and Bea was also, typically, put off by math. No one told
her that the math and science requirements were minimal for social work,
or, indeed, that she only needed to pass them, that she didn't need to
excel, that grades in the seventies were fine, or that she might do a lot better, in fact, than her science teacher (a woman, incidentally) predicted.

After being "pushed" by her husband (a school teacher, now retired),
Bea acquired the thirty college credits she needed to become a school secretary. Not only did she fulfill this requirement, much to her surprise, but
she took additional classes at Kingsboro Community College. Bea then
became personal secretary to the principal of Thomas Jefferson High
School, where she and most of the Brownsville girls had gone to school,
and she held this post for twenty years, until her retirement.

Anyone who knows how the informal system of public schools
operates can appreciate the importance of that position. Bea, informally,
performed many school social work functions for the students, parents,

and even teachers. She was someone they could count on to help them find solutions or to find others who would be able to help them; she researched regulations; she called for information and gave advice; she helped with job referrals; she was someone to whom they could always talk, explain their problems. Bea was their sounding board.

It wasn't until her retirement party that Bea first began to understand how highly valued she had been, not only for her excellent secretarial and administrative skills, but for what she called the human relations aspect of her job, a part of the job that she was not required to perform but which she did instinctively. Bea was not a social worker, but she was a facilitator in the best social work tradition. She says:

> When I retired, people said things to me. One parent said, "I can't thank you enough for what you did for my daughter"; another said, "Don't you remember when you made those phone calls . . . ?"

At first it was difficult for Bea and some of the other women to see the connections between their girlhood ambitions and their eventual careers. Of course, their skills did not conform with the full range or depth of the skills they would have acquired through professional training or schooling, but they had achieved an impressive degree and range of competence through experience, and had managed to engage in some aspects of the work they had wanted to pursue as young girls.

Jean Bleckner and Terry Apter never became the teachers they'd hoped to be, but they did work as teacher aides, and a good part of their jobs turned out to involve teaching. Flo Grosswirth didn't become a nurse, but she did work with brain-damaged children. Bea Siegel did not design clothes, but she designed custom-made furniture for the family business. Fayge Lubin designed clothes. Bea Larkin did some of the tasks she would have performed as a social worker. But the women's skills were never validated by a credential or legitimated by an external authority, and it's difficult to believe that one can teach or design, or do social work, or nurse, if there is no Wizard of Oz awarding a diploma that says "Teacher," "Designer," "Social Worker," or "Nurse."

The women achieved status in their occupations without the benefit of college degrees. Claire Moses did take some courses but dropped out. Others, too. None of the Brownsville women in this study who began college after graduating from high school in the 1940s stayed to complete their degrees. Three of the women, however, later became college graduates, one after her children were fully grown, for her own personal satisfaction, and the others to pursue professional careers.

Sarah Lieberman moved to Montreal when she married, in 1947. When her children were young, like the friends she had left behind in Brooklyn, Sarah immersed herself in their lives, was involved with their school, supervised a group of Girl Guides, the Canadian counterpart of the Girl Scouts. "Living was good," Sarah says. It was not difficult to be an observant, orthodox Jew in Montreal; it was a city with a substantial Jewish community. Sarah became occupied with the B'nai Brith organization and became president of an active chapter. She had "a happy life"; even so, when the last of her four children left home for college, "I felt a gap. I wanted to do something for me, something was unfinished." Sarah had always wanted to go to college and finally did. She earned her bachelor's degree in Liberal Sciences at Loyola University (a division of Concordia).

Eleanor Chernick did not wait quite as long as Sarah had. When she joined the navy she didn't see the world, but she did reap the benefits of the GI Bill of Rights, which paid for schooling for returning veterans. As a girl, Eleanor fought bitterly with her mother over taking an academic course in high school. Unlike most of the other women I interviewed of this forties group, all of Eleanor's friends simply took it for granted that they were going to college. She thought it was because they were not quite so poor. "Some lived in one family houses," Eleanor says, as proof of their slightly higher social class.

> I set my sights on college, they pulled me along. One of the girls even had a sister who was a college graduate. If it weren't for my friends I would have done what my mother said: "Take the commercial course, get married, have babies."[9]

The rift with her mother was so great over this that Eleanor left home and went to live with her older sister even before she graduated from high school.

In 1946, after her discharge from the navy, Eleanor was determined to use her GI benefits. She enrolled at Brooklyn College as a biology major but switched to education when she met her husband. Eleanor graduated and married in 1949. She taught for only one year before the first of her three sons was born but she didn't regret leaving her job; she loved being a mother, she says. Fortunately, she had already established the basis for a teaching career when her marriage "got rocky."

In 1961 Eleanor returned to school, this time to Hofstra University, where she became "fascinated with how children learn to read." She earned a master's degree, became a consultant and reading specialist and began to teach courses at CUNY's York College in Jamaica, Queens. "I loved teaching at the college level," and, realizing she would need a doctorate, she returned to Hofstra.

Consistent with her lifelong interest in the sciences, Eleanor's doctoral dissertation, which she researched at the Nassau County Medical Library, was a study of the effects of a specific diet on hyperactivity, a pre-ADD (Attention Deficit Disorder) condition that was believed at that time to be an emotional, rather than a chemical disorder. Eleanor was on the cutting edge of research into understanding the relationship between diet and a lack of ability to concentrate; it was a time when few were taking the connection between diet and behavior seriously.

"I continued, little by little," Eleanor says, "to do what I wanted to do." In 1979 she became Dr. Eleanor Chernick; she had earned the degree of Doctor of Education. Since then she has worked as an adjunct instructor at various colleges in the Long Island area and supervised student teachers. We wondered how much farther she might have gone in her career if she had started earlier. There was a book written some time ago with the sensitive title, *The Hidden Injuries of Class*. How many women, like Eleanor, also suffered the hidden injuries of gender?

Educated women, it has long been noted, have ambitions that make them less than satisfied with being "just a housewife." They threaten the conventional wisdom about what a woman might expect to achieve; they challenge the status quo (of both cultures, Jewish and American). Therefore, while it had been a struggle for women to break down the barriers to higher education, it was even more difficult for them at professional schools. Women who did receive their degrees and tried to enter nontraditional professions were still swimming upstream. Consequently, like Eleanor, most chose "fields that were hospitable to women."[11] Florence Kusnetz chose to do otherwise, and entered the fray.

Florence graduated from Thomas Jefferson High School with an academic diploma in 1946. During a two-week orientation period to Pratt Institute's dietician program, she agonized over whether to enroll. She never did. When the time came for her to pay the tuition she couldn't bring herself to ask her parents for the money. Instead, she took a business course and worked as a secretary and bookkeeper until 1950, when she married and left New York for Detroit. Her husband's work with the Public Health Service meant that her family had to move fourteen times over the next twenty years. (With an admirable generosity of spirit she says, "It was hard to move, but on the other hand, I made friends all over the country.")

By 1966, when she was living in Baltimore, Florence's two sons were eight and ten years old. For a while she'd felt she needed to do "something out of the house," and had been searching for what it might be. "I was sure my brain had atrophied," she says. Since she had taken some college courses before she moved from New York, Florence decided to go back to school.

In the days of the Cold War, when Florence was first contemplating a career, "family life" was the necessary condition for a "free society." Women were discouraged from higher education or were shunted into programs, with the exception of teaching or nursing, that were tailored to prepping them for their domestic roles. Recently, I saw an advertisement in the *New York Times Education Supplement* for "Adult Degree Programs" at Brooklyn College, including a "weekend college" that offers special programs in the Liberal Arts and Sciences, Business, Education and Computer Science, convenient class schedules (including evenings and weekends,) counseling services for adults returning to school, financial aid for part-time students, and so on. What a stunning change![12]

Florence began her return to school, twenty years after her high school graduation, very tentatively. In the mid-sixties, there were no programs designed to accommodate Florence and other *returning* women; that is, women re-entering college after a long hiatus.[13] Such programs would not emerge until at least a decade later. It was still very unusual to find a mature woman in a classroom during the regular day session. Not only were the students young, Florence says, but it wasn't until she was in her forties and had been back in college for five years that she had a teacher who was older than she was.

Although she had been tenth in a class of six hundred when she'd graduated from Jefferson, Florence couldn't believe her "great grades." In spite of A's, and loving school, she was afraid to take on more than a couple of courses each semester. She also worried about not being there for her boys, and struggled to find courses that would get her home no later than four in the afternoon. To her great relief, when she finally gave them their own keys they behaved responsibly and were proud to be trusted.

Florence finally enrolled full-time when she moved to Cincinnati. She achieved membership in the honor society, Phi Beta Kappa and, in

1970, completed her degree in political science. By this time she was confident of her ability but unsure about what field to pursue in gradu- ate school. She had applied for a fellowship in urban planning but, although she didn't know anything about it, thought she might like to study law. Florence sat in on a class in contracts at the University of Cincinnati Law School—and was, she says, hooked.

In a replay of the conflict she had experienced over whether to attend the dietician program at Pratt or to be practical and take a busi- ness course, Florence almost didn't allow herself to follow her desire to study law. She was offered the fellowship in urban planning, which car- ried a stipend, and if she went to law school she would have to bear the cost of tuition. Her husband helped her make the decision. He asked, "If the money was removed from the picture, which would you choose?" Unhesitatingly, she said, "law!" And the decision was made, although yet another move would intervene. However, it would prove to be the last. Florence found herself in a place where she would not only succeed in her career, but would make an enormous contribution to the judicial system of the fourth most populous city in the country: Houston, Texas.

Florence was fortunate that her credits from the University of Cincinnati Law School were transferable to the Law School at the Uni- versity of Texas. In Cincinnati she had become somewhat of a celebrity when she had appeared on a television interview as one of eleven women attending the law school and, at forty-one, the oldest, but in Houston, she says, "no one took us seriously." In fact, one day a professor declared that it was "Ladies Day," and proceeded to direct all his ques- tions to the three women in class.

It was not only most of her professors and many of her classmates who did not take her seriously, but her parents, the people she especially wanted recognition from, did not comprehend why she had returned to college at all. "What for?" they asked. Her husband and children, how- ever, did understand. At her graduation they applauded and called and shouted "Mom! Mom! Mom!" with such exuberance that the dean, teasingly, accused her of bringing along her own cheering section.

Florence started her own practice in general law in 1973, after a $250–a-month internship, and as time went on she became a specialist in family law. By the early 1980s she had become extremely upset, "dis- gusted," she says, with the way women were treated in the divorce courts. It was so adversarial, she says, that "every case was a battle." It was "bloodshed in the divorce courts" that made her look for alternatives, and took her to Virginia to train as a mediator with another attorney who was developing a divorce mediation system there. When she returned to Houston as the first trained mediator in the state, she established a "parallel practice," separate from her law practice. As a family mediator she became involved with a national mediation organization and began a statewide mediation system to keep women, if possible, out of the court system. It was such a new concept that her mediation practice was listed in the 1981 Houston phone book under "Meditation," in the same section as Yoga.

Although she did not know it, in establishing a mediation system Florence was following a cultural tradition: the system of *bet din,* of courts established in the *shtetlach* to settle acrimonious domestic disputes. In *Battered Jewish Wives,* Mimi Scarf wrote:

> In 1920, the New York Conciliation Court was founded by Louis Richman (a lawyer) and Samuel Buchler. Its purpose was to deal with matters of special Jewish concern that might be incomprehensible to non-Jewish judges. These included moderating agreements between individuals and their synagogues, dealing with messy disputes between Jews to keep them out of public civil proceedings, making peace between disputants, and dispensing justice. Most of the arguments were carried on in Yiddish . . . half the cases [were] disputes between husbands and wives.[14]

Florence said that the family court system in Houston was dominated by (the same phrase Claire Moses used) "an old boys network" of referrals and cliques. Mediation was a way to avoid the courts but it didn't do anything to alter the system, which needed reform. It was later exposed as thoroughly corrupt, in a political battle in which Florence played a key role.

For her pioneer work in establishing a mediation system, for her advocacy and legal work, for "outstanding contributions," Florence was voted one of ten "Women on the Move" in the state of Texas (out of a field of several hundred nominees). The award was sponsored by a number of organizations, among them Texas Executive Women and the editors of the *Houston Post.* When she was interviewed, she was asked about her particular sensitivity in her work in family practice. Florence said, "I was a grownup before I was a lawyer."

Florence retired from a career of remarkable achievement in 1992, but she would not have a placid retirement. Soon afterward, no longer bound by issues of confidentiality or conflict of interest, she became a vocal advocate for reform of the family court system, although, in spite of her groundbreaking work, she still didn't see herself as a leader. "Who am I to take on the establishment?" she thought. She was called on, however, by an FBI agent who was pursuing an ongoing investigation of the activities of some of the family court judges, and was put in touch with another activist. Although the federal investigation was eventually dropped, a core group was formed who established a registered Political Action Committee, raised $80,000, hired consultants, targeted particular judges who were running for reelection, found candidates to run against them, mounted a full-fledged political campaign, and replaced seven of the nine entrenched judges with reform candidates.

Florence stayed with the campaign in spite of threats of physical harm. She is now getting ready to challenge those remaining judges who might be foolish enough to run in the next election. Whether she has been motivated by it or isn't even familiar with it, Florence's life exemplifies a well-known saying from the *Mishnah*: "It is not incumbent upon you to finish the task, neither are you free to give it up."

The women highlighted above, and many other Brownsville women of the forties generation, overcame immense barriers imposed by immigrant, working-class, and cultural norms to achieve significant levels of success in the public world. Eleanor Chernick and Florence Kusnetz went still farther by attaining professional status, although, in this respect, they were more like the younger Brownsville women than their contemporaries.

The contrast between the two groups of women who came of age in Brownsville over a period of less than twenty years (1940–1958) is striking with regard to their educational achievements and, consequently, the work to which many of them returned. More than half of the fifties women earned degrees, not only bachelor's but master's degrees (almost four times as many as the forties women who participated in this study), and more than half of the fifties women are professionals—psychotherapists, teachers, and nurses—compared with only two professionals (that is, with earned college degrees) in the forties group.[15]

The forties and fifties women are from the same culture: they are second and third generation Eastern European Jews. They come from the same mix of orthodox, "partially observant," and secular families.

The women are from the same community, which was changing in the 1950s but still dominated by the Jewish culture. They are basically from the same class, that is, working-class, backgrounds. But all of these elements differed in sufficient degree between the two groups to have a major impact on the life chances of each.

The women of the forties generation were subject to the traditional Jewish cultural norms and attitudes that were still being enforced by the immigrant (first) generation. In this tradition, women were never the scholars, *der lamdn*. These attitudes, together with working-class poverty, made it difficult, if not impossible, for the forties women who did want to go to college to pursue their goals. In addition, the desire to emulate the norms of middle-class American society severely limited their choices. At that time, middle-class women were expected to be housewives. It was a mark of middle-class status that the husband was the breadwinner, that the wife didn't have to work. If women worked after marriage it was only for pocket money or for extras, because surely their husbands were able to support the family. Therefore, it was argued, why prepare girls for anything more than a temporary worklife before marriage?

For the younger women, the experiences of the immigrant generation were in the more distant past. More of their parents were the children of immigrants and thus second generation. In their case, the relaxation of Jewish cultural norms and the growing acceptance of higher education for American women were joined. Their families experienced relatively greater affluence during the war and during the postwar boom, and could afford college for the girls who wanted to attend. This combination of factors gave more of the fifties women a share of the Jewish men's "right" to an education. As they reentered the world outside of their homes and sheltered communities—and entered a decade characterized by norms, values, and attitudes that were deliberately counter to the repressive and conservative culture of the fifties—these influences gained additional weight.

However, like the forties women, few of the younger women initially made conscious choices or decisions. They use almost the same words as the forties women:

- Lila Perlmutter: "I never thought I had a choice. I was molded into a pattern and didn't deviate too much."

- Dolores Plaxen: "You just accepted that this is what you do; the value was family. I never thought I needed a career."

- Linda Brasco: "*He* would make the living."
- Lillian Wellen: "I wanted to be taken care of but I had children right away."
- Doris Levinson: "House, children, do some kind of charity work."

This was the fifties woman's image of the future, with a Jewish touch.

Growing up in the forties and fifties, "life was predetermined," Isabel Cohen says. Her mother was a college graduate (the only mother among the Brownsville women who was), but it was her father, an attorney, who influenced Isabel to go to college.[16] Isabel was not, however, encouraged to choose her profession; teaching was "a given," still the one acceptable profession for Brownsville women. "If I had a choice," Isabel says, "I think I might have done something different."

> The stereotypic image that we all had at that time was that we would do something after college but it would be an interim kind of thing—that you got married and you had children—that's as far as I got.

By the fifties, a college education was becoming acceptable for Brownsville girls, and not only for girls like Isabel whose parents were educated. Even some of the girls from working-class families expected to go to college and, fortunately, could attend the tuition-free colleges of the city university system: Brooklyn, Hunter, City College. Roslyn Bowers's brother attended a college in Alabama, but, "It never occurred to me to go to an out of town school," she says. Harriet Portnoy used the expression that was common in Brownsville but that I had not heard in many years: an "away school."

The women, like Isabel, who went right on to college after their high school graduations prepared themselves for careers in teaching: Ruth Berman, Doris Levinson, Martha Opitz, and Roslyn Bowers. Roslyn, in contrast with some of the other women, was the only one of her group of friends who went to college. Roslyn's mother told her to go into teaching. "You come home at the same time as the children," she said. Teaching was considered the best career for a woman, and it continues, even more than nursing, to be the career they believe is most compatible with family responsibilities (drawbacks being the relatively low pay scale and pay ceiling).

After the homemaking "interim," when they felt their children were old enough, the women returned to teaching and went on to earn advanced degrees. Ruth Berman became an administrator, a "Chairman" at Edward R. Murrow High School; one of her accomplishments was the development of the first coeducational Special Education Phys. Ed. program. Isabel Cohen, also in Special Education, developed one of the first resource rooms in the New York City school system.[17] None of the women regret having spent so many years of their lives in this immensely important, if undervalued, profession (although some did choose other, second careers later on).

Nursing, although it could provide the kind of flexible schedule that was manageable for women with school-aged children, was not highly sought after by the Brownsville girls of Thomas Jefferson High School in the 1950s. (Only two percent of those graduating cited nursing as their professional goal in the yearbooks covering 1950–58.) Rhoda Nemerofsky was an exception. She was five when she had her tonsils were removed. "The nurse was awful!" she says. "I remember going home saying when I grow up I'm going to be a nurse to be kind to little children." Rhoda decided "then and there and it stayed with me. I never had any doubt in my mind." And Rhoda did follow her own mind, over her mother's objections. "She was very upset that I wasn't bringing money into the house." Her mother also protested that nursing was not for Jewish girls; it was menial; it was for *schvartzes*, for blacks, her mother argued. (By the 1950s the perception was that it was no longer Irish but black girls who became nurses, although there were several other Jewish girls in Rhoda's nursing program.)

Rhoda was very good at her job. At Beth El Hospital, she soon found her area of specialization in surgical nursing. "It was like coming home," she says. She became head nurse after only two years but, meanwhile, she had met her husband, a biologist. They moved to Rochester before he settled into the science department at a State University College in New York and Rhoda settled into mothering (two daughters), homemaking, and various community activities.

The rest of the fifties women returned to clerical or secretarial work. Bea Benjamin did not have children but did have a successful, uninterrupted career with a firm where she's remained for more than thirty years. Bea began as a secretary and now is senior office manager.

Some of the women sought part-time work after their children were in school. Lillian Pollack and her sister offered themselves as a pair for job sharing, an idea that would reappear as an innovation some twenty years later. Lillian says:

> I did it for mental stimulation. My sister and I lived together
> in a two-family house. We got a little *noodgy* [restless] so we
> decided to go and register with a temporary agency and just
> play around, working here and there. If they wanted one of
> us to come in for a second day we said, "I can't but I'll send
> my sister."

Many of the women held various positions to which they were not
particularly committed: they just took one job or another. Arlene Feldman "did some real estate, sold jewelry, got a job as a secretary." Then
something happened.

What happened was, as Rochelle Feld explains:

> Women of our generation came into their own in a very pecu-
> liar manner. All of a sudden we stopped and said, "Wait a
> minute, I can do it!"

Like her friends, Norma Ellman talked about her second becoming;
not the one she experienced in adolescence but in midlife. She says:

> I'm a very independent person, I'm perfect for the ad, "You've
> come a long way baby." My mother taught me you've got to
> obey your husband, that was it. I've become more of my own
> person. I realized there was a personality of "me" that had to
> come out. I had the right to expression, the right to feelings.
> That happened to me when I got my financial independence,
> when I went back to business.

And (in exactly the same words that her namesake, Bea Larkin,
used) Bea Benjamin says, "We became our own person."

Whether what happened was "all of a sudden," or the result of
slowly changing perceptions that finally erupted into consciousness,
some of the women began to realize that they could make meaningful
changes in their lives, and they set about doing so.

In some ways, the Brownsville women who came of age in the
fifties were like the midwestern women Dinnerstein described in
Women Between Two Worlds who also married and started their families soon after graduation from high school. They had all been
inducted into the fifties "cult of domesticity"; but when they were
ready to return to the workplace, the women were still in their thirties,
a time in their lives when they could profit from the changes that were
taking place for women.[18]

As it did for the forties women, work offered them something that they hadn't quite expected. It provided them with greater self-esteem and a degree of financial independence that they came to value. Doris Levinson says:

> I never felt so good as when I went back to work and had my own money; it gave me a sense of independence that I hadn't had since I married. It felt good to be able to contribute in extras.

Sylvia Zinn says, "I liked it. I got dressed in the mornings. I got out." Sylvia has held various interesting jobs. She began her clerical career during high school but not, like the others, simply to have spending money. Because of her "terrible home life," Sylvia left as soon as she graduated, to live with a girlfriend, but her mother begged her to come home; she was the "intermediary" in the family. She soon married, however, and did get away.

After about a dozen years of homemaking Sylvia wanted "desperately to be out." There was no career she was interested in, but she needed the money and, she says, "another kind of stimulus." Sylvia went back to a series of clerical jobs, which she describes as nondescript. "I started doing serious work," she says, "when I moved out of New York." Sylvia had taken courses in stained glass but it wasn't until she moved out of Brooklyn to Woodstock, in upstate New York, that she began to design and fabricate stained glass pieces, sometimes working with home builders. At the same time she began to deal in oriental rugs.

Sylvia thinks of herself as a bit of a dilettante, but I see her as an intuitive salesperson and entrepreneur. In time she became involved with the real estate market, and, finally, became a trader in the stock market. She has also returned to her interest in crafts; she sells handcrafted wooden footstools, exquisitely upholstered with unusual fabrics and designs.

Zena Bloom, who lives in Dutchess County in upstate New York, was one of those women who was not interested in a career. She "didn't see herself working." But in the early sixties she took a keypunch class and then a civil service test, and she got a job in the early days of data processing. She worked for a local school district where she "met a lot of IBMers" and decided to apply for a job with them, to do more challenging work.

Her first assignment, although she was working on the first generation of supercomputers, was not exactly what she had hoped: She said that she made "widgets." She became so good at what she did, however, that she became a trainer in new technologies and developed orientation packages for new employees. Zena went on to middle management and became an expert and trainer in OSHA regulations (which had been, coincidentally, developed by Florence Kusnetz's husband). She tracked trends related to safety and health. Zena was in a high-echelon position; she reported directly to upper-level management. As an interesting sidelight, which became part of her job, she was an official Tour Host for IBM. This responsibility began when a group of Israeli government and sales people visited the IBM facility. Since Zena was the only Jew working at her level of management (and a woman?), she was asked to be their hostess.

Elaine Cohen was my classmate in the rapid advance class in junior high and took an academic course in high school, but she graduated with a general diploma (what someone called a "no-no"). Elaine failed a regents exam, without which she couldn't get an academic diploma, but she "didn't bother" to re-take it. She was getting married; she wasn't going to college. Elaine worked as a saleswoman for several months after her graduation, because she wasn't trained for clerical work.

Elaine was raised with the belief that married women don't work. Now she has some regrets:

> I didn't see married women in business in my family; not my older sister or sister-in-law. I was told, "don't work, stay home, your husband earns a living for you." I lost out on a lot of things. We would have had more money, I would have been out there, met more people, had more worldliness.

As a suburban housewife, Elaine spent her time playing canasta, Mah-Jongg, shopping. It wasn't until her children were in high school that she went to work, "slowly," in sales, the work in which she'd had her brief experience. Today Elaine is a salesperson, the "top in twelve stores" in an upscale designer clothing store chain. Although she feels the stress of having to "keep up her image," she says, "it's worth it." It has been critical in building her self-esteem:

> I never had the accolades that I have now. If I started twenty years ago, I don't think I would have had the confidence. I was quiet, timid. I didn't contribute to conversations. I was afraid to say the wrong thing. It's a good feeling. I feel independent. I feel more secure. Now I'm not scared. I've been able to do something on my own. How did I get here? I pinch myself sometimes.

A number of the women, as Ruth Kesslin did, focused on finishing unfinished business by earning their degrees. When Ruth had to go back to paid work because her family needed the additional income, she took various jobs, none of which were satisfying to her. At last, she decided to try college, and graduated *summa cum laude* at the age of forty-five, did some postgraduate work and, in 1984, began a successful private practice as a clinical psychotherapist.

Like Ruth, Lila Perlmutter and Martha Opitz became psychotherapists. Lila Perlmutter married at eighteen and proceeded to raise both her own two children and a sister's child. As a teenager, although her parents "weren't interested in school," Lila says, she did attend college briefly. When Lila returned to school after her children were born, she studied, over an eight-year period, until she earned her bachelor's and master's degree in social work. "It worked out perfectly," Lila says. "I had my family when I was young and was prepared for an empty nest."

Initially, Martha Opitz was "drawn into working with the emotionally disturbed" through her teaching. She began a masters degree in Special Education, worked in recreational therapy with geriatric schizophrenics, and worked in an adolescent day treatment center. But she wasn't satisfied. "I felt as if I'd thrown myself away," she says. Finally she completed her MSW program, and is doing work that is meaningful to her. She has worked with families with problems and with foster care placement on the very streets of East New York on which she played as a young girl. And, like Lila and Ruth, she has a private practice. When I interviewed her, Martha was attending the Psychoanalytic Institute for advanced study.

"I must have done something wrong, because you don't want to stay home and take care of the house and raise your family," was her mother's response. Rhoda Nemerofsky, already a nurse, was trying to explain why she was going back to school. Rhoda says:

> The expectation was that I was going to stay home and raise my children. I hated it. I had to come up with something. I wasn't happy. The smart thing to do was to go back to school. I worked out a plan, one course per semester. It would take me nine years. I remember thinking, in nine years I'll only be thirty-four and my children will be grown. I managed to do it in seven.

Rhoda was not one to be put off. She not only completed a bachelor's degree but later earned a master's and began a second career in teaching, as a school-nurse teacher and health educator at the campus laboratory school. Health administration would have been more lucrative but, Rhoda says, as a school nurse teacher she was "able to be home with the children." Her last job before her recent retirement was at the campus health center.

Rochelle Feld also became a nurse. Rochelle became enamored with the poster image of nurses when she was a schoolgirl but, unlike Rhoda, didn't think she would ever become one. Rochelle graduated from high school in 1952. She enrolled in college in 1972. Several years later Rochelle began her nursing career. "I remember thinking," she says, "there's got to be more than this, there has to be more. There was some kind of anxiety, restlessness." She was finally inspired to return to school by women she saw on television who were "doing other things," and by new concepts, "a new vocabulary I didn't know before." So Rochelle went back to school, "as a married woman with two children, a dog, a cat, a house, and a car."

Some of the Brownsville women, like Harriet Portnoy, went back to college to become teachers. But Harriet, "a kid that always played school," is unique among the fifties women in that she is the only one to have pursued a science major.

> I was raised to believe that family comes first. I didn't have a
> problem with that, providing I finished school and had a
> career. I wasn't the type to stay home and scrub my floors. All
> my friends went on to college; many of them are teachers. I
> was going to college pregnant and having babies.

Harriet went to school at night, having her children "in between." She was an A student, accused of "breaking the curve" by two male classmates. "They told me I was taking their A's away, they had to get into medical school."

Harriet got her degree in biology nine years after she graduated from high school but found that she "loved geology" and eventually became an earth science teacher. When she was in undergraduate school she knew nothing about careers in geology for women. "Maybe somebody should have told me girls could be geologists," she says. When she decided to go on for postgraduate work it was in geology. She took a year off, not only from her job, but from her family as well. Her sons were in college, her daughter was a high school senior. With her family's encouragement and support, and with frequent visits from her husband,

Harriet spent a year at the University of Miami, studying oceanographic geology, as a "core controller." She monitored and distributed core samples from the ocean floor.

In addition to her teaching, Harriet also coaches girls' soccer and field hockey at her school. She was one of the tomboys, she says; she played stickball, handball, and other street games. Harriet never questioned why there was not a swim team while there was a water ballet "team" for the girls; she just took it for granted that sports were for boys. (There were no competitive girls teams at Brooklyn College either, Harriet says.)

Arlene Feldman, now a seventh grade English teacher (and a writer who recently had a short story published) was advised, like so many of the other girls, to take the commercial course. It was a mistake, she says, but you can "go crazy by dwelling on 'what ifs.'" Arlene worked in a series of office jobs, as a health aide and then as a school secretary. She got her degree in 1991 after having "realized the accomplishment of a good marriage and children," without which she does not believe she could have been content. She has now completed a Master of Fine Arts program at Brooklyn College, in fiction writing.

Of a total of twenty women in this study who came of age in the 1940s, all graduated from high school and a few began college, but none completed their degrees. The women all worked in clerical jobs after (some during) high school. They all quit their jobs soon after they married and remained at home until most of their children had completed grammar school. Only three of the women, Lorraine Nelson, Sarah Lieberman, and Irma Greenbaum, never returned to paid work; at some point, even if only part time or for a short while, all of the others returned to clerical jobs, and some of the women attained managerial positions. Three of these twenty women, Sarah Lieberman, Eleanor Chernick, and Florence Kusnetz, eventually earned college degrees; Eleanor and Florence went on to attain postgraduate degrees and to pursue professional careers.

Of the twenty-one women in this study who came of age in the 1950s, all graduated from high school. Five went on to college and completed their degrees in teaching: Roslyn Bowers, Ruth Berman, Isabel Cohen, Doris Levinson, and Martha Opitz. One of the women, Rhoda Nemerofsky, became a registered nurse. All of these women returned to their professional careers after their children entered school.

A total of eleven women of the fifties group, more than half, became college-educated professionals. All but one earned master's degrees.

Harriet Portnoy, who had continued her studies throughout the early years of her marriage and child raising, earned her teaching credentials. Others went back to school to earn college degrees, Arlene Feldman in teaching, and Lila Perlmutter and Ruth Kesslin in psychology. Martha Opitz reschooled and retrained, also for a career as a psychotherapist. Rochelle Feld returned to school to become a nurse.

Other women in the fifties group have had successful business, office, or sales careers. Lillian Pollack chose to remain primarily a homemaker but had a steady part-time job as a bookkeeper throughout her homemaking career. Only Linda Brasco did not return to paid work.

When she was still in PS 184, Linda had discovered a love of art. One of her teachers encouraged her to prepare a portfolio for the School of Industrial Arts, but her parents wouldn't allow her to attend. Instead, she took a commercial course at Jefferson; but Linda continued to draw and paint. She started a sewing club because she could create her own designs and she joined the Yearbook art committee. Like the famous caricaturist, Al Hirschfeld, she hid her friends' initials in the drawings. "I thought I pulled off a great coup," she says.

Linda has "done art" throughout her life. It's been her "medicine" and "escape hatch," but she became a professional artist in the late 1980s. She was commissioned to decorate the lobby of a building on Greenwich Street in Manhattan, near the World Trade Center. It took two and a half years for Linda to install nine hundred handmade tiles.

Today, Linda has remodelled part of her home to use as a studio. She no longer needs "affirmation from outside." Linda has, she says, "her place."

The Brownsville women—those who came of age both in the forties and in the fifties—managed to have successful careers outside of their domestic spheres, by overcoming the barriers that had been constructed by both culture and society. They have achieved a great deal, and some, quite appropriately, have been formally recognized for their achievements by their peers or other professionals.

But success has to be defined in different terms for those women whose careers could not hope to compete with the obligations of family life (Valerie Greenberg had a handicapped son; Lois Rusakow's daughter was disabled as the result of having been hit by a truck.) Success can't be measured by the same criteria for women whose careers took a clearly secondary place and for those who remained primarily homemakers; their lives were limited to the domestic realm. If we define suc-

cess as only that which can be achieved in the public world, we are eval-
uating "successful" women by the same inappropriate criteria against
which feminists have been battling. There are few awards for women
whose successes are confined to the domestic realm and little recognition
for domestic achievement beyond the obligatory Mother's Day card and
"dinner out." Claire Moses measured herself against the male standard
of achievement and accepted the unfortunate but prevalent denigration
of homemaking and child rearing when she said that she had spent, "too
much time not doing anything too important."

Fortunately, as will be shown in the concluding chapter, the
women's lives, even those women who had various and casual jobs, or
those who were "just" homemakers, were enriched by a variety of charitable activities, by their involvement in transmitting a sense of
Yidishkeit to their children and grandchildren, by their lifelong friendships, by their long-lasting marriages, and by a wide range of self-edu-
cational and cultural activities. They look back and tell about these in
the following chapter.

CHAPTER SEVEN

Conclusions

Looking Back

We were different from our parents like night to day because we were the first ones in the mold trying to break away.

—Katie Tepper Stavans

W hat were the women doing, what were their lives like? What can we learn from as well as about them? Aren't women's lives worth knowing about?

I was initially guided in this study by these questions, suggested by the philosopher Elizabeth Minnich,[1] and they remained at its core as I focused on the forty-one Brownsville women. As they talked about their lives, and as they and I together explored their life histories, the questions were answered. I did learn what they were doing, what it was like to come of age in Brownsville in the 1940s and 1950s, and how their lives were permanently influenced by their early experiences in the neighborhood. These women are worth knowing about, and learning from—and, because these second- and third-generation Brownsville women represent working-class, Ashkenazic Jewish-American culture at mid-century, they also tell a larger cultural story. In the telling, the women confirmed some but negated other assumptions I held when I began the interviews.

There was an additional question with which I began and which, in fact, sparked this study. I wondered whether Brownsville had been the kind of "nurturing neighborhood" for the women that it had been for the men. Sorin convincingly demonstrated the men's success in terms of education, careers (professional or commercial), and their consequent rise in socio-economic class. He also cited their long-term marriages and the upward mobility of their children as measures of their success. All of these standards can be applied to the women as well as the men. However, their relative weight has to be gauged quite differently, and inversely.

It is altogether remarkable, given their life chances, that criteria related to educational and professional achievements can be used at all to measure success for many, indeed, for so many of the women. Brownsville women were not nurtured, as the men were, for educational or professional accomplishments or for leadership roles.[2] The full range of possible achievements was limited for these Jewish-American women, as traditional and parochial community values, coupled with contemporary middle-class values, directed their behavior. To move beyond their constraints, to have choices, the women had to reach into the deeper, more fundamental value system of the Jewish culture. They had to claim, if tacitly, that they, and not only their brothers, were entitled to be educated and to earn the respected status, or *yikhes,* one acquires through education. They had to assume that a commitment to *takhles,* meaningful goal-directed activity, and to *tikn olam,* the improvement of the world, went beyond both charity, *tsedakah,* and their homemaking responsibilities. In this respect the women's achievements in education and their careers were accomplished in spite of their having been raised in Brownsville.

But at the same time, Brownsville served as the medium through which profound cultural precepts were transmitted. It was in Brownsville that the women, unselfconsciously, were immersed in the Jewish culture, in *Yidishkeit.* It was there that they learned to shun idleness. It was there that they developed a social consciousness and a sense of responsibility for the welfare of their family, friends and the community. And it was in that thoroughly Jewish community that the women came to know and to internalize these values, to believe, as Harriet Portnoy says, that "Jewish *people*"—she includes women—"have the sense that no goal, intellectual or career, is out of reach." The answer, then, to the question of whether Brownsville was a nurturing neighborhood for the women is not yes or no but *yes and no.*

The women believe that Brownsville was a nurturing neighborhood for yet another reason. It was there that they acquired their highest value: family. And with it a clear understanding and acceptance of their "most important" role. Even in the face of evidence to the contrary provided by their own working mothers, the ideal image of the *baleboste* persisted in Brownsville. Like the *shtetl* ideal, the Jewish wife was not supposed to have a life outside of her home, except as the charitable one, *eyshit chayil*, the woman of valor who "stretcheth out her hand to the poor . . . reacheth forth her hands to the needy."[3] In this respect I agree with the women; Brownsville did prepare many of them well—for their *gendered* role, the role of the Jewish woman, *baleboste* and *Yidishe mama*.

Determining how well a Jewish woman performs her role is subjective. It's not quantifiable. The measures are imperfect, internal, and intuitive: longlasting marriage, lifelong friendships, the educational and material success of their children, their participation in *Yidishkeit*, their sense of mutual obligation, expressed as "giving back" through work in the helping professions and through charity, their affirmation of the value of affiliation, as shown through the reestablishment of community as they moved from Brownsville to other areas.

Brownsville women performed their traditional role but also did more, as the broader ethical precepts of Jewish culture overrode the parochial and as the changing nature of American society (in which opportunities for women were dramatically expanding) provided a counterweight to the inertia of tradition. Once their primary responsibilities of home and children had been adequately secured and they had discharged their clearly defined "women's" responsibilities, the women looked outside of the home for new goals, to find meaningful work and to evade dreaded idleness. Norma Ellman says:

> You're busy, busy, busy. Then, all of a sudden, the babies are
> going to school. There are no more diapers around. You say,
> "Hey, it's time I got out a little bit."

It was not only paid work that drew the women out. Those who did not return to the workforce tried to find other meaningful outlets for their energies. Most often this meant charitable, volunteer work. Sydelle Schlossberg said that the revival of the Brownsville Boy's Club Alumni Association itself came after a long period of inactivity, as the indirect result of such an effort. As Sydelle recounts the story, there was a "friends club" of fourteen Brownsville couples that had begun "because these BBC men and their wives had a bond that they didn't want to lose." They met in each other's apartments every other month. Then, when one of the original members died, at the age of thirty-nine, they decided to get in touch with as many Brownsville people as possible to start an educational fund for his children. Before that, the Alumni Association was "in name only; there was nothing going on," Sydelle recalls. But then, "The men took the bull by the horns and got in touch with others. In 1964–65, the Alumni started."

The men began to send out newsletters. They got the Alumni organized, but the educational fund never was created. The women then decided that if they were going to collect money for charity in the name of the Brownsville Boys Club, they needed a more formal group. By the time the "women's group" of the BBC started, Sydelle had moved away, but Bea Siegel and Terry Apter continued as founders and leaders.

Even Brownsville women who did return to the workforce were actively involved with charitable organizations. Doris Levinson, who had a full-time teaching job, became Secretary of B'nai B'rith's District 1, which covers New York State and New England, only the second time a woman was elected as an officer in 148 years. It is her way, she says, of giving back, to the community.

"Giving back," the expression that the women use to explain the social consciousness that has taken them into many of their commitments, also took the form of advocacy. Roslyn Bowers and Sylvia Zinn were actively involved with the civil rights movement and, as I was in the sixties, with efforts (by organizations like SANE, Ban the Bomb, and the Women's Strike for Peace) to halt nuclear testing. Roslyn participated in the Democratic Reform Movement, both on a national level and locally. Ruth Berman was a member of a community "watchdog" committee when there was a threat of pollution in her neighborhood. Some of their volunteer work was unusual and unexpected. Lois Rusakow joined the auxiliary police in her neighborhood, Marine Park. "I walked the beat," she says. Zena Bloom was an "ORT" fundraiser for Israel (an organization for research and training).

Lorraine Nelson has engaged in a lifetime of giving back. When I interviewed her, Lorraine was worrying about a dinner that the synagogue was giving in her honor, as Woman of the Year, because of her service to the community. I was impressed with her gentleness. While I was talking with her, two Jehovah's Witnesses came to the door. Lorraine sent them on their way without impatience, in a considerate manner. "We are observant Jews, we follow our religion," she said. "Maybe you can find others who don't."

Lorraine is involved with many activities: fundraising, charity, the sisterhood, Hadassah. She has spent many hours preparing immigrants for their citizenship test. She has been involved with *Deborah*, a fund that manages health care for the poor. She was worrying about the dinner because it was going to be expensive for some of her friends: "I don't want to obligate them to spend money to come to a big dinner. The synagogue said that I could invite some guests, so they wouldn't have to pay, but there are better uses for the money." Lorraine describes herself as a "humble woman." It would be a contradiction of her values to take pride in having been charitable. Some of the other Brownsville women, however, are not quite so modest. They feel good about themselves, they've done good work, they've heeded the admonition to be the good Jewish woman, the *eyshit chayil*.

Like Lorraine Nelson, the few who did not pursue careers (although they may have taken occasional jobs) expressed few regrets with the direction their lives have taken. The women internalized the values, taught if not modelled by their mothers, of the patriarchal Jewish culture; they are satisfied to have been the proverbial "woman behind the man." They were taught that their husband's needs came before their own, the quid pro quo being implied, if not as explicitly stated as it was by Bea Siegel's mother, who said: "You take care of him and he'll take care of you." It was accepted that this "lifeboat" carried *men* and children first. As Sydelle Schlossberg says: "I'm like my mother. She was happy; she took care of her family. That was my whole life and I was rewarded for this."

Some of the women have had successful careers. Some have gone back to school and have earned not only bachelor's but advanced degrees. Still, when I asked them to talk about their achievements, what they value most, even those who had enjoyed significant professional accomplishments inevitably answered in terms of relationships: children, family, friends. Typical of their generation, their most meaningful successes (and conversely, what they see as their most devastating failures) have been within the sphere of their personal, private, domestic lives.

In looking back, most of the women take the longevity of their marriages as the single most important measure of their success. Most have been married for more than forty, some for more than fifty, years. The women are proud that they are not like young married people today. Norma Ellman says, "We had staying power." But, "They're not good at it," Rae Mirsky concludes.

Sorin has credited the men of the Brownsville Boys Club, with building "fulfilling, enduring marriages."[4] Of course the men were partners in the good marriages, hard-working, loving and supportive husbands.

But it was the women who dedicated themselves to their marriages and their households.[5] In the early years, when homemaking was their only full-time job, their lives mimicked the historical ideal of the *baleboste*, the archetypal "mama" captured perfectly in a lyric from the musical *Fiddler on the Roof*: "Who must tend the family and run the home, so papa's free to read the *Holy Book?* . . . the mama!" Ironically, in the new country, many of the immigrant mothers of the Brownsville women, strong adherents of the European orthodox tradition, were no better able to play their traditional roles than they had been in the *shtetlach* of Europe. But their modern, middle-class daughters were. The Brownsville women took care of all household concerns so that their husbands could pursue their schooling and careers in the same way that the traditional, if idealized, wives freed their husbands from household concerns.

Even when their children were older and most of the women had second jobs outside the home, family continued to be their most important consideration. "Women have less constraints and restrictions today," Claire Moses says. "Whatever I did, I had to come home and discuss it with my husband and we had to decide how it would affect the family."

The women worked hard at their marriages. Even those they considered "the best" had their frustrations. Some of the women are still regretfully but totally dependent upon their husbands. "I never saw myself as making a career . . . I didn't feel I was the breadwinner. Now, what is mine?" one woman laments.

Some of the women felt inadequate: feelings that were reinforced by men, who made all the decisions. Katie Stavans says:

> What I got from my mother was bad. My mother was the type
> that never stood up for herself. That's the reason my house
> was so harmonious. She never stood up for what she wanted.
> I am the same way; only it worked against me in my marriage.

Male dominance, which is, of course, not limited to the Jewish tradition, was reinforced by the women themselves. They complied by accepting sexist stereotypes, such as "emotional equals irrational," when their husbands casually dismissed their opinions:

> He's a perfectionist. No matter what I would do, it couldn't
> please him; he's so much more capable than I am. In handling
> finances, he's on top of everything. My responsibilities were
> managing the home: to cook, to clean, to make appointments.
> But the nitty-gritty, that was him. I couldn't fight much with

> him because he's a very logical person and I'm not. It's easy
> for me to listen to him. I'm a very irrational person, I get very
> emotional. He thinks before he talks. Sometimes I would
> want something and he would say, "What do you need that
> for?" It would bug me.
>
> And that was a very common phrase. I felt inadequate over it.
> There are some things I had to get over in my life, that was
> one of the big things. There were some times when I'd start to
> scream and yell because I would get crazy. He handled the
> money, and I didn't know what I could spend and I what I
> couldn't spend. I get a household allowance, and sometimes I
> would go over that allowance so I would have to explain why
> I went over that allowance and that used to bug me. That was
> his macho control.

Although many of the men supported the women's decisions to go back to school, or to work, some blocked their attempts. One of the women says: "It was very subtle. He was very proud and supportive but felt competition for my time as his companion." Another said her husband was "resentful, threatened" when she advanced from sales to become a district manager and began to have real success in her job. His blocks were overt; he played upon feelings of guilt, accusing her of neglecting her family, her primary, domestic responsibilities. Yet another of the women, Ruth Kesslin, understood: "My husband was genuinely conflicted about my growing and changing."

If their husbands' jobs demanded it and they had to move, their lives changed dramatically. Some of the women found new communities bewildering. During her husband's brief assignment there, Rhoda Nemerofsky found herself in the deep South. One of the first things she looked for when she arrived in Atlanta with their infant daughter (in those days before disposables) was a laundromat. When she found the laundry and it had a "Whites Only" sign on the door, she thought: "Where do people do their colored wash around here? It's a good thing I only have to wash diapers."

The story may seem naïve or even a bit disingenuous, but the meaning of the sign didn't register immediately. Rhoda knew about Jim Crow laws, she knew about segregation, but only as an abstraction. There had always been black people around the neighborhood and in school. She was a nurse; her closest friends in nursing school had been a group of black women; black women were her colleagues in the hospital. The move took some getting used to.

Since their connections were so strong, for some of the women, such as Flo Grosswirth, moving to strange communities, away from friends and family was painful:

> I was mad when we moved away. I didn't really know how to be . . . I didn't know it was okay to be angry that my nest was disturbed, my life was disrupted. I felt as if I'd been thrown to the wolves.

Sydelle Schlossberg says: "Every time I moved, that was traumatic for me, but it was the right thing to do each and every time." There was no discussion. It was best for the husband, for his job or career, and therefore it was best for the family. Florence Kusnetz moved fourteen times in twenty years. The women made their adjustments: they taught themselves to become more independent, learned to drive, joined the temple, became part of their new communities.

The women might do some things very differently today. They believe they would be more assertive, but in looking back, none of the women who are still in long-term marriages admit to any regret in having stuck it out, even through the most difficult times. One woman, whose marriage is less than satisfactory, has "thought about divorce," she says. "We don't share the same interests." When I asked what has stopped her, she answered, "In part it was loyalty, but more it was part of growing up, of your values, you just don't leave." Lila Perlmutter, who was about to celebrate her fortieth anniversary when I interviewed her, said: "No matter what fight we ever had, no matter how big it was, divorce was not an alternative; working it out was the only alternative." Some women, Norma Ellman thinks, "felt they owed a certain allegiance to their children no matter what the situation, so they stuck it out because of the children." And then she adds, a bit cynically, "or they thought, maybe next door it's worse."

But numbers alone can tell a misleading story. A striking characteristic of this generation was the determination to stay together at all costs, which often included "day to day misery for one or both partners."[6] Katie Stavans was one of these women, who remained in her marriage long after it probably should have ended. She says:

> All my children came out damaged from my marriage. When I had one child my mother said, "Leave your husband"; and later on my children wanted me to leave!

And marriages did, of course, end. Four of the Brownsville women who married in the forties were divorced; two of them later remarried. There is a higher number, as we would expect, among the younger couples. Six of the fifties women have been divorced, for a total of ten of the forty-one.[7] Some of the women spoke candidly about their problems; some wouldn't discuss the divorce at all; some would, but only "off the record."

It was very difficult for the women to face the censure of their families and community. Dolores Plaxen says, "I was always made to feel that I was the first person in the world to get divorced. It was such a *shande* that my mother wouldn't let me tell my family about it." For some time afterward she pretended that she was still with her husband. Another woman is now in a long-term, successful, second marriage but for her the *shande* is still potent; she wouldn't talk about her divorce and had to be reassured that I would not name her. She not only "took all of the responsibility for the failure of the marriage" but when her daughter was divorced, took responsibility for that as well. She felt, she says, as if she were "looking in the mirror."

Most of the women who are divorced are defensive; none of them were raised at a time, or in a culture, that permitted them to be casual about divorce, and they regret that they couldn't live up to the ideal. But they feel that they did all they could to save their marriages. Divorce, in the end, was the best, sometimes the only, decision that could be reached. When her husband's extreme manic episodes threatened to endanger the children, Raye Cohen had to, finally, give up on keeping her family together. "It was very difficult," Raye says, "Divorce was very extraordinary in my family." Rochelle Feld allowed herself to be exploited by her first husband, who could never find a job because, it seemed to her, he never looked for one. After a year Rochelle realized that she didn't have to put up with it. She wasn't afraid to go out into the world. She saw that she could make it on her own and asked for a divorce. (Rochelle remarried five years later.) And there are other stories of philandering, compulsive gambling, abuse.

Whatever the reasons for the divorce, in addition to the feelings of failure and shame, the women were left with the burden of earning an income, even if they had some financial support. Some still had young children at home and few were prepared to earn more than a clerical worker's wage. Some of the women were fortunate that their mothers were close by to help care for the children. But with the breakdown of the extended family system others, such as Dolores Plaxen, had no one to turn to. Her husband had put everything in his own name. "He tricked me," she says. "I was left even without my home." But Dolores not only repaid the money she had borrowed, "to buy him out"; she found a way to support herself and put her three sons through college. She says, with understandable pride, "I did it alone."

Katie Stavans finally extricated herself from her emotionally abusive marriage. She summoned the courage to risk being on her own at midlife:

> I walked out before too, but forever, after thirty-six years. I stayed because I was insecure, I never gave myself credit for anything. Maybe I didn't want to fend for myself.
>
> Finally, I could do it because when you're ready, you're ready. Now I feel like I'm a new person. After the divorce, when I went to buy furniture I wouldn't take a soul with me. I wanted to get what *I* liked.
>
> If I left sooner I could have had a new life, but I survived.

Divorce was an imperative for another Brownsville woman, Ruth Berman. Ruth is a lesbian.

When Ruth was coming of age, all homosexuals were considered "perverts"; no distinction was made between homosexuals and pedophiles. In a recent letter to the *New York Times* a writer said that lesbians still suffer the "double abhorrence," of being lesbian and female but in American society in the 1950s homophobia was perhaps at its most extreme. Psychoanalysis had provided labels; it was widely accepted that homosexuals were deviant and maladjusted. They were considered so unstable that President Eisenhower banned them from holding federal jobs.

At a time when the family was being hailed as the most powerful defense against communism, in rejecting the sanctified role of wife-and-mother, lesbianism "offered the most profound challenge to the family" and also challenged the male supremacy upon which traditional family values are based.[8] Both American and Jewish society repudiated any alternative to the ideal of the traditional family. As discussed earlier, in Jewish society homosexuality was disparaged and female homosexuality was not even acknowledged; lesbians and lesbianism do not even appear in the literature. Since it is logical to assume that Jewish lesbians existed in the same proportion as in society as a whole, the subject must have been taboo.[9] Therefore, even if it had occurred to Ruth Berman that she might have been a lesbian, she literally banished the thought.

Ruth was reasonably happy as a teen "because of friends" who have remained close to this day. They celebrated their sixtieth birthdays together as they had celebrated their sixteenth. When they were teenagers the girls of Club Emanon met after school every day, whenever they were free. They went to the Young Women's Hebrew Association, they played ball in the park, they went to the movies and the theater (Ruth and Lillian Wellen, a childhood friend who was present during the interview, burst into "Texas Little Darling," a song from the first show they had ever seen).

Ruth took an academic course in high school ("I hated the idea of secretarial work") and went on to earn her degree at Brooklyn College. Like her friends, Ruth dated. "I knew I was fitting into something I didn't enjoy but I was born too soon," she says. "You didn't have a choice, you had to be attracted to a boy." Ruth met her husband when they were both teaching at the same school and, although she had only been working for one year, like her contemporaries Ruth conformed to social and community pressures concerning marriage and family. She remained at home until her youngest child was four. She never considered that there might have been an alternative.

For most of the eighteen years that it lasted, Ruth had a "model marriage," raised "three outstanding children," and had a busy life. Ruth had been raised in an orthodox, observant home, so it was natural for her to became involved with the temple. She was also an activist, a member of a mother's action committee in "the co-ops" (cooperatively owned apartments). Ruth says: "It was a real community, primarily Jewish, on Twenty-Sixth Avenue and Bay Forty-Third Street in Brooklyn—but something was missing; I never felt totally myself." When Ruth was "about forty," the psychological repression, she believes, finally took its toll in a physical illness, ileitis.

Although Ruth said that she was initially "repelled" by and "struggled" with her sexuality, in time she came to accept her lesbianism. Now, she celebrates it. She has a cordial relationship with her ex-husband, and her children have come to accept Ruth's partner of almost twenty years. Now, Ruth says, she is "a whole person."

"Domestic partner" is one of the unsatisfactory terms for a person in a gay relationship. There are others—friend, house mate, lover—equally unsatisfactory because they don't express the full range of partnership implied in "marriage."[10] There is a word list that has been created by *Yugntruf,* a Jewish cultural organization, so that we can have a Yiddish vocabulary with which to speak about such relationships. The word that is cited is, I believe, the most sensitive: *gelibte.* It means not lover, but loved one.[11]

Today there are laws that ban the kinds of discrimination that we took for granted in the fifties.[12] Ruth is one of those responsible for the change. Still the activist, she has fixed her focus on Gay Rights. Because of her work as a member of the Lesbian/Gay liaison, Ruth was recognized by the Brooklyn Attorney General's office for the role she played in winning spousal benefits for domestic partners who are city employees and retirees. In 1994, both Ruth and Connie Kurtz, her *gelibte,* were honored at the "Festive *Simcha*" celebrating the 21st Anniversary of the Gay and Lesbian Synagogue, the Congregation *Beth Simchat Torah* in New York's Greenwich Village. They received an award "for Pursuit of Justice" not only as "champions in the pursuit of spousal rights for gay and lesbian couples," but for being "founders of gay and lesbian 'coming out' workshops."

Ruth and Connie's activism has taken them in numerous directions. They are co-directors of a counseling center; they publish ♀*utspoken,* a newsletter for women; they are speakers and workshop leaders for numerous organizations; they have co-hosted a radio show, "Women Talking Women Talk"; and they share in an unambiguously political business enterprise. They sell T shirts, sweatshirts, hats, buttons, and bumperstickers which not only bear slogans supporting women's, children's, and human rights but, at the same time, expose smokescreens in popular slogans (one of my favorites is a "An Oxymoron a Day Keeps Reality Away").

While she rejects what she calls "the patriarchy of Judaism," Ruth accepts its morality of "justice and equality." Ruth and Connie were among the first women congregants at Congregation *Beth Simchat Torah* which is led by a dynamic young Rabbi, Sharon Kleinbaum (who is also a lesbian), and where, on her sixtieth birthday, Ruth became *Bat Mitzvah.*

In keeping a kosher home, Ruth has reaffirmed one of the obligations that she had abandoned many years before. But Ruth does not see her observation of *kashruth* as a religious obligation, but rather as a ritual or custom, part of her identification as a Jew. "Being Jewish doesn't allow you to let go," Ruth says. "I'm constantly drawn to it. I *can't not* say I'm a Jew, but I came back on my own terms."

Like almost all of the Brownsville women, Ruth has grappled with what Irena Klepfisz calls the one fundamental question: "How am I a Jew?"[13] And Ruth has defined the parts of Judaism and *Yidishkeit* with which she can identify and to which she can remain faithful, particularly its commitment to "caring, nurturing, and responsibility." Ruth's attachment to Judaism, which she says goes "beyond pride," is a sentiment shared by all but one or two of the women.

There are, characteristic of Jewish-American culture today, as many variations and degrees of religious observance as there are women in this study. The women range from the observant and orthodox to those who reject Judaism and have turned to the nonobservant or secular aspects of *Yidishkeit*, what has been described as a "difficult-to-define sense of group awareness: a shared history, shared understandings, a Jewish ethnic identity." It has also been less generously described as a most curious phenomenon, Jewishness without Judaism, or at least Judaism as traditionally conceived.[14]

Even those women who consider themselves primarily secular and assimilated have a deep sense of pride and affiliation. Raye Cohen, who rebelled against her orthodox upbringing, says:

> I'm Jewish minded, Jewish conscious. I admire anybody who does practice; it must be very rewarding for them. I didn't find it satisfying to me, or necessary, but I love what it represents.
>
> Do I believe in God? I think, I don't think so. I don't think you need to believe in God if you don't do such horrible deeds as would bring the wrath of God upon you. If there is a God, he's forgiven me for my little indiscretions. In my heart I feel I've done good.

Bea Benjamin used the same expression as Raye. What she meant by "Jewish minded" included pride in the culture, in the accomplishments of Jews in the arts and sciences, and particular pride in the accomplishments of Jews in Israel.

Dolores Plaxen identifies with "the plight of Jewish people." Persecution was an explicit part of her family history; her grandfather's parents had been killed in a pogrom. "He killed someone in retaliation and was shipped off to America with a cousin." Perhaps predisposed by this personal history, Dolores was profoundly affected by the stories of the Holocaust. "I thought, if I was a young girl, what would have happened to me?" Dolores is not observant although she celebrates some holidays and won't eat *khomets* (leavened food that is not kosher) for Passover. She "loves being Jewish," admires "what Jews are supposed to be": their morals, ethics, and values. This theme was often repeated. Minette Cutler, who was raised in an orthodox family, says, "They may call me a hypocrite but there are certain things you can't let go of."

Isabel Cohen was "turned off to Judaism" when she was young. Her extended family included her grandmother, who was observant and demanding. It was unfortunate, Isabel says, because living with her grandmother should have been an introduction to the religion, but Isabel only knew, and resented, the restrictions.

"You couldn't eat this, couldn't do that. 'You used the wrong towel to wipe the dishes and silverware.'" Still, when her children were growing up she felt that she needed to observe the holidays to give them a sense of their Jewishness. Some of the other women, too, who are not otherwise distinguishable as Jews, still attend services on the high holy days and continue to fast on *Yom Kippur*.

Harriet Portnoy accepts one of the common explanations for *kashruth*: that it has its roots in the prerefrigeration sanitary and health needs of the early, middle eastern Jewish culture.[15] Harriet says:

> Because I'm a scientist, I realize milk and meat were kept separate for health reasons and it became a tradition. Now there's no problem of contamination when you put the dishes in the dishwasher. Consequently, it is no longer necessary today.

Harriet doesn't keep a kosher home but has passed on other rituals. Her daughter (who was *Bat Mitzvah*) still "changes over" that is, she uses a different set of dishes for Passover. And Harriet's "kids still won't drink milk and eat meat in the same meal."

Some of the women made concessions to ritual out of respect for their parents. Claire Moses kept a kosher home, she says, so that her "parents could eat in her house." Raye Cohen did the same. "Even though I wasn't religious from the age of fifteen on, when I got married I kept a kosher home out of deference to my parents and my family, who were religious." But, she admits, "they wouldn't eat in my house anyway because they didn't trust me, so I stopped." (I could identify with Raye; I had a similar experience and finally resorted to serving on paper plates.)

"I came out of a Jewish household," Roslyn Bowers says, "but I rejected it all." Perhaps no one became more assimilated than Roslyn. She was brought up in a family that was typical of Brownsville of the

1940s and 1950s in that they were "partially observant." They "kept kosher, they didn't cook or write on the Sabbath, they observed the holy days." Roslyn did not have any religious education but, of course, was expected to (and did) marry a Jew. Otherwise her parents would have disowned and mourned for her. "They would have sat *shiva.*"

As an actively involved participant in the Civil Rights movement of the sixties, Roslyn saw religion "as the greatest divider of humankind." Today Roslyn acknowledges that she did not, in fact, "reject it all," because she sees her involvement with Civil Rights and the Freedom Party, community politics and the Democratic Reform Movement on the Upper West Side of Manhattan, as part of her Jewishness. "There is some connection about being Jewish and being involved and being concerned for others," Roslyn says.

When Israel was censured in the United Nations, Roslyn attended a protest rally in the garment district, and this event sparked her return to *Yidishkeit.* Roslyn realized that she wanted "to learn more about being Jewish." She visited the Lubavitchers in Brooklyn.[16] She attended lectures. She learned to read, write, and improve her spoken Yiddish, and to read Yiddish literature. She learned to read Hebrew. She visited synagogues when she travelled overseas. She sent her daughters to Hebrew school, began to celebrate Chanukah (they had previously celebrated the holiday season with a Christmas tree). One of her daughters designed a *Hagadah* (the story of the Exodus recited at the Passover *seder* meal) which Roslyn treasures. Her connection with Judaism is cultural and historical, "but I am Jewish," she says. Finally, Roslyn Bowers, like Ruth Berman, decided to become *Bat Mitzvah.*

Lila Perlmutter is the only Brownsville woman in the fifties group who has remained orthodox and observant. At eighteen, when her mother died "too young" after a terrible illness, Lila wasn't sure about her faith. But she made a conscious decision to remain observant and orthodox.

Like her mother, Lila had been observant while she was growing up, although neither her friends nor any other members of her family were, not even her sister. Lila's father, who left the family on the day she was born, came to visit from time to time, usually on Saturdays. She says:

> He watched TV and would deliberately leave the set on when
> he left, knowing that we wouldn't be able to turn it off until
> sundown. One time, he had some furniture delivered to our
> house on a Saturday. My mother was so humiliated and
> embarrassed!

Being observant had its cost. For Lila, one price that she had to pay
was that she wasn't able to become a medical secretary. The certification
examination was given by the Board of Education, but only on Saturday
mornings, "and I was a Sabbath observer," she says. "That was it!"

A couple of incidents preceded her reaffirmation. The first occurred
right after her mother died:

> I remember laying in bed, angry with God to do this to some-
> one who believed in Him, yelling at Him, "You'd better have
> a good reason," and realizing, I must believe in Him and He
> had His reasons. And I thought, if I believe, I should serve
> Him the way orthodox people believe He wants them to serve
> Him, by keeping the laws. If I'm right, I'm doing the right
> thing. If I'm wrong, who does it hurt?

The second incident occurred when Lila decided that she would
say *Kadish* for her mother, the mourner's prayer for the dead. It was
something orthodox women did not do, she said, but, "My mother
didn't leave sons, she had a husband who was a bastard; who would
do it?"

"I knew," Lila says, "that there was nothing that says I have to, but
I wrote to a Jewish organization to ask if there was anything that says I
can't." They replied that they didn't know of a prohibition against it if
there was a *minyan*, the ten Jewish males that constitute a quorum for
prayer, although as a woman she couldn't be part of the *minyan*.

Fortified with her letter, Lila went to the synagogue at six o'clock in
the morning, before she went to work. There was a *minyan* praying in a
small room, so she stayed outside of the doorway and prayed along with
the men. "They were unhappy to see a young woman saying *kadish*, but
they didn't stop me." In fact, they wouldn't have been able to stop her.

> When they told me I couldn't be an astronomer, I said okay.
> When they told me I couldn't be a medical secretary, I said
> okay. But if they told me I couldn't say *kadish*—no, sorry, I
> had to. I had a fire in me, there was no question.
>
> On the third day one of the men asked, "are you going to do
> this every day?" I said yes! The next day when I came back
> they had built a *mehitzah* for me, a wooden screen with white
> curtains, and they left one chair with a *sider* [the Jewish daily
> prayer book] on it. I was so touched: they made room for me,
> they accepted me.

When Lila bought her own home it was two blocks away from a synagogue so that she could walk to services and, although her husband wasn't religious, she "put her foot down" and insisted on her sons going to a *yeshiva*. She believes women have a special place in Judaism because they "raise the next generation." She wanted her sons to be raised to be Jews, to marry Jewish women. "Living an orthodox life," Lila says, "can only be a positive thing to do morally and ethically, a good way to live with my fellow human beings."

For at least one of the women, however, Jewish pride has crossed the border into chauvinism. "I'm very Jewish," she says. In her definition, Jews claim high moral ground: "To be a Jew is to be good in your heart." But, surprisingly, she didn't see that her own definition was compromised when she accompanied it with the denigration of "every *shvartze* [black] in the neighborhood" who drove the Cadillacs she coveted, or the denigration of the *shiksa*, the non-Jewish woman, her son married. Unlike my old clubmate, Elaine Cohen, she must not even recognize her prejudices. Elaine was forced to face her own prejudices when her son not only married outside the faith, but married a black woman. "I was brought up to be almost a racist," Elaine says. "My mother told me blacks were bad people; I had a fear of them." She admits that she had a great deal of difficulty accepting her daughter-in-law, although she has grown to love her. Guilelessly, she says: "She's very light skinned, I don't see her as a black girl."

Intermarriage is a common concern among most of the women, with varying degrees of intensity. None of them married out of the religion. The only woman in this study who is married to a non-Jew is Linda Brasco, the product herself of a Jewish father and Russian Orthodox mother. Her sister, Arlene Feldman, converted to Judaism when she married. (Sadly, Arlene's mother refused to invite her family to the Jewish wedding, but over the years she has "mellowed.")

Like Elaine Cohen's son, many other children of the Brownsville women have married non-Jews. This is a reality with which most of the women are not comfortable, but which they have had to accept. They accept it with difficulty, even when their daughters- or sons-in-law have converted into the Jewish faith. Although they are obliged by Judaism to do so, the women don't fully accept the convert. They would agree that, "at best the convert is a palimpsest," a term that literally means parchment or vellum that has been written over but on which the "old writing will always bleed through."[17] They don't believe that someone can "really" become a Jew, particularly when their definition of Jewishness is so culturally and historically determined.

Intermarriage hinders a task which the Brownsville women take seriously and for which they claim full responsibility: to pass *Yidishkeit* on to their grandchildren. Since, a recent article reported, "more than 50 percent of Jews intermarry and few children from such bonds are raised Jewish,"[18] the women have ample reason to believe that intermarriage not only threatens and dilutes *Yidishkeit* but that Judaism itself is in jeopardy. Even if that figure is exaggerated, the problem is substantial. Minette Cutler asks, not comprehending: "Why can't the Jewish people stay together? There's too much assimilation."

Sydelle Schlossberg describes herself as "very Jewish," which she defines as "outgoing, showy, comfortable with children, bonding." Her American-born parents weren't observant: "They were socialists." Although they did observe the holidays and Sydelle went to *shul* with her grandparents, she was never religious. Sydelle was stunned, however, when her son told her that his fiancée wanted to have a church wedding. "That was going too far," she says. Because she refused to attend the wedding, it was agreed, finally, that it would be performed by a Justice of the Peace.

It was a great blow to Minette Cutler when one of her sons intermarried. "It was my background. I didn't like it when my son did it," she says. "I almost disowned him. I couldn't accept it even though she converted and I wouldn't ever have accepted a reform conversion." Minette confides, "I was very mean to this woman he married." It took some time for her to come around but she did: "You wouldn't believe how close I am with her today," she says.

Intermarriage is not only troublesome to the women because of their loyalty to Judaism; they also believe that intermarriage makes the necessary adjustments to marriage more difficult, and that their children already deal with many problems, in some respects many more than they did.

Toward the end of the interviews I asked each of the women how they would assess their lives in comparison with the lives of their mothers and their daughters (and women of their daughters' generation). Who had an easier time? Whose lives were—are—more fulfilling, more meaningful?

With regard to their mothers, the answers came almost without hesitation. As Flo Grosswirth says, "We are the lucky ones, we had it the best." In comparison with their mothers, their lives have been much easier; in comparison with their daughters' generation, their lives have been much less complex. Not surprisingly, the women could readily enumerate why, in most respects, their lives have been better than their mothers' were and are much easier now that they are at or nearing retirement age.

Unlike their mothers, the women in this study are financially secure. They may not be rich, but they are not poor, by any historical or contemporary measure. The women are able to make full use of their leisure time. They participate in a wide range of cultural activities and some have travelled extensively. They enjoy many luxuries and advantages of which their mothers could not have dreamed. Sydelle Schlossberg recounted a story, with some embarrassment, about her search for a condo in Florida. She and her husband found one they liked except for one drawback: it had only one bathroom. When she told the story she laughed at herself, saying, "Listen to me. When we were growing up we thought we were lucky to have a bathroom down the hall, now I can't manage without two."

It is only when they are overcome with feelings of nostalgia for a simpler time that the women feel that their mothers had it better. Some, such as Isabel Cohen, say that their mothers' lives were "predetermined, but easier." Because their mothers had even less choice than they had, as the women see it, their mothers had less conflict. They knew their role, they accepted it. "They weren't spread so thin." Some also believe that their mothers had a sense of security, in living within the safe haven of the extended family, that they themselves haven't felt since they left the neighborhood. But overall, given this reservation, the women believe that their lives have been much better, materially and emotionally easier, culturally richer and more satisfying in most respects than their mothers' lives were.

Perhaps it should not be surprising either that, although the assessment is more complex, they feel their lives have also been better than the lives today of their daughters, daughters-in-law, and the women of their daughters' generation.[19] This is despite the fact that their daughters are better educated and have had vastly greater life chances and choices than they had. In fact, almost all of their daughters and daughters-in-law are not only college graduates but have advanced credentials or professional degrees.

The women are grateful that their daughters had so many more career options than they had (and that they can and do engage in a wide assortment of careers). While the women do not call themselves feminists, (they actually tend to use the outdated expression *women's lib-bers*), they believe that this is due, in great measure, to the women's movement.[20] Claire Moses says:

> The women's movement helped raise women's expectations, that's not negative. It's easier for women today; they can do what they want to do, they can be a free person in the sense that you know what is out there and you're doing what you want to do.

Their lives are easier too, Roslyn Bowers says about her daughters' generation, because they grew up "expecting sharing" in their marriages. Eleanor Chernick, somewhat romantically, agrees: "The women's movement helped our daughter's lives; they have a partnership in planning their lives, implementing their careers, raising their children." Surprisingly, Lorraine Nelson, who has lived the exemplary life of a traditional, orthodox Jewish woman—"school, job, marriage, housewife"—sees the change through a somewhat unrealistic (and very middle-class) lens. "Careers are wonderful for women," Lorraine says. "They don't have to give up anything today; they give up TV. They have housekeepers; the husbands help with the kids."

Their daughters were socialized into an American culture in which women's options were expanding—and are continuing to expand—and in which it was no longer taken for granted that a man could have it all but a woman could not. Rochelle Feld says:

> You were brought up with the thought that you would get married like your mother and have babies like your mother and have a household like your mother. This generation, they think they're going to have that and still do work. And they don't have to be nurses and teachers and social workers, what we were ingrained to be. They can be oceanographers and Diane Fosses.

"They have *real* choices," Sally Forman says, somewhat enviously. But Sally and most of the women believe that choices have not made life easier for their daughters. Katie Stavans says, "We were sheltered; it was much easier. It's much harder for them because the world is more open, they have a bigger scope than we did; our world was very limited." But, as Rochelle Feld says, "Harder doesn't necessarily mean less happy. It may be more fulfilling." Rae Mirsky echoes this: "It's still better; they're more self-confident, they're more fulfilled. You're not sitting back and letting someone take care of you." She adds: "Good luck to them."

It was certainly not a new phenomenon for daughters to grow up wanting to lead lives that were radically different from the lives their mothers led. Many of the Brownsville women had that experience themselves. Katie Stavans says, "We had a big generation gap. We were different from our parents like night to day because we were the first ones in the mold trying to break away." But what was unique to their daughters' generation, coming of age in the sixties and seventies, was that they were the first who "had the *opportunity* to act on these dreams and aspirations and to make them a reality."[21]

The women are witnessing their daughters having both family and career at the same time, not "either-or" and not putting one off for the other. "I had high aspirations, I wanted to be a professional," Claire Moses says. She thinks that if she had been born into a later generation she would have done her own thing first, and would have been "like modern women today who go out and have a career and get married at thirty-five."

Claire took it for granted that she would marry, but another change that the women are seeing, which is very baffling to them, is that their daughters are deciding whether to marry or to devote themselves exclusively to professional careers. The women can't comprehend how their daughters can consider such a choice. Valerie Greenberg's daughter told her, "I don't need a man to make me happy," and like her, although not necessarily by choice, a number of the daughters in their late twenties and thirties are still single. Some of the women with single daughters fault women's liberation and the sexual revolution. In this area they judge feminism harshly. The women say: "Why should a guy get married? Women have given up their bodies"—"The freer life style, the sexual experimentation is scary"—"Sometimes it's more than they can handle"—"It's hard for young people, they have to worry about staying alive"—"Women's lib screwed up a lot of girls with too much freedom."

Linda Brasco says, "God knows it's a crazy place, I always hold my breath."

Some of their daughters share apartments with domestic partners, a practice that concerns Minette Cutler: "I'm old fashioned when it comes to this business of living together. Even my oldest son got married from the house, and girls have a lot more to lose."[22] As Shirley Donowitz says, they, particularly the forties women, came from a time when parents not only had influence but still had control: "my father would tell me who to go with, who not to go with." Clearly (perhaps it's too much to expect of them), most of the women don't share Sylvia Zinn's open-mindedness; her daughter is "looking for the perfect mate," Sylvia says, "but meanwhile she's living!"

Sydelle Schlossberg doesn't agree; she doesn't envy the women of the next generation at all. Compared with her daughters-in-law, Sydelle believes that her life was much easier. "They both are juggling careers," in teaching and law, "at the same time that they are trying to raise their families. Their husbands are also busy and so they spend more time on their own." Their daughters, also "the daughters of feminism," are heir not only to its successes and benefits but to its struggles and to its failures.[23] The women believe that their daughters' "advantages" have come at too great a price.

Even supporters of the feminist movement such as Claire Moses and Roslyn Bowers, are critical. Claire says that she thought women "would do better; the standards of salary and the standard of working conditions have not been equalized." And furthermore, she thinks feminists have not been sufficiently diplomatic: "The women's movement made men more wary. Male chauvinism shows in places it might not have showed in other times; they've become defensive. Women get in their own way."

Lillian Pollack has serious reservations about affirmative action. She says, thoughtfully and without animosity:

> I do believe there is such a thing as a glass ceiling but women have other things. There are so many opportunities open that were even unheard of, even professions that weren't even around when I went to school. Women are placed in jobs just because they're women. You're using a person's gender, race, etc. to make up for past abuses, but then you're creating a different class of people who are being discriminated against; that would be people with merit.

Lillian concludes, pensively, "Whenever there's a change, unfortunately, it swings too far the other way."

Rhoda Nemerofsky, too, thinks the women's movement has gone too far, although she was speaking about a different issue; she thinks the issue of having choices has been turned on its head. Rhoda says:

> We took options away from them, we fought so hard for our
> options we never gave our girls the option. We say, "What do
> you mean they're getting married and staying home?"

But Rhoda understands that it is not only because of feminism that "the young girls of today have no choice; they have to go to work." The women correctly see that many of their married daughters work, even those with very young children, because they require two incomes to maintain the standard of living in which they were born and raised.

Harriet Portnoy brought all of the issues together when she articulated why she believes she "had it all." Harriet was born in a tenement apartment in Brownsville. "From the time I was born until I was eighteen, I probably went as far as New Jersey," she says. But, like her Brownsville peers, Harriet spanned an enormous distance during her lifetime, in much more than geographic terms. "My daughter's life," Harriet says, "began where mine left off." For Harriet's daughter and other daughters like her, it is a great struggle to maintain that taken-for-granted level of comfort. Harriet says:

> When I was first married, it was only two people and one
> child. I didn't think I needed a four-bedroom house, a big
> house on a big piece of property. My daughter was born in a
> big house with a big piece of property so when she got mar-
> ried, that's what she needed right away.

Rhoda Nemerofsky agrees but adds the element of impatience:

> Something we waited twenty-five years to have, they want now.
> Today every kid gets married, they live in an apartment for a
> day and a half and they have to buy a house. That was the fur-
> thest thing from our minds. Nobody owned their own house.

Whether it is, as Lillian Pollack says, that "kids live over their heads," or as Terry Apter says a bit more kindly, that "they need a lot more than we did," the women find it regrettable that their daughters have to work in order not to fall to a lower station in life. It is ironic, in the sense that they have to work, that their daughters are more like their immigrant grandmothers than like their own mothers. Roslyn Bowers regrets that "we've raised a generation who can't 'top' their parents." She asks, "How much farther can they go?

As the women judge their daughters' generation according to their own subjective criteria, the things that they value highly and that have given meaning to their lives, the women conclude that they have had better lives not only than their mothers had but than their daughters are having today.

The women believe that their lives have been, and still are, meaningful. They are conscious of the leap they've made in social class in the course of one generation. They were all born into a poverty-ridden community and suffered not only the "hidden injuries of class," but of gender. They had all of the disadvantages that their life chances imposed on them. But, as Norma Ellman says, simply, "We've come a long way." And, although they have already accomplished a great deal, their plans are far from over.

A few of the women, Rhoda Nemerofsky is one, still have heavy demands placed upon them by tending to both their grandchildren and elderly parents. She is part of the phenomenon that has been characterized as the "sandwich generation." Rhoda says, although not at all begrudgingly, "I'm retired but I'm doing the job I gave up twenty-plus years ago to go to work: cooking, cleaning, caretaking."

Others are still looking toward retirement. They expect to travel, to move, to reestablish ties with old friends and make new ones, to have more time for their grandchildren, to continue their civic or charitable activities, to be physically and mentally active. Minette Cutler thinks that she may finally fulfill her desire to go to college when she retires but she's not sure when that will be. "After all these years of working can you just come home and sit?" she asks. Next year she will celebrate her fiftieth year with the same firm, and then, Minette says, "I'll think about it."

Bea Larkin has been taking courses at Kingsboro Community College. Jean Bleckner would like to go back to school to fill "a void," she says. The Brownsville women of the forties who are already retired defy the stereotype of the "empty-nest syndrome":

> The traditional woman bases her self-esteem on a role, motherhood, that she must finally relinquish. Some do this with ease; some others . . . cannot. But the problem is not hers alone; society has provided no guidelines, for her, no rites of passage. There is no *Bar Mitsvah* for menopause. The empty nest, then, may prompt the extreme feelings of worthlessness and uselessness that characterize depressives. One can think of these women as overcommited to the maternal role and then, in middle age, suffering the unintended consequences of this commitment.[24]

Although they were certainly devoted to their children, the description is not a good fit for any of the Brownsville women in this study. Perhaps it is because, except for the time when their children were very young, they were never totally immersed in the housewife/mother role. They went on to lead active lives. They worked, they were involved with charitable organizations and with community activities, they travelled, they took classes, they maintained close friendships. They still do.

The women are not mourning their empty nests. On the contrary, they're finding this period in their lives liberating. Norma Ellman rarely babysits: "I've got my own life to live right now," she says. "I've done my job." Norma, who sings with the Long Island *Yidish* Gilbert and Sullivan Opera Company had the lyrics of *The Pirates of Penzance* and a rehearsal schedule on her sidetable when I interviewed her. She was settling down to study them when I left.

Shirley Donowitz never thought she had any talent, but in 1965 her brother gave her "a canvas and a couple of paints" so she started to paint. "I loved children," Shirley says. "Teaching was in the back of my head because whenever we played school, I was always the teacher." Not only is Shirley still painting and displaying her work, but now Shirley is teaching art classes.

The women have much to do. I know, because of how difficult it was to make appointments with them. They seem to be constantly busy with something, often Jewish cultural activities. Jean Bleckner and some of her friends have formed a Yiddish club. They read books, listen to Yiddish music, speak to each other in Yiddish. She has a "sense of joy in being able to speak and understand the language." Zena Bloom knows Yiddish. She learned to read and write when she went to the *shule* on Stone Avenue in Brownsville. Like Jean, Zena attends monthly Jewish study groups (one is held in Yiddish) which meet in people's homes in her upstate New York community.

Although her daughters didn't appreciate it, I loved the message on Roslyn Bowers's answering machine: "I'm out spending my daughters' inheritance." At least some of it was going to be spent on an upcoming trip to Morocco. But Roslyn, who lives in Riverdale, doesn't limit her outings to exotic places. She subscribes to the opera and ballet. She has many friends, and they go to shows, museums, films, shows. They take walking tours all over the city. She goes to the gym a couple of times a week and was taking a class at NYU in "Political Conspiracy."

Many of the Brownsville women have moved to southern Florida along with their friends of more than fifty years. Many others join them during the winter months. Though the move away from their children was difficult for them, they have each other. The women are proud of having achieved close, lifelong friendships. They have gone through every passage in their lives together. In Florida, Sally Forman says, "I feel as if I've come back home." Through their relationships with each other they retain their connection with Brownsville and with their early, shared experiences in the neighborhood.

It was in the community of Brownsville that the values of the Jewish culture became permanently integrated with the women's personal value systems. I believe that the part of their character that is enabling them to have rich and fulfilling lives in their retirement was formed there, the part that never says "I am finished." There is optimism in these women, something they absorbed into their personalities that never stops striving for more, for a better life for themselves and their children, for greater personal fulfillment and achievement, even to improve the world. I don't believe it is accidental that there is, in this group, a striking absence of those symptoms of despair and depression that can overcome women in the later years of their lives.[25]

I am certain that the most difficult thing I asked the women to do was to identify their most significant personal success, to talk about what they are proud of about themselves; not about their children, or their husbands, or their material successes, or even their marriages. This was not due just to modesty. It was enormously difficult for them to define themselves in the first person, as "I," alone and separate. They didn't know how to think about themselves as separate and to find their value in their own qualities, their own selves. When they finally thought about it in this way they were able to say that they are most proud of simply being good, warm, caring, charitable, and loving people; of having been hard workers, willing to struggle, both inside and outside of their homes, both physically and emotionally to provide support for their growing families; of having retained their values and of passing *Yidishkeit* on to the next generation. And shouldn't they be proud? They have valuable personal and social qualities that are becoming more and more rare; they have made a contribution as role models to their contemporaries, to their children, and to their grandchildren.

In listening to their collective story I learned how the Brownsville women, "the girls," overcame their circumstances and their life chances;

how they were socialized, acquired their values, defined and redefined them, made choices, did not make choices, and make choices still. There are differences between the experiences of the women who are separated in age by only five to ten years, with regard to their education, careers, and domestic lives but great similarities as well.

Each time I completed an interview I left with the feeling that these are ordinary, but also extraordinary, women. And at the risk of being accused of sounding overly sentimental and having fallen into the "nostalgia trap," I must say that I think our society will be poorer, indeed, when they're gone.

I also, always, came away wondering how different my life might have been, how much more like theirs, if I'd grown up a few years earlier. A few years later. A few more blocks to the east.

Daughters

New Dilemmas

You have to be a superwoman now. No one thinks its cute to be dependent.

—Dolores Work Plaxen

R ecently, an article appeared in the Jewish weekly newspaper, the *Forward,* entitled "A Mystery Story,'The Jewish Mother' Has Disappeared." A report issued by Hadassah's National Commission on American Jewish Women informs us that "many women shun motherhood" or hold jobs that prevent them from "hovering over the *kneidelach*" (those succulent dumplings some of us remember from our youth), and from hovering over the children.[1]

The Brownsville women, all but two of whom were able to remain home when their children were young, did not need the 1990 National Jewish Population survey to tell them that "fewer than one-third of Jewish mothers with children under six" are full-time homemakers.[2] These "Jewish mothers" are their daughters.

The Brownsville women understand the issues, they know why their daughters work. They work due to a collision of factors: changes in cultural norms for American Jews, the women's movement, which opened educational and career opportunities for women, changes in technology and in economic conditions. All of these now-familiar elements, and many others as well, have provided their daughters with educational opportunities and career options that were unavailable to the women themselves. "Now girls have the option to be everything and anything," Lillian Pollack says.

The women understand that their daughters are in the workplace in such large numbers for various and complex reasons. Certainly, one reason is that their education has prepared them to pursue professional careers, careers that require them to remain in the workplace without a lengthy "time out" to raise a family. On the contrary, for young women today, remaining at home is often a brief time out from their careers. A woman can't drop out of law or computer-related work for ten years and keep up with changes in the field.

"It goes without saying that a woman will be educated today," Dolores Plaxen says, and indeed, women's educational gains have been enormous in recent decades. In 1960 only thirty-five percent of American women enrolled in colleges, compared with forty-six percent of young men. By 1986 women had caught up with men, as more than fifty percent of both women and men were enrolling in college.[3] By the end of the decade women's enrollment had surpassed men's. Women were receiving not only baccalaureate but advanced degrees: in 1992 women received thirty-eight percent of the 38,000 doctorates that were conferred.[4] These figures are not abstractions to the Brownsville women. Their daughters' educations confirms the data. Doris Levinson and her husband were born during the Depression into typical Brownsville families. Doris says:

> My husband and I have come very far from my roots. My
> daughter graduated from Duke University. She is an attorney,
> a lobbyist. It's just one generation removed!

Their daughters grew up in middle-class households with expectations of a level of comfort throughout their lifetimes that they took for granted, but which, because of a steady decline of men's real wages over the past fifteen years, their households cannot maintain without a second income. A decade ago, Congress proclaimed that working women were preserving family living standards: "It is their working wives who have maintained what prosperity the family has."[5] As Fayge Lubin says, "It's harder than it was for me, keeping up with material things." Added to this is the phenomenon of continually rising expectations stimulated at least in part by the media and advertising. It is ironic that these middle-class, professional women don't have the choice of whether or not to work; like their immigrant grandmothers, they *have* to work. Terry

Apter says, "they grew up having a lot and they compete with others who have more. They borrow; it's tough to pay back."

It is not only because their daughters need the income, or even because they are educated for professional careers that they are working mothers. There is yet another reason. Since Freidan located the "problem that had no name" in the homemaking role, that was "seen as the key to women's subordination." Untying the apron strings became the apparent signal of liberation.[6] If domestic work is low-status work, then housewives' work, since it is unpaid, is devalued even further to the status of non-work, particularly in a society that values money as highly as the United States. American society, including the woman who describes herself as "just a housewife," persists in this faulty judgment in spite of the fact that we have been forced to see how truly valuable housework is, and how expensive and difficult the services of the housewife are to replace.

Rhoda Nemerofsky believes that one of the most egregious problems created by the women's movement is that we took the choice of being a traditional housewife away from our daughters. Most of the women agree. They believe their daughters are missing something that they recall with nostalgic pleasure, an important part of their most important role. The women wish their daughters could experience, as they believe they did, the satisfactions of being home with their babies. "Before, women enjoyed being home," Terry Apter says, and then adds, "but of course we didn't know better."

In the same *Forward* article, a member of the Hadassah commission warned against "getting too sentimental about the disappearance of the Jewish mother of old," because for many women, she said, being home all day with toddlers is "boring" and "draining."[7] Many of the women did, in fact, eventually get bored but, as Flo Grosswirth says, "The same way you remember childbirth, you remember the good parts, the important parts."

There *were* good parts—but the women also hold onto the belief that it was right to have stayed home when their children were young. "Raising the next generation is one of the most important things a Jewish woman can do," Lila Perlmutter says. Being the good mother, putting the children's needs before their own, was a highly valued virtue. Because they thought it was right, if they chose work or a profession such as teaching, it was one that would allow them to put family first. Being the good mother became the core of their identity. The women's sense of self-worth is validated in some basic respects, even today, by what they gave up to be successful mothers; their self-image and self-esteem still, to a large extent, depend upon how well they believe they performed the mother role. And, "Experts agree that there is probably no other role with less latitude"[8]

Success as a mother is a very difficult thing to measure, but there were mothering "rules." One of those rules was that you stayed home when the children were little. For Brownsville girls, the image of the perfect mother who was at home was reinforced by the Jewish culture and by the intense idealization of the family in the postwar and Cold War eras. And this was despite the fact that many of their own working mothers did not have the luxury of staying home to model the ideal role. Minette Cutler is one of the women who had to go back to work before her children were in school. Minette's mother cared for the children, but even so, she says, "I was considered not a good mother by many of my peers" (although she added, "If I had been a professional it would have been okay").

Their daughters are not playing by the old rules, and the women worry about who is raising their grandchildren, not only because they know how inadequate day care is in this country but because they believe that the children should be with their mothers.[9] The mythology persists that mothers are the best ones to raise their children as if intuitively, magically, they can do the best job of it; yet in individual cases we have ample evidence to the contrary. And we don't know if having a working mother is bad for even very young children. There are studies that say yes, others that say no. One study "proved" that children didn't suffer any ill effects if their mothers worked, and three months later another contradicted those findings. An interesting study of African-American full-time working mothers has shown that their children perform better on IQ tests and have higher self-esteem.[10] Some of the women are not resolved within themselves; they can argue both opposing views. Eleanor Chernick thinks that the final verdict has not come in. She believes that "children's lives are not contingent upon the lives their mothers are leading but on the quality of the relationship between their parents. We have to wait to see how these kids turn out."

The Brownsville women have a range of opinions about their daughters as working mothers of young children. Lillian Pollack says:

> They make a lot of money. They have a baby and give it to someone else to watch. Women are missing out, the child misses out, and they don't know it.

The women deplore the phenomenon of "latch-key children," those children who come home from school and spend many unsupervised hours alone. But Claire Moses has another point of view. She is adamant, speaking not only from her own experience as a working mother, but from her own childhood:

> I don't believe that working or being productive or doing something that requires an education or skills has a negative effect on anybody. What was I, not a latch-key child? My mother and father had a store, so what was I? I still had to go upstairs, I still had to stay in the house by myself, I still had to find a book to read . . . and there was nothing wrong with my children. They came home for lunch, it was left ready for them, and they came home after school and went to Hebrew school.

Although they worry about their grandchildren, they don't want to turn back the clock. None of the women want their daughters to give up their careers but most think they should take a longer hiatus from work, as they did, for child rearing. They are very proud of their daughters who are psychologists, guidance counselors, and teachers. Lillian Pollack had the highest average in both math and Spanish. She "earned both medals and should have gotten both," she said, but didn't; the math medal went to a boy. When her daughter *did* win a math medal, an old friend of Lillian's said to her, "You see, she got your medal for you." Now Lillian's daughter is a math teacher. "The better part went through me to her," Lillian says.

Only one of the daughters of the Brownsville women is a nurse and only one is a social worker; one of their daughters is a paralegal. A relatively large percentage, however, have become attorneys, as law, along with medicine, is losing its male domination. Some fear that these professions are becoming feminized; it's a far cry from the days when Rhoda Nemerofsky said that medicine "wasn't a girl thing." In 1994, half of the medical school applicants were women.[11]

The women relish the fact that their daughters and daughters-in-law are in an array of fields that are unusual or nontraditional for women (and certainly for Jewish women): Swedish massage therapy; computer engineering; the culinary arts (one studied at the Cordon Bleu to become a chef); horticulture therapy; biotechnology; bartending; lobbying. A number are involved with the media arts: one is in film production, another is an agent for a film art director, another is a singer. My daughter took her degree in theater arts. Her first job, straight out of college, was as an assistant to the wardrobe mistress in an "extravaganza" theatrical production in Reno, sewing molted feathers back onto dance costumes. Then she was a singing waitress for a brief time until she settled into a career, working primarily with the entertainment industry, as a travel consultant.

We know that these represent only some of the occupations in which women have made substantial gains. There are many others. And more women are in the sciences.[12] Unlike Harriet Portnoy who "came to earth science late," somebody is telling girls that they *can* be geologists. Harriet's daughter is an engineer.

Lila Perlmutter wanted to be an astronomer. She had been told that as a woman and as a Jew it was totally unrealistic. Several years ago Lila saw a woman astronomer interviewed on PBS. At first she was "furious" (but not, as she should have been, with her advisor, culture, society). Lila says:

> I was furious with myself. I let myself drop out of the race. I was compliant. All I had to do was try? In the interview the woman said, "Everyone told me I shouldn't do it."

> I told everybody. I told my son, "Oh, you should have seen this woman, she's an astronomer." I told my daughter, I told my nephew, I told my husband, I told my friends, I told everybody. I told everybody that this woman made it.

Their daughters are "making it" too. The women are witnessing their daughters having both family and career at the same time, not "either-or": something women of their generation and social class did not attempt. However, in spite of their educational accomplishments, the women and many others believe their daughters have not been provided with the skills (or the props) they need in order to perform the delicate balancing act of work and family. "You have to be superwoman today," Dolores Plaxen says. The women believe that there is a great deal of stress placed upon the marriage and family, although some researchers disagree and claim that the media has fostered a false and exaggerated notion of the working mother.[13] Whichever assessment is correct, as working mothers of the nineties, their daughters are being challenged with new dilemmas.

It is only necessary to spend a short time at the library computer to generate an enormous bibliography on the subject of managing work and family. There are books and articles pro and con. Some deal with all the now-old issues and some with new ones such as "eldercare programs in the workplace." (Jean Bleckner and Sally Forman would have benefitted from such a program. They retired from their jobs to care for their elderly parents.) There is advice; there are handbooks and manuals. There is at least one "Taxonomy of behavioral strategies for coping with work-home role conflict."[14] There is a facilitator's manual, with "step by step" instructions for a program designed to help participants learn effective skills for managing multiple roles and for balancing work and family issues. Some of the work on "current issues" goes back at least twenty years.[15]

Phyllis Moen's conceptualization of "three separate but intertwined realities" is helpful in understanding why change is so slow. First, new institutions are not yet in place since we are still in the midst of change. The "second reality" has to do with profound beliefs about the meaning of family and issues related to separate spheres for men and women. The final, third reality, is that there is a "mismatch" between the way our institutions operate and the needs of women, particularly the needs of working mothers. The intractability of these obstacles to change were not fully appreciated in the early days of the women's movement when Elizabeth Cady Stanton optimistically predicted, more than one hundred years ago, that women would have a "more enlightened public sentiment for discussion"; it could not have been clear how deeply embedded the obstacles are and the profound effect they have upon public policy.[16]

These lead to another reality: the daughters of the Brownsville women lead vastly different lives from the ones their mothers led. Few of the Brownsville women have daughters who are following the old, traditional pathways. Even Lorraine Nelson's daughter, who is orthodox and raising four children, went to college and earned a teaching degree in Special Education.

The Brownsville women realize that their daughters not only can have careers and marriage simultaneously rather than sequentially, as in the past, but they can decide whether to marry at all or to devote themselves exclusively to professional careers. It is one of the most difficult things for the Brownsville women to understand, that their daughters might choose to be single. They can't believe that a woman can lead a rich and fulfilling life in ways other than through marriage and family (and they don't begin to comprehend lesbianism). However, some of their daughters not only have not married but will not marry or have children. Others, like the daughter of one of my friends, will not marry but will have a child.

Women who are seriously competitive about their careers try to follow a career trajectory that is similar to the one followed by almost all
men. Many "career women" delay marriage and family until their late
thirties or early forties, believing that they should firmly launch their
careers before they have to deal with the difficult issues related to managing home and work. If they have children they either return to
employment quickly, or never take time out at all. As men have always
done, young women today expect to be able to have a career that is not
compromised by the demands of either children or a spouse. Elaine
Cohen's daughter, a national sales manager for a designer company, is
an example.

We know that demands can be onerous for women in dual career
families. If a move has to be made to another location, it is usually the
husband's career that takes precedence. Women need to be "available"—for a dinner party or for other functions at which wives are
expected to appear. It is tacitly understood that it is the woman who will
stay home if a child is too sick to go to day care. There can be competition over status, arguments over housework.[17]

The image persists that their husbands will willingly share the
burden of the "second shift," that is, the work to be done at home
after the nine-to-five job, but the reality is something quite different.[18]
Women's participation in the workforce in record numbers, particularly married women with young children, may represent a revolution
outside of the home but there has been a "stalled revolution" in the
home.[19] Domestic responsibilities, especially child care, have primarily, if not exclusively, remained the woman's second job. Motherhood
and all that implies remains the "sorest point" of feminism. For some
women it has been so difficult to "follow male career patterns while
mothering, that a retreat into traditional roles is sometimes a tempting solution."[20]

In *Working Women Don't Have Wives,* the writer, Terri Apter (not
Brownsville's Terry Apter) explains that what would be ideal for
women, as for men, is "a partner who looks after their domestic needs,
cares for their children, accommodates their changing occupational
needs, and puts family responsibilities first and foremost . . . takes care
of everything else, so that the man can concentrate on his career."[21] A
perfect description of the perfect Jewish wife and mother.

Even for the women who have made the adjustments to their
careers, who have resolved the problems of the children and the "second

shift," sexism is still prevalent in many professions. Few today seriously attempt to explain women's absence from particular fields in terms of gender preference, as the college President Lyn White did in the 1950s,[22] but rather attribute it to gender bias. At first it seemed obvious that what was needed was equality in the workplace and the full force of the women's movement was exerted to address this problem. When it soon became apparent that "equal" treatment in the workplace would result in "unequal" outcomes, the issue shifted to one of equity which might be characterized as unequal treatment to achieve equal—or at least fairer—outcomes. Practices that have evolved for a male work force do not work for women with child-care responsibilities and who "don't have wives."[23]

Although social policy legislation helps to a degree, as we have seen in other areas of civil and human rights, practice remains resistant to change in the United States and elsewhere. Even in places where there has been "ideological" support of equality for women, such as in Scandinavia and the former Soviet Union, habitual biases are deeply embedded in the society.[24] In these countries, women still dominate the service sector, and some professions have become feminized. In other professions there are still job segregation and wage differentials.

Apter wrote, "In the economist's sense of rationality wherein an individual's choice is based on good value for money" it is clear that "the traditional division of labour . . . is efficient and rational."[25] A brief discussion with a former member of an Israeli kibbutz illustrates the validity of her conclusion. In its attempt to deal humanely with conflicting parenting and work responsibilities, women not only have work leave after the birth of a child, but various other provisions have been made for the primary caretaker to spend time with preschool children. Sometimes it is the men, but usually the women who visit the day care center, often at bath or mealtime. They also spend part of their workday doing housework, preparing the evening meal and being available for the children when they arrive home from school. They are fully paid for this time, but since the kibbutz is work driven, that is production driven, the policy presents problems. Time out from productive (as opposed to service) work is expensive; time out for children and family life is expensive; it reduces the income of the kibbutz. The women resist quite a bit of pressure to return to full-time "productive" work, and, because the kibbutz places a high value on family and domestic service, it does continue to pay the cost.

The United States stands out in contrast not only to the kibbutz described above (as well as others in Israel), but to some European countries which provide children's allowances, maternity benefits, and paid parental leaves of absence. As Moen has noted, our society pays "lip service to the importance of families and children" but we have been "notably reluctant to pay the costs of significantly expanded government benefits and services for women, for working parents or for families."[26]

Sadly, it is now more than thirty years since *The Feminine Mystique* was published, and women are still knocking at corporate and other doors with the same suggestion boxes, but few have been implemented. Most of the more common strategies—part-time work, job sharing, flexible time, home work, leaves for women (rarely for men)—although welcomed by women during their child-rearing years, have disadvantages. Career paths are still geared to the male model of continuous employment. There are also some newer ideas, such as telecommuting, or flexible work space.

Telecommuting is a newer form of home work which may seem better suited to professional women's needs, but it, along with other forms of work at home, has serious pitfalls. Women find that they can't identify strictly separate work time, their work is not seen as "real work," they're interrupted by husbands and children, they miss the workplace, they may be forgotten or overlooked because they are not present when some immediate decision has to be made. One among a plethora of books for the working mom advises, simply, "Don't do it."[27]

Some analysts such as Alice Kessler-Harris are optimistic. "If we begin," Kessler-Harris wrote,"with the assumption that both work and family are desirable and necessary for men and women, then we will ultimately find answers that are respectful both of women's desire for autonomy and of their capacity for nurturing."

The Brownsville women express concerns about their daughters choices, they worry about the quality of their daughter's lives, they worry about adequate child care, about stress and pressure, and about divorce; and they are highly critical of the women's movement for exacerbating the new dilemmas their daughters are facing as working mothers and career women. Yet they applaud and support the gains that women have achieved, which they believe have come about as a result of "women's lib." It is a very interesting contradiction.

When I asked my final question, "What advice would you give to your granddaughter?," they answered:

- "Don't be just a housewife, get a career."
- "Go to college, get an education, don't be a follower."
- "Have a family but learn to earn a living on your own, don't let things stand in your way."
- "Find a career and have children but only if you want to."
- "Have as much input as your husband, have as much rights."
- "Find a career, a job, something you love to do."
- "Get married, have children, but don't rush in. You can be anything you want to be."

One of the women could have been speaking for all of the Brownsville women when she said, simply: "Go for it!"

Appendix

The primary sources for this book were the women. I conducted interviews with them, mostly in their homes, over a period of five years; I conducted only one extensive telephone interview. Each interview took two to three hours, occasionally there were two or more women present. I did telephone some of the women for updated information.

Initially, I contacted many of the women through the Alumni Association of the Brownsville Boys Club. These were women who had experiences that were parallel to those of the men. And because Thomas Jefferson, the local high school for Brownsville youth, also has an active Alumni Association I was able to contact other women who were interested in being interviewed and through whom I was referred to friends or relatives.

Prior to the interviews I sent the women a questionnaire (interview protocol) so that they would have time to think about the issues I was going to raise with them. Although the interviews took on the form of a natural, rambling conversation, the protocol enabled me to check from time to time to see that we had touched upon key points. I taped each of the interviews so that I could refer to specific remarks or details as I collated the information. Sometimes I followed up with phone calls for additional material or for clarification.

INTERVIEW DATES

Terry Guberman Apter	6/12/92
Jean Kanowitz Bleckner	2/24/91
Eleanor Schwartz Chernick	10/12/94
Raye Roder Cohen	2/23/91

Minette Zharnest Cutler	3/28/92
Shirley Hershenson Donowitz	2/24/91
Norma Fuchs Ellman	4/25/91
Sally Stern Forman	2/26/91
Irma Meyerson Greenbaum	10/13/94
Florence Bain Grosswirth	4/27/91
Florence Moglinsky Kusnetz	10/1/95, 3/22/96
Bea Finkelstein Larkin	4/6/92
Sarah Barbanel Lieberman	8/19/91
Frances Rosenthal Lubin	3/27/91
Rae Margolis Mirsky	1/26/91
Claire Spielman Moses	2/26/91
Lorraine Zakow Nelson	10/13/94
Sydelle Koran Schlossberg	2/25/91
Bea Meiseles Siegel	1/9/91
Katie Tepper Stavans	2/24/91
Bea Gable Benjamin	5/18/94
Ruth Green Berman	5/4/93
Zena Kusher Bloom	10/8/94
Roslyn Wohl Bowers	11/18/94
Linda Gralla Brasco	1/24/94
Elaine Epstein Cohen	4/6/92
Isabel Herman Cohen	4/25/91
Rochelle Skoble Feld	5/4/94
Arlene Gralla Feldman	1/24/94
Valerie Gordon Greenberg	1/24/94
Ruth Charney Kesslin	5/4/94
Doris Davidson Levinson	4/26/91
Rhoda Bratkowsky Nemerofsky	4/21/95

Martha Yoelson Opitz	11/13/93
Lila Herman Perlmutter	10/12/94
Dolores Work Plaxen	4/26/91
Lillian Gross Pollack	10/11/94
Harriet Potashman Portnoy	11/17/94
Lois Berman Rusakow	11/12/93
Lillian Pomerantz Wellen	5/4/93
Sylvia Albert Zinn	2/22/95

THE GIRLS

NAME	HS*/GRADUATION	MARRIED	OCCUPATION	HIGHER EDUCATION
Terry Guberman Apter	J/1943	1946	Secretary	
Jean Kanowitz Bleckner	J/1943	1947	Secretary	
Eleanor Schwartz Chernick	J/1941	1949	Bookkeeper/Teacher	Ph.D.
Raye Roder Cohen	J/1943	1950	Secretary	
Minette Zharnest Cutler	J/1947	1949	Office Manager	
Shirley Hershenson Donowitz	CC/1946	1947	Secretary	
Norma Fuchs Ellman	T/1943	1952	Secretary	
Sally Stern Forman	J/1945	1949	Bookkeeper/ Office Manager	
Irma Meyerson Greenbaum	J/1944	1956		
Florence Bain Grosswirth	J/1946	1952	Sales	
Florence Moglinsky Kusnetz	J/1946	1950	Attorney	LL.D.
Bea Finkelstein Larkin	J/1947	1949	Secretary	
Sarah Barbanel Lieberman	J/1947	1947		B.A.
Frances (Fayge) Rosenthal Lubin	N/1940	1943	Seamstress	
Rae Margolis Mirsky	J/1945	1949	Office Work	
Claire Spielman Moses	J/1945	1946	Administration	
Lorraine Zakow Nelson	J/1949	1953		
Sydelle Koran Schlossberg	CC/1945	1948	Bookkeeper	
Bea Meiseles Siegel	J/1945	1948	Bookkeeper	
Katie Tepper Stavans	J/1945	1947	Office Work	

Name	School/Year	Year	Occupation	Degree
Bea Gable Benjamin	J/1952	1962	Office Manager	
Ruth Green Berman	J/1951	1956	Teacher/Counselor	M.A.
Zena Kusher Bloom	J/1952	1954	Manager	
Roslyn Wohl Bowers	J/1959	1965	Teacher	M.A.
Linda Gralla Brasco	J/1958	1959		
Elaine Epstein Cohen	T/1952	1953	Sales	
Isabel Herman Cohen	T/1951	1957	Teacher	M.A.
Rochelle Skoble Feld	J/1952	1953	Nurse	
Arlene Gralla Feldman	T/1957	1959	Secretary/Teacher	M.F.A.
Valerie Gordon Greenberg	J/1958	1962	Secretary	
Ruth Charney Kesslin	J/1951	1956	Psychologist	M.A.
Doris Davidson Levinson	T/1953	1957	Teacher	M.A.
Rhoda Bratkowsky Nemerofsky	J/1956	1960	Nurse	M.A.
Martha Yoelson Opitz	J/1956	1963	Psychotherapist	M.A.
Lila Herman Perlmutter	J/1953	1954	Psychotherapist	M.A.
Dolores Work Plaxen	J/1955	1957	Office Work/Model	
Lillian Gross Pollack	J/1950	1951	Bookkeeper	
Harriet Potashman Portnoy	J/1955	1957	Teacher	M.A.
Lois Berman Rusakow	J/1952	1957	Office Work	
Lillian Pomerantz Wellen	J/1952	1958	Secretary	
Sylvia Albert Zinn	J/1951	1952	Varied/Entrepreneur	

* J—Thomas Jefferson High School   T—Samuel J. Tilden High School
N—Needle Trades High School   CC—Central Commercial High School

Notes

There is considerable and legitimate concern among historians over the scholarship (as well as the politics) of oral history, particularly over projects that record and interpret the words of women, for women: What should the role of the interviewer be? Should the questions control and direct the interview or should they allow the interview to take its own path? Can we be sure questions are not leading? Can we trust self-reporting? Can we trust memory? Can we trust the process? That is, does it evoke truthful responses?

These and other questions present many dilemmas to the researcher, in part because there are no definitive answers to them. We can only approach historical "truth" by finding some consistency among responses in each historical circumstance. We must structure, that is, reasonably direct the interviews in order to arrive at a kind of critical mass of responses, otherwise we can't know if a response is representative or simply idiosyncratic. The more responses to a particular question or issue—that is, the more data—the better. But the realities of time constraints upon the researcher, the oral historian, make vast numbers and in-depth interviewing mutually exclusive. I muddled through these and many other questions and issues to arrive at a balance; my choice was for greater depth and more limited, although not meager, numbers.

The process of selection does raise some methodological questions. Although I chose individuals at random from a much larger number of interested women than I could have managed to interview, all the women are self-selected; they are women who wanted to talk about their lives. They are also women who haven't separated themselves from Brownsville; they have remained affiliated.

I believe, to some degree, that these factors are meaningful, since the population *is* somewhat skewed. The women who have retained an attachment to their former community through various school or other organizations, by definition, do not include those who, for whatever reasons, have lost touch. It is possible to speculate, for example, that those who agree to be interviewed, those who remained affiliated, had more positive experiences in Brownsville than others. But there is no way to verify such speculation.

In spite of the limitations, the validity of this study is affirmed because the women's experiences closely match and corroborate what has been reported in numerous other studies and in related literature. In many instances, the

Brownsville women and the women interviewed by Myra Dinnerstein, Brett Harvey, Corrine Azen Krause, and others used exactly the same words to describe their experiences. The similarities are striking.

CHAPTER 1

1. Two of the fifties women, Linda Brasco and Arlene Feldman, are sisters, offspring of an intermarriage between their Jewish father and their Russian Orthodox mother (rare in those days and rarely encountered in Brownsville.) I didn't know this when I arranged to interview them. However, I found that they fit the profile of Brownsville women as closely as any other. They may have had other cultural factors added to the mix but they are most definitely Brownsville "girls." I didn't see any reason to exclude them from the study. On the contrary, I think that their experiences, which so closely match the others', attest to the strength of the Brownsville culture.

2. The other major Jewish subculture is the Sephardic, the *Sepharadim*, whose ancestors lived in the countries bordering the Mediterranean: southern Europe, north Africa, and the Middle East. Their common language, the written version of which, like Yiddish, uses the Hebrew alphabet, is the Spanish-based ladino, sometimes called Judaismo.

3. David Elkind, *All Grown Up and No Place to Go* (Reading, Massachusetts: Addison-Wesley Publishing Company, 1984). Although the book is somewhat dated due to such unfortunate occurrences as the growing incidence of AIDS among teenagers, I think it is still one of the best for understanding the process of "coming of age."

4. To avoid awkwardness, I sometimes use the term "Brownsville women" without qualifiers such as "these" or "the women of this study."

5. Gerald Sorin, *The Nurturing Neighborhood: The Brownsville Boys Club and Jewish Community in Urban America, 1940–1990* (New York: New York University Press, 1990), 6. Sorin believes that Brownsville was unique because similar neighborhoods did not produce a similar institution, nor did Brownsville itself, in the 1960s and 1970s, when it had become a predominantly black community. Ibid.

6. Taken from "News from New York University Press," promotional literature for *The Nurturing Neighborhood*.

7. "Are 51 Percent of the Stories Missing?," *On Campus with Women* 20, no. 3 (Winter 1990): 1.

8. Alter F. Landesman, *Brownsville: The Birth, Development, and Passing of a Jewish Community in New York* (New York: Bloch Publishing Company, 1971). Landesman not only was Executive Director of an important community

organization, the Hebrew Educational Society, he also helped initiate the Brownsville Neighborhood Health and Welfare Council and represented Brownsville on twenty or more civic organizations.

9. Carol Gilligan, "On *In a Different Voice:* An Interdisciplinary Forum," *Signs: Journal of Women in Culture and Society* 11, no. 2 (Winter 1986): 325.

10. Elizabeth Kamarck Minnich, *Transforming Knowledge* (Philadelphia: Temple University Press, 1990), 38 and 27. Minnich raises numerous other questions regarding the discipline of history, and particularly ways in which we must think about new paradigms, not just "add women and stir" models.

11. Linda Wagner-Martin, *Telling Women's Lives: The New Biography* (New Brunswick, New Jersey: Rutgers University Press, 1994), 4.

12. Nancy F. Cott, ed., *A History of Women in America* (Westport, Connecticut: Meckler, 1994). A collection of key articles that have appeared in numerous journals over the past twenty years, organized in topical volumes.

13. Gerald Sorin used the term "consciously, compensatory history" (but it was not negative criticism,) in a review of *World of our Mothers* (New York: Schocken Books, 1988).

14. Shulamit Magnus, "Out of the Ghetto: Integrating the Study of Jewish Women into the Study of 'The Jews,'" *Judaism* 39, no. 1 (Winter 1990): 33.

15. Henry L. Feingold, *A Time for Searching: Entering the Mainstream, 1920–1945* (Baltimore: Johns Hopkins University Press, 1992). The series was published by Johns Hopkins University Press. See also, S. Henry and E. Taitz, *Written Out of History: Our Jewish Foremothers* (New York: Biblio Press, 1990).

16. Edward S. Shapiro, *A Time for Healing: American Jewry since World War II* (Baltimore: Johns Hopkins Press, 1992), 249. In fact, in February 1997, a conference of orthodox women was held to discuss many outstanding issues. It was provoked by a recent, controversial, ban against women's prayer groups by rabbis in Queens. Toby Axelrod,"Staking a Claim to Tradition," *The Brooklyn Jewish Weekly* 209, no. 43 (February 21, 1997): 1+.

17. Wagner-Martin, 6.

18. Mary Blewett, "Good Intentions," *Women's Review of Books* 9, no. 5 (February 1992): 10. Attributed by the writer to Marie-Françoise Chanfrault-Duchet in Blewett's review of Sherna Berger Gluck and Daphne Patai, eds., *Women's Words: The Feminist Practice of Oral History* (New York: Routledge, 1991).

I agree with Blewett/Chanfrault-Duchet, that one of the jobs of the oral historian is to be an interpreter of events: to place individual stories in a larger context and to provide a bit more objectivity, even sometimes to contradict the more subjective or "perceived meaning."

19. Jenna Weissman Joselit, *The Wonders of America: Reinventing Jewish Culture, 1880–1950* (New York: Hill and Wang, 1995), 133.

20. Sorin, *Nurturing Neighborhood*, 189.

21. See Notes on Methodology.

22. Landesman, 95.

23. Corrine Azen Krause, *Grandmothers, Mothers and Daughters: Oral Histories of Three Generations of Ethnic American Women* (Boston: Twayne Publishers, 1991).

24. Kate Simon, *Bronx Primitive* (New York: Viking Press, 1982).

25. Henry Roth captures this in his story of Jewish immigrant life earlier in the century, *Call It Sleep*. However, I remember exactly the same comments, expressions, and denigrations of non-Jews being used when I was growing up. Henry Roth, *Call It Sleep* (New York: Robert O. Ballou, 1934).

26. Deborah Dash Moore, *At Home in America: Second Generation New York Jews* (New York: Columbia University Press, 1981), 3.

27. Landesman, 66. See chapter 21, "The Glory of the Community."

28. Philip Roth, *Portnoy's Complaint* (New York: Random House, 1969).

29. Lillian S. Robinson, "Foremothers to be proud of," *Women's Review of Books* 11, no. 3 (December 1993): 16.

30. Naomi Shepherd, *A Price Below Rubies: Jewish Women as Rebels and Radicals* (Cambridge: Harvard University Press, 1993), 32.

31. Elizabeth Cady Stanton, *The Woman's Bible* (Ann Arbor, Michigan: Northeastern University Press, 1993). Also, Cullen Murphy, "Women and the Bible." *Atlantic Monthly* 272 (August 1993): 39–64. Among the noted biblical scholars, whose fascinating stories Murphy cites, are Bernadette Brooten, Elaine Pagels, Elizabeth Schüssler Fiorenza, and Phyllis Trible.

32. See Shepherd. Also see Irena Klepfisz, "*Di Mames, Dos Loshen*/The Mothers, The Language: Feminism, Yidishkayt, and the Politics of Memory," *Bridges: A Journal for Jewish Feminists and Our Friends* 4, No. 1 (Winter/Spring 1994/5754): 20.

One of the earliest American feminists was a Polish immigrant, Ernestine Rose, who was a signer of the Declaration of the Rights of Women in 1848.

33. Elaine Tyler May, *Homeward Bound: American Families in the Cold War Era* (New York: Basic Books, Inc., 1988), 12–13.

34. Richard Fein, *The Dance of Leah: Discovering Yiddish in America*, (Cranberry, New Jersey: Associated University Presses, 1986), 92.

35. Moore, 234.

CHAPTER 2

1. Sorin, *Nurturing Neighborhood,* 1.

2. Moore, 62.

3. Ibid., 69.

4. Ibid., 70.

5. Joselit, 4.

6. Landesman, 8.

7. See Jerre Mangione and Ben Morreale, *La Storia: Five Centuries of the Italian-American Experience* (New York: Harper Collins, 1992).

8. Sorin, *Nurturing Neighborhood,* 11.

9. Landesman, 95.

10. Ibid., 38.

11. Ibid., 29.

12. The parents of younger people today use Yiddish, if they use it at all, "when they don't want their children to understand what they're talking about." Scott Heller, "Rescuing Yiddish Books," *Chronicle of Higher Education* 42, no. 4 (September 22, 1995): 11(A).

13. Leo Rosten, *Hooray for Yiddish* (New York: Simon and Schuster, 1982), 241, 103, 148. There is a more recent book of Leo Rosten's, *Joys of Yinglish* (New York: McGraw Hill, 1989), devoted to this topic, as well as another, scholarly, discussion in *Anglish/English* by Gene Bluestein (Athens: University of Georgia Press, 1989).

14. See Richard Fein's, *The Dance of Leah,* for a moving account of a third generation Jew rediscovering and mastering the language.

15. Deborah Sontag, "Oy Gevalt! New Yawkese, An Endangered Dialect?" *The New York Times,* February 14, 1993, sec. 1, p. 1+.

16. See Herman Galvin and Stan Tamarkin, *The Yiddish Dictionary Sourcebook* (Hoboken: Ktav Publishing House, Inc. 1986) and "Campuses See Revival of Interest in Yiddish as Field of Study," *Chronicle of Higher Education* XLII, no. 4 (Sept. 22, 1995): A18.

17. Later the H.E.S. played an important role in the lives of Brownsville youth, including many of the girls. They took music lessons there, they studied Hebrew, they participated in cultural and sports activities and went to the H.E.S. summer camp. Today its active alumni association is located in Canarsie.

18. Landesman, 69–71. To put the amount in perspective, $30 could pay for about three months' rent at the turn of the century.

19. Dr. Levine is one of the few women mentioned by Landesman in his chapter entitled," The Glory of the Community." The information concerning the Sanger clinic is taken from Landesman, 121–123 (he refers to Sanger's memoirs), and from *Famous American Women: A Biographical Dictionary from Colonial Times to the Present*, ed. Robert McHenry (New York: Dover Publishing Company, 1980), 368.

20. Sorin, *Nurturing Neighborhood*, p. 14.

21. Joselit, 55.

22. Sorin, *Nurturing Neighborhood*, 14.

23. Ibid., 71.

24. Ibid., 20.

25. Landesman, 327.

26. Moore, 5.

27. David Gonzales with Garry Pierre-Pierre, "Little Sympathy or Surprise," *The New York Times*, November 21, 1993, p. 44.

28. Sorin, *Nurturing Neighborhood*, 14.

29. Moore, 101.

30. Ibid., 98–99.

31. Ibid., 62.

32. Ibid., 233.

33. Ibid., 127.

34. In a curious turnabout, Raye's youngest daughter, perhaps out of the same rebelliousness, decided at the age of twelve that she *was* going to be observant. She moved away from home and, until her marriage, lived with orthodox families and was brought up by them in the traditional manner.

35. Joselit, 174, noted that "eating *out*" was a phrase riddled with transgressive implications.

36. Joseph Berger, "As Delis Dwindle, Traditions Lose Bite," *New York Times*, May 15, 1996, B1+. According to this article the number of "authentic kosher delicatessens" in New York City and the suburbs has declined to thirty-five; their decline has followed that of Jewish communities in the city. Since 1950 the Jewish population in New York has decreased from more than two million, to one million.

37. Landesman, 12

38. See Joselit, 229–243.

39. Sorin, 160–161. West Indians also began to migrate to New York in the 1960s, most of them settling in Brooklyn. Today there are between 500,000 and a million West Indians in New York. See Philip Kasinitz, *Caribbean New York: Black Immigrant and the Politics of Race* (Ithaca, New York: Cornell University Press, 1994).

40. Kazin, quoted in Moore, 64.

41. Krause, 10, and Moore, 48.

42. Landesman deals, mournfully, with the loss of the Jewish community in his book, but it was written in 1970. In the final chapters of *The Nurturing Neighborhood* Sorin discusses the changes in the population and the community.

43. Sorin, 161–163.

44. In another ironic twist, Elaine's son married a black woman, putting her humanity to the test.

45. Landesman, 371.

46. For what a reviewer described as an engrossing first book and one that conveys the atmosphere of Brownsville today, see Greg Donaldson, *The Ville: Cops and Kids in Urban America* (New York: Ticknor & Fields, 1993).

47. Felicia R. Lee, "Despair Grows in Brooklyn," *New York Times Book Review*, Sunday, November 28, 1993, p. 25.

48. Sorin, 60.

49. Of course the women I contacted through the Alumni Association of Thomas Jefferson high school were graduates but so were the women I met through the BBC alumni association.

50. Sorin, 90.

51. Ibid., 6.

52. Ibid., 1. As Stephanie Coontz pointed out in the *The Way We Never Were: American Families and the Nostalgia Trap* (New York: Basic Books, Inc., 1992), ix, when we look back, "The actual complexity of our history—even of our own personal experience—gets buried under the weight of an idealized image."

CHAPTER 3

1. "Alone" meant that she wasn't travelling with family. It is likely, as was common practice, that she had joined with a group who were led to the port city by a guide.

2. It was known, but ignored by rabbis and others, that both as prostitutes and white-slavers, Jews were notoriously prominent in the trade, but Jew-

ish leaders feared publicly admitting Jewish participation because they knew it carried political risks. Naomi Shepherd, *A Price Below Rubies: Jewish Women as Rebels and Radicals* (Cambridge: Harvard University Press, 1993), 238.

3. Irena Klepfisz, "Recognizing Yiddish Literature's 'Nameless Soldiers,'" *Forward* (October 20, 1995), 11–12. See also Klepfisz's introduction to *Found Treasures*.

4. Blu Greenberg, *On Women and Judaism: A View from Tradition* (Philadelphia: The Jewish Publication Society of America, 1981), 43. Greenberg organized the recent conference of orthodox women. See Axelrod, "Staking a claim to tradition."

Judith Plaskow also believes that the role of women in Judaism is a "theological issue," although Cynthia Ozick disagrees; she thinks that it is "a sociological fact." See their debate in Heshel, 218, 123.

5. There was (still is) a contribution made to the synagogue for a "seat" during the high holy days. The top two floors housed a bigger and more elaborate room and had a balcony (actually the third story) where the women sat. Seats there were more expensive.

6. Oren Rudavsky and M. Dawm, *A Life Apart*, 1997. The film tell the story of an ultra-orthodox religious sect, holocaust survivors who came to America after WWII, and their progeny. The *Hasidim* live in segregated communities and resist acculturation.

7. Susannah Heschel, *On Being a Jewish Feminist: A Reader* (New York: Schocken Books, 1983), xxii.

8. Adrienne Baker, *The Jewish Woman in Contemporary Society: Transitions and Traditions*(New York: New York University Press, 1993), 51. Their exclusion from *halakhic* education keeps them from participating in the debates through which the law is re-interpreted. Along with that of the minor, the idiot, and the deaf mute, the testimony of women is not accepted in religious courts since women are considered too emotional, not reliable witnesses.

9. See Axelrod, "Staking a claim to tradition."

10. Baker, 35.

11. Ibid., 34.

12. Schneider, 121. The preference for male children is certainly not exclusive to the Jews or to the orthodox community but exists in many cultures today. It was reported in a news broadcast on CNN NEWS, May 6, 1992, that the Indian government has had to take steps to prohibit abortion clinics from informing women of the gender results of amniocentesis since only one out of eight thousand abortions in 1991 was a male fetus. They doubted that the prohibition would be successfully enforced.

13. Adler, in Heschel, 13.

14. Ibid, 3. In "The Jew Who Wasn't There: *Halakhah* and the Jewish Woman," Adler relates one of the *Midrashim,* Jewish cautionary tales, which tells about Adam who is parted from Eve and encounters a demon, a "Lilith" figure. Adler offers an alternative interpretation.

15. Some restrictions are meant to ensure *kvod hatsibur,* or public decency, and to suppress a woman's sexuality: a woman must cover her hair and her arms and legs. Because her voice can lead to licentiousness, there is the injunction against women singing in the presence of men: *kol ishah ervah.*

16. Baker, 69.

17. In ancient times women participated in many of the occupations mentioned in the Bible; farming, buying and selling land, weaving and selling textiles are just a few.

18. Baum, Hyman, Michel, 15.

19. Interview with Bessie Trachtenbroit (December 5, 1995), who came to America in 1922, not quite sixteen. She has vivid recollections about life in the Russian *shtetls* of Kheshovete and Taraschete before and during the Revolution and the Civil War. Jewish immigrant women did go to school in America, however. They made up forty percent of New York's night school pupils in 1910–11.

20. In her discussion of Jewish women's education, Adrienne Baker explains that Maimonedes, the distinguished Jewish sage of the twelfth century, suggested that "the majority of women were not prepared to dedicate themselves adequately to such study, therefore they would gain only superficial knowledge." But it was a "circular argument," as Baker points out, because "if women did not have the opportunity to study, they could hardly be expected to study in depth." Baker, 50–51. It is an example of the kind of circular reasoning to which Elizabeth Minnich refers (in *Transforming Knowledge*) and which has typically been used to limit women's access to particular areas of study, as it was used by White in *Educating Our Daughters.*

21. The literal translation is *Come Out and See.* This book was published first at the end of the sixteenth century but there were thirty editions printed within a century, and more than two hundred more by the 1800s. It is still read today.

22. Shepherd, 53–54.

23. Ibid., 249.

24. Earlier in this century the Jewish mother had a "double responsibility," as she was responsible for inculcating not only Jewish but American values in her children. Joselit, 71, 134.

25. Ibid., 134.

26. Shulamis Berger, "The Making of the American *Balebostel* Housewife." Paper presented at *Di Froyen, Women and Yiddish*. Conference on Tribute to the Past, Directions for the Future. Jewish Theological Seminary, October 29, 1995.

27. Sydney Stahl Weinberg, *World of Our Mothers* (New York: Schocken Books, 1988), 114–120.

28. Joselit, 38.

29. Adler, in Heschel, 13.

30. Schneider, 22.

31. Baker, 2.

32. Baker, 135.

CHAPTER 4

1. Blu Greenberg, *On Women and Judaism: A View from Tradition* (Philadelphia: The Jewish Publication Society of America, 1981), 123.

2. Phyllis Moen, *Women's Two Roles: A Contemporary Dilemma* (Westport, Conn.: Auburn House, 1992,) 6.

3. Joselit, 6.

4. Shonie B. Levi and Sylvia R. Kaplan, *Guide for the Jewish Homemaker* rev.ed. (New York, Schocken Books, 1964), xv. First published in 1959 by Farrar, Strauss and Co.

5. Ibid., 27. Books such as *The Three Pillars* by Deborah Melamed of the National Women's League of the United Synagogue of America were recommended in the listing on p.235.

6. Elizabeth Hale Gilman, *Things Girls Like to Do* (Philadelphia: Uplift Vocational Books, 1917). This was contained in Part I of the volume: Housekeeping. Part II was devoted to Needlework and was written by someone with the delightful name of Effie Archer. There was also a companion volume, *Things Boys Like to Make*. The choice of titles makes a subtle, but clear, distinction between the passive "do" for the girls' book, and the more active "make" for the boys'. Also, note the name of the publisher.

7. Typical holiday dishes. *Latkes* means pancakes. *Tsimes* is a dish usually made of cooked carrots, sweetened with raisins.

8. Levi and Kaplan, xv. This is in the introduction, which was written by S. Gershon Levi.

9. Baker, 143–4.

10. Hollywood, light years removed from the realities of Brownsville life, nevertheless insinuated itself into the lives of the girls in many significant ways since, by the 1940s, Hollywood had already taken on the role of a major, if not *the* major sociocultural and informal educational institution among the media.

11. Susan M. Hartmann, *The Home Front and Beyond: American Women in the 1940's* (Boston: Twayne Publishers, 1982),164–165. What she calls the wartime's "younger and hastier marriages," may also have contributed to the rising postwar divorce rate.

12. Baker, 147.

13. Susan Weidman Schneider, *Jewish and Female: Choices and Changes in Our Lives Today* (New York, Simon and Schuster, 1984), 300.

14. Hartmann, 164.

15. In American society in the forties and fifties, few writers, mostly of fiction, were sympathetic with lesbian relationships or portrayed them in a positive light. This was also the case in film. *The Celluloid Closet,* a recent film history of the portrayal of homosexuality by Hollywood shows that, if gays and lesbians were portrayed at all (rather than just hinted at, which was more common in the 1940s), the women were shown as deviant, tortured, and suffering, not because of society's ill-treatment but because of their "abnormality." Gays and lesbians were shown as dangers to unsuspecting women and children; no distinction was made between homosexuality and pedophilia. Rob Epstein and Jeffrey Friedman, *The Celluloid Closet*, United States, 1995. This film is based upon a book by Vito Russo.

In the Jewish culture, lesbianism was considered so rare that there are few mentions of it in the *Talmud* and none in the Bible. Even today, because it is such a taboo subject, the incidence of lesbianism among Jews is not known, although Baker makes the reasonable assumption that it is not different from society as a whole: probably about ten percent of the population. Baker, 166–167.

16. Florence Kusnetz' husband gave up the idea of becoming a doctor because he didn't think he could get into medical school. He became an engineer instead, specializing in health and safety in the workplace, and became one of the authors of the original OSHA, Occupational Safety and Health Administration, regulations.

17. Schneider, 242.

18. Sorin, *The Nurturing Neighborhood*, 30–31.

19. Greenberg, 28.

20. Stephanie Coontz, *The Way it Never Was* (New York: Basic Books),2.

21. Edward S. Shapiro. *A Time for Healing: American Jewry since World War II* (Baltimore, Johns Hopkins Press, 1992), 139. See also the oral history

written by Myrna Katz Frommer and Harvey Frommer, *It Happened in the Catskills* (Orlando, Harcourt Brace Jovanovich, 1991).

22. An interesting recent book is Judy Barrett Littof and David C. Smith, eds., *We're in This War, Too: World War II Letters from American Women in Uniform* (New York: Oxford University Press, 1994). Also, see Hartmann, chapter Three, "Women in Uniform."

23. Thomas Blaisdell, "Education for Parenthood," *The Annals* 67 (September 1916): 47. Dr. Blaisdell was the Dean of the School of Liberal Arts at Pennsylvania State College for Women.

24. Some sociologists and economists discriminate between semiprofessions and professions in considering such issues as level and length of specialized education, autonomy, income, status, etc. Teaching and nursing are generally considered semiprofessions. I am using a looser interpretation, however, and, for the purposes of this discussion calling them all professions. I am distinguishing, however, between job and career; career being something that required more extensive preparation, expected to have a trajectory and to be a long-lasting, if not lifetime committment.

25. Moen, 4.

26. Greenberg, 51.

27. Hartmann, 22.

28. Russell Freedman, review of *Rosie the Riveter: Women Working on the Home Front in World War II*, by Penny Colman, in the *New York Times Book Review*, September 10, 1995, 35. For information regarding women's work, an extensive collection of records and documents of the Women's Bureau of the U.S. Department of Labor related to women's labor during World War II is available through University Publications of America in Bethesda, Maryland.

29. Carol Hymowitz and Michaele Weissman, *A History of Women in America* (New York: Bantam Books, 1978), 323.
There were some major changes in the 1940s, including the opening up of some careers such as medicine which had been almost exclusively male dominated. Hartmann, 94, 104.

30. A recent article commemorating the fiftieth anniversary of a high school in Elizabeth, New Jersey, might have been written about the Brownsville women: "The goals listed beside the yearbook portraits of Battin High School's all-girl class of 1944 repeat themselves like memorized verse: secretary, typist, bookkeeper, receptionist, stenographer . . ." "50–Year Retrospective," 4(B).

31. Greenberg, 25.

CHAPTER 5

1. Among the teachers of the senior class of 1957 at Thomas Jefferson High School were ten women, five men. There was only one non-Jewish name in the group.

2. Betty Freidan, *The Feminine Mystique* (New York: W.W. Norton, 1963).

3. Susan Brownmiller, *Femininity* (New York: Linden Press, 1984).

4. Nancy J. Cobb, *Adolescence: Continuity, Change, and Diversity* (Mountain View, California: Mayfield Publishing Company, 1995), 340.

5. *Aurora*, Thomas Jefferson High School Yearbook, 1958, 7.

6. Even later, in college, the only girls' sports were fencing, tennis and other non-team sports.

7. Elayne Rapping, "A World Well Lost," *The Women's Review of Books* 10, no. 12 (September 1993): 11. Review of Brett Harvey, *The Fifties: A Women's Oral History* (New York: Harper Collins, 1993).

8. Stephanie Coontz, *The Way We Never Were: American Families and the Nostalgia Trap* (New York: Basic Books, 1992), 25. Coontz claims that the fifties was not a "return" to basic family values at all, but a time during which that myth was created. Her book clearly is a response to the reassertion of "family values" by American conservatives and an attempt to expose the fifties myth as a fiction.

For the first time in more than one hundred years, the age for marriage and motherhood fell, fertility increased, divorce rates declined, and women's degree of educational parity with men dropped sharply. In a period of less than ten years, the proportion of never-married persons declined by as much as it had during the entire previous decade. Ibid., ix–x.

9. In fact, historians generally refer to it as the "cult of domesticity." See Virginia Sapiro, *Women in American Society* (Mountain View, California: Mayfield Publishing Company, 1990), 348.

10. Elaine Tyler May, *Homeward Bound: American Families in the Cold War Era* (New York: Basic Books, 1988), 10. This book is a thorough and convincing discussion of the relationship between domesticity and the Cold War ideology.

11. Ibid., 7, 11.

12. Ibid., 23.

13. Harvey, 71. Eugenia Kaledin, *Mothers and More: American Women in the 1950's* (Boston: Twayne Publishers, 1984), preface.

14. Freidan, 209. By 1956 there were 20,000 sets sold daily, and more than five hundred stations; by the end of the decade Americans were watching fifty million TV sets. Kaledin, 2.

15. Kaledin, 184.

16. Jean Kilbourne, who lectures extensively on this topic, has produced a series of films and articles about women and advertising. The first was titled "Killing Me Softly."

17. The exhibit, on tour from the American Advertising Museum in Portland, Oregon was held in New York City in November, 1995. Stuart Elliott, "Advertising," *The New York Times*, November 3, 1995, D18. Coontz wrote that advertising increased by four hundred percent between 1945 and 1960, 171.

18. Elliott, "Advertising."

19. Berkshire Conference on the History of Women. Vassar College, June 11–13, 1993. "Getting Married in a Nation of Plenty: Weddings and Consumerism in Postwar America." Presentations by Sally McMurry, Penn State University, and Regina Lee Blaszczyk, University of Delaware.

20. Through such devices the home furnishing trade expanded and companies such as Fostoria, Corning, Owens, and Lenox cleverly developed a demand for their products. These companies became the largest suppliers to young brides. Regina Lee Blaszczyk, "It's a Cinderella Story: The Home Furnishings Trade, Brides-to-be, and the Construction of Domesticity, 1945–60," paper presented at the Ninth Berkshire Conference on the History of Women, Vassar College, June 11–13, 1993, in a session entitled "Getting Married in a Nation of Plenty: Weddings and Consumerism in Postwar America," June 11, 1993.

21. Joselit, 22.

22. Katherine Jellison, "From the Farmhouse Parlor to the Pink Barn: The Commercialization of Rural Weddings in the Postwar Midwest." Berkshire Conference, op. cit.

23. Harvey, xv.

24. The latest contemporary figure for teen pregnancy is about one million per year. About half that number of babies are born to single parents. Coontz suggests that one reason is that the new economic situation of the nineties makes "early marriage less viable," 39.

25. Harvey, 8.

26. May has an interesting discussion of sexuality in the context of "containment." See chapter 5.

27. The photos are also reproduced in May, 4–5.

28. Carl Bernstein, *Loyalties: A Son's Memoir* (New York: Simon and Schuster, 1989).

29. For a full discussion of American-Jewish radicals, see Sorin, *Prophetic Minority*.

30. I disagree with Barbara Sinclair Deckard that, by a combination of prosperity and anti-Red hysteria in the fifties, "the possibilities for a revival of the women's liberation movement were cut off," Barbara Sinclair Deckard, *The Women's Movement: Political, Socioeconomic, and Psychological Issues* (New York: Harper and Row, 1983), 305. The women's liberation movement was an offshoot of Civil Rights in the same way that the first wave of feminism occurred in conjunction with the abolitionist movement in the mid-nineteenth century. I agree, rather, with Stephanie Coontz who wrote that although it would take ten more years for Freidan's notion of the problem that had no name to resonate with thousands and thousands of women, *The Feminine Mystique* was a product of the 1950s (37). Furthermore, it was in 1952, in *The Second Sex: The Classic Manifesto of the Liberated Woman,* that Simone de Beauvoir crystallized the powerful concept of woman as other. She wrote: "One is not born, but rather becomes, a woman. No biological, psychological, or economic fate determines the figure that the human female presents in society; it is civilization as a whole that produces this creature, intermediate between male and eunuch, which is described as feminine. Only the intervention of someone else can establish an individual as an *Other.*"

31. As Oakley explains, Brownsville girls like Elaine were "inducted" into the domestic role by an apprenticeship that is informal but does have "regular procedures," beginning with their imitating their mothers. Ann Oakely, *The Sociology of Housework* (New York: Pantheon Books, 1974), 113–114.

32. Jonathan Rosen, "A Dead Language, Yiddish Lives," *The New York Times Magazine,* July 7, 1996, 26.

33. There are, of course, one or two women in each of the groups who fit the characteristics of the other group. In any case, categories are almost always arbitrary. They can only be useful if it is understood that there are exceptions, but without the categories we can't see patterns or make generalizations.

34. By the late 1950s enrollment had gone from forty seven percent to a little more than thirty five percent. Kaledin, 36.

35. Ibid., 53–54.

36. Sorin, *Nurturing Neighborhood,* 162.

37. Ibid.

38. It was interesting to see that there was a higher percentage of female to male graduates overall. But among blacks, females consistently exceeded male graduates by at least 2:1.

39. Freudian psychology, by its focus on the individual, deflected the focus of attention from broader social/gender issues: if there were problems, they were located in the psyche of women, not in the structure of society. And feminists

from Mary Wollstonecraft to most of the suffragists, were charged with being the source of women's problems because they encouraged women to pursue higher education and to entertain the idea of careers. The old turn-of-the-century warhorse claiming that educated women have sexual disorders was neighing once again as women who looked outside marriage for their fulfillment were charged with being "unwomanly," a euphemism for lesbianism. Deckard, chapters 2 and 3, and Kaledin, chapter 9. Passim.

40. May, 20.

41. Although the TV division of the advertising industry was expanding enormously, it wasn't the only exploiter. When Freidan's search through "issue after issue" of popular magazines such as *McCall's, Woman's Home Companion, Life,* and the *Ladies Home Journal* resulted in not finding "a single heroine who had a career, a commitment to any work, art, profession, or mission in the world, other than 'Occupation: housewife,'" she became among the first to alert women to the way they were being depicted in the pages of these magazines. Freidan, 116.

42. Lyn White, *Educating Our Daughters: A Challenge to the Colleges* (New York: Harper and Brothers, 1950), 17–26, passim.

43. Quoted in Harvey, 73.

44. Even though the boys' choices don't cluster in few areas, there were clear trends and preferences. Accounting and business were the clear favorites in 1941 but by 1954 they were overtaken by engineering, which remained the most popular career choice. Contrary to conventional wisdom, the Jewish boys did not aspire to become doctors and lawyers—at least not yet. Few chose these professions, perhaps because it was understood that there were quotas, if not formal, for admission to medical and law schools.

45. May, 20.

46. By 1956, Brooklyn College had begun special programs to attract women into teaching in order to help alleviate the teachers' shortage. One program that was actually aimed at women with school-aged children offered classes during the hours when their children would be in school. Another was a Masters of Art in Teaching program for women who already held liberal arts degrees. Kaledin, 35–40.

47. Among them were: the first female doctor and paratrooper in the army and navy; a savings and loan president; a trader on the floor of the merchant's stock exchange; a woman elected to the American Institute of Banking; and Hanna Arendt who became the first woman, in 1959, to attain the rank of full professor at Princeton and Cecilia Payne-Gaposchkin at Harvard. Kaledin, 77.

48. Harvey, 174.

49. Dinnerstein, ix–x.

CHAPTER 6

1. Deckard, 317. There had been a gradual increase in the number of women in the workforce, from about twenty percent around the turn of the century to about twenty-five percent by the time that World War II started. During the war years, the female labor forced increased by more than fifty percent. Coontz wrote: "Three-fourths of the new female workers were married, and a majority were mothers of school-age children" (159).

It has been suggested, and I agree, that the image of women staying at home with the children, at least until they are school age, was one of the things that prevented the development of an adequate early childhood and day care system in the United States, as exists in most European countries.

2. Moen wrote that women "typically left work when they were in their late twenties; but, by their late thirties and early forties, half of them held jobs once again" (13).

3. Moen, 11.

4. Deckard, 305. By 1970, three-fourths of all clerical workers were women.

5. Moore, 64, 234. One of the reasons that Jews tended to cluster in new neighborhoods, Moore said, was "residential exclusion," the informal practice of "redlining" that kept Jews out of particular neighborhoods.

6. Freidan, Chapter 10.

7. Curiously, Minette Cutler never learned to drive. Having someone to drive her around, she said, was her "one luxury in life."

8. Levi, 182.

9. I was struck by the intensity of Eleanor's belief. Lila Perlmutter also believed that it was her group of friends who influenced her choice of study, but in her case it was to pursue the commercial course. I agree with them. I've said almost exactly the same thing about my own experience. I, too, was in a rapid advance, college bound program and my friends, all of the "Jills," spoke of going to college as if it were inevitable. However, unlike Eleanor's, few of my friends enrolled and completed their degrees. I did not complete my degree either until, like Eleanor, I returned to school years later.

10. Toward the end of the nineteenth century a woman was permitted to go through the program at Harvard Medical School but only with the understanding that she would not, in the end, receive a degree. Even as we entered the second half of the twentieth century, access to professional colleges was extremely limited for women.

11. Harvey, 174.

12. *New York Times Education Supplement,* April 7, 1996. Current attention to adult students (more than half of whom are women) is not only a great change from the days of watered-down curricula for women; it is even a great change, philosophically, from Brooklyn College's first "special program for mothers," which was started in 1956 to help alleviate the teacher shortage.

13. There has been a good amount of research in the field of adult education on the special needs of "returning women." Some are caused by negative experiences women had, particularly with math and science. These subjects have been called a "critical filter" by Sheila Tobias and others, since they keep women out of a variety of professions.

But there are other areas of need for "returning women" as well. These include flexibility of study and class time, ability to withdraw without penalty (when there is a family emergency, for example), smaller study groups, effective mentoring and counselling services, credit for life experience learning, etc.

14. Mimi Scarf, *Battered Jewish Wives: Case Studies in The Response to Rage*: (Queenston, Canada: the Edwin Mellen Press, 1987), 53.

15. In my own family there was the perfect example of this phenomenon. My sister Doris, older by nineteen years, would have been the one to have her doctorate if our birth orders had been reversed. As it was, she didn't even graduate from high school. But when she retired she earned her General Education (equivalency) Diploma, went on to complete a bachelor's degree and was doing her master's degree in women's studies when she passed away.

16. The importance, encouragement, and approval of significant males, fathers and husbands, is a consistent theme in the literature about women of previous generations who have had successful careers. The message from the men, "I believe you can make it in a man's world," could only rarely have been given by a woman, certainly not by a Jewish woman, except in those rare instances where a woman had already broken the rigid gendered boundaries.

17. For those readers who are unfamiliar with educational jargon, a resource room is an area, often in a school library, in which there are special materials, "resources," for children with special needs and specially trained teachers and aides.

18. Most of the women in Dinnerstein's study became professionals in various fields. Dinnerstein, 8.

CHAPTER 7

1. See Minnich, *Transforming Knowledge*. She was rethinking a classic problem that has been raised in the academic world once again, this time by feminists: What knowledge is of most worth?

In a curriculum that is already full, we have to constantly reevaluate what is taught by returning to this criterion. If we agree that women's experiences are worth knowing about, and we include women's studies in the curriculum, what do we give up?

For at least two decades, because they have to make choices, departments of history and the other social sciences, philosophy, literature, the behavioral sciences, the "pure" or hard sciences have been trying to decide how to transform their curricula to include groups who have been traditionally underrepresented in the disciplines. But there is resistance to perspectives that represent the work and points of view of ethnic minorities, both native and immigrant, as well as women, gays, physically handicapped, and others.

2. This is less true, as Bea Benjamin understood, for the women of the fifties than the forties. She said, "there is a big difference between women ten years older and our age. In the fifties and sixties women started to do their own thing."

3. Proverbs 31–10.

4. Sorin, *Nurturing Neighborhood*, 190.

5. Coontz wrote that success "was often achieved at enormous cost to the wife, who was expected to subordinate her own needs and aspirations to those of both her husband and her children" (36).

6. May, 204.

7. Sorin's figures show that the men of the BBC had very few divorces: nine percent. Sorin surveyed most of the alumni of the BBC, however, a much larger group. Among the women of this study the rate is higher, perhaps because of the younger average age: twenty percent for the forties women, almost thirty percent for the women of the fifties group, an average of twenty five percent.

8. Harvey suggests that, perhaps on a more fundamental level, lesbianism seems even more threatening than male homosexuality because a lesbian's "sexual satisfaction" does not "come from a man" (178).

9. Baker, 166–171.

10. At one time there was even a (fortunately failed) attempt to use the acronym POSSLQ, taken from the census category: Persons of Opposite Sex Sharing Living Quarters.

11. They have translated a number of contemporary words and expressions into Yiddish, not only those dealing with gay life.

12. Harvey, 199.

13. Klepfisz, *Di Mames*, 14.

14. Baker, 93, 92.

15. An alternative explanation, which is accepted by some anthropologists, is that kosher laws are simply a way of forming a bond through common practice, ritual, and prohibition and is not related to scientific explanations. *Kashruth*, for the observant, is simply a matter of law; it is written!

16. Richard Fein described a similar experience in *The Dance of Leah*, cited in the bibliography.

17. Stephen J. Dubner, "Choosing my Religion," *New York Times Magazine*, March 31, 1996, 36+.

18. Philip Lopate, "In a Strange Land, Act Strange," *New York Times Magazine*, March 26, 1995: 20.

19. Clearly, the daughters might disagree with many of the points, but this is written from the perspective of the women who were interviewed and is not meant to represent any "objective truth." This is a tempting follow-up study. A recent publication, *Her Face in the Mirror: Jewish Women on Mothers and Daughters*, ed. Faye Moskowitz (Boston: Beacon Press, 1994), represents a number of well-known daughters' perspectives.

20. In this way they are like the women surveyed in a 1992 CNN poll, which found a seeming contradiction. Almost all "espoused feminism's goals," but less than one-third considered themselves feminists. Leora Tanenbaum, "Divide and Conquer," *The Women's Review of Books* 12, no. 9 (1995): 5.

21. Berg, 40.

22. It has even carried over to her own generation. "Friends of mine," Minette Cutler says, "are living with men; it goes against my values."

23. Rose L. Glickman, *Daughters of Feminists: Young Women with Feminist Mothers* (New York: St. Martin's Press, 1993), xiii.

24. Cited in Baum, 242. This quotation is taken from the sociologist Pauline Bart's, "Mrs. Portnoy's Complaint: Depression in Middle Aged Women."

25. As discussed in notes on methodology, factors related to affiliation and self-selection need to be considered.

EPILOGUE

1. *Forward*, December 1995. A suggestion for the "harried Jewish mother" that was made to alleviate stress was "*Shabbat* in a bag" a takeout Friday night dinner for the family.

2. By 1980, "a landmark year . . . the dip in the women's labor force participation during the childbearing stage had disappeared. By 1990 over half the mothers with infants under 12 months of age were in the labor force, as were three out of every five mothers of 2-year-old toddlers." Moen, 15.

3. Moen, 25.

4. *WAC Stats* (New York: The New Press, 1993), 45, 62. These statistics compiled by the Women's Action Coalition are attributed to a variety of sources including government and industry documents.

5. Studies cited in Terri Apter, *Working Women Don't Have Wives: Professional Success in the 1990s* (New York: St. Martin's Press, 1994), 20, 143.

6. Ibid., 56.

7. *Forward*, 5.

8. Barbara J. Berg, *The Crisis of the Working Mother: Resolving the Conflict between Family and Work* (New York: Summit Books, 1986), 27.

9. It's interesting that in the publicity surrounding the recent "nanny case" in which a young au pair from England was accused of battering the child in her care to death, most of the rhetoric lamented the fact that the mother (although a professional) was not at home with her children, rather than the issue of adequate day care.

10. Apter, 95. It is speculated that because black mothers lift their family above the lower twenty percent income level of their community and because the morale of the working family is higher, their working has an overriding advantage.

11. According to *WAC Stats*, p 60, in 1989 women received forty percent of law degrees. In 1989 women were awarded one-third of all medical degrees, up from just over ten percent in the early seventies. Because so many medical school applicants are women, some are concerned that medicine may, in fact, be well on its way to becoming a feminized profession, as in the Soviet Union.

12. Since 1975 the number of female economists has almost tripled, as has the number of mail*carriers*. Twenty years ago there were no women commercial pilots or firefighters (only fire*men*) and only a small number of architects. In 1975 only 4.3 percent of architects were women, as compared with 14.6 percent in 1988.

13. Roslyn C. Barnett and Caryl Rivers, "The myth of the miserable working woman," *Working Woman* 17, no. 2 (Feb. 1992): 62+. Also see Coontz.

14. Donna L. Wagner and Gail G. Hunt, "The use of workplace eldercare programs by employed caregivers," *Research on Aging* v.16, 1 (March 1994): 69+ Discusses workplace elder-care programs, which have become a more common component of the work-family benefit package of employers in recent years.

Susan Chira, "Still Guilty after all these years: a bouquet of advice books for the working mom," *The New York Times Book Review,* May 8, 1994, 11.

Uco J. Wiersma, "A taxonomy of behavioral strategies for coping with work-home role conflict," *Human Relations* v.47, no. 2 (February 1994): 211+.

15. In 1975 Rosabeth Moss Kanter was one of those already writing on this issue. See *Work and Family in the United States: A Critical Review and Agenda for Research and Policy* (New York: Russell Sage Foundation, 1977).

16. Moen names these three realities: 1) a transition in progress 2) deeply entrenched ideologies 3) structural lag. Moen, 5–7, Passim.

17. Housework has been so exclusively women's work that in Britain, in 1970, a couple was unsuccessful in its claim that the househusband should be allocated dependent wife benefits. Apter, 58.

18. Berg, 159.

19. Apter, 9. She quotes A. Hochschild.

20. Ibid., 53–54.

21. Ibid., 1.

22. See *Educating our Daughters*.

23. Moen, 7. Phyllis Moen offers what she refers to as a "life course solution" to the problems faced by women who want to have careers and a family life, a solution that would change the structure of work for both women and men so that women are not disadvantaged in their careers and so that men and women can share more equally in the work of the household. Her suggestion goes beyond solving problems for working mothers. She believes that training and retraining through life are essential for the workforce (129–130).

24. Apter, 155.

25. Ibid.

26. Moen, 7.

27. Leslie Garner, *How to Survive as a Working Mother*, quoted in Apter.

Glossary

I used two primary references for Yiddish: Samuel Rosenbaum, *A Yiddish Word Book for English Speaking People* (New York: Van Nostrand Reinhold, 1978), which uses the YIVO transliteration scheme and Herman Galvin and Stan Tamarkin, *The Yiddish Dictionary Sourcebook* (Hoboken: Ktav Publishing House Inc., 1986). I also consulted two learned friends: Lillian Burd for Yiddish; Dorothy Ross for Hebrew.

Although Yiddish has almost disappeared from everyday use, there are some major efforts underway to keep the language from being lost to all but some dedicated scholars. The *Chronicle of Higher Education* claims that "it is finding new life as a scholarly field of study." This is an interesting irony since one of the previous times that Yiddish was threatened with extinction was during the *Haskalah* when the *maskilim*, Jewish intellectuals, deprecated Yiddish as a *zhargon*, a "linguistic pastiche." They wrote in Hebrew, the sacred language or *loshyn-Koydesh*. Whatever its intellectual merits, Yiddish has a unique expressiveness and richness, a texture and color upon which I've drawn quite liberally.

It is sad to see the language succumbing to disuse as the Yiddish speaking generation passes on. Yiddish came to America as the living language of the central and eastern European immigrants. But, Jonathan Rosen (an editor at *The Forward*, a Yiddish language newspaper) wrote, "Yiddish came to have the same effect on many American Jews that kryptonite had on Superman—it was a piece of the place they came from and therefore the one thing they could not abide."

Many women Yiddishists attended a recent conference on "*Di Froyen*, Women and Yiddish," at the Jewish Theological Seminary in New York City. These well-known Jewish scholars, many of whom are secularists, consider Yiddish to be an essential part of the Jewish culture, and particularly of Jewish women's history and culture. They are trying to revive the use of the language, along with, among others, the

199

YIVO Institute, the Workman's Circle, and *Yuguntruf*, a Jewish cultural organization. In this technological age, Yiddish is also being kept alive in cyberspace through "Mendele," an online Internet Yiddish language and culture discussion list, and "Virtual *Shtetl*" on the World Wide Web.

Wherever possible, the spelling of Yiddish words conforms to the transliteration scheme of the YIVO Institute for Jewish Studies. But I have retained the more familiar spelling for some Yiddish terms. For example, the YIVO transliteration for *maven* is *meyvin*; it seems very odd to me. Consequently, there is some inconsistency. Also, I used Hebrew terms when they seem to be more appropriate. I use the Hebrew for *Bat Mitzvah* for example, rather than the Yiddish *Bas Mitsve*. What follows is a glossary of both Yiddish and Hebrew terms that are used repeatedly but defined only the first time they appear. In the glossary, the terms are Yiddish unless otherwise indicated.

Ashkenazim (Hebrew): Eastern European Jews (from *Ashkenaz*, Hebrew for Germany).

Baleboste: Homemaker (literally, mistress of the home).

Bar Mitzvah: (Hebrew) The ceremony in which a thirteen-year-old male reaches adult status in the Jewish religion (literally, son of the commandment).

Bat Mitzvah: Coming of age ceremony for girls. In Yiddish it is *Bas Mitzve*.

Deborah: A charitable medical/health organization.

Eyshit chayil (or *Ayshit chayil*, Hebrew): Woman of valor. In Yiddish it is *eyshis chayil*.

Hadassah: International Jewish Women's organization.

Halakha (Hebrew): Jewish law.

Kashruth (Hebrew): Kosher, referring to the dietary laws. In Yiddish it is *kashres*.

Kheyder (Hebrew): traditional Jewish religious school (literally, room). The usage comes from the one-room school where boys began their religious education.

Mehitzah (Hebrew): The partition behind which women are segregated in the orthodox synagogue.

Mitzvah, Mitzvoth (pl.) (Hebrew): Commandment, good deed, ethical obligation. There are 613. In Yiddish it is *mitzve*.

Sefardim: Mediterranean and southern European Jews (from *Sefard*, Hebrew for Spain).

Shabes: The Sabbath. In Hebrew it is *Shabbat*.

Shande: Shame, humiliation.

Shtetl, Shtetlach (pl.): Small eastern European village or town.

Shul: Synagogue.

Shule: School.

Takhles: (Hebrew) Orientation to ultimate outcomes; meaningful, goal-directed activity.

Talis: Prayer shawl. In Hebrew it is *talit*.

Talmud (Hebrew): Commentary, analysis, and legal debates of Jewish scholars concerning the application of Biblical principles to every aspect of Jewish life. It is the basis for Jewish law.

T'filin (Hebrew): Phylacteries. Small cases worn in prayer by orthodox Jewish men.

Tikn Olam (Hebrew): Improvement or repair of the world.

Tsedakah (Hebrew): Righteousness, justice. Used to mean charity. In Yiddish it is *tsedoke*.

Torah (Hebrew): The first five books of the Bible, or the Pentateuch. Also called the Books of Moses. In Yiddish it is *toyre*.

Yarmulke: Skull cap.

Yeshiva: A school of intensive Jewish study of the Torah, Talmud, Jewish law and ritual, previously limited to male students.

Yidish: Yiddish in *Yidish*.

Yidishkeit: Jewishness, Jewish culture, and Judaism.

Sources

Adler, Rachel. "The Jew Who Wasn't There: *Halakhah* and the Jewish Woman." In *On Being a Jewish Feminist: A Reader*. Susanna Heschel, ed. New York: Schocken Books, 1983.

Apter, Terri. *Working Women Don't Have Wives: Professional Success in the 1990s*. New York: St. Martin's Press, 1994.

"Are 51 Percent of the Stories Missing?" *On Campus with Women* 20, no. 3 (Winter 1990): 1.

Axelrod, Toby. "Staking a Claim to Tradition." *The Brooklyn Jewish Weekly* 209, no. 43 (February 21, 1997): 1+.

Baker, Adrienne. *The Jewish Woman in Contemporary Society: Transitions and Traditions*. New York: New York University Press, 1993.

Barbre, Joy Webster, et al. *Interpreting Women's Lives: Feminist Theory and Personal Narratives*. Bloomington: Indiana University Press, 1989.

Baum, Charlotte, Payla Hyman, and Sonya Michel. *The Jewish Woman in America*. New York: Dial Press, 1975.

Berger, Joseph. "As Delis Dwindle, Traditions Lose Bite." *New York Times*, May 15, 1996, 1+(B).

Berg, Barbara J. *The Crisis of the Working Mother: Resolving the Conflict between Family and Work*. New York: Summit Books, 1986.

Berger, Shulamis. "The Making of the American *Baleboste*/Housewife." Paper presented as part of the conference on *Di Froyen, Women and Yiddish: Tribute to the Past* at Conference on Tribute to the Past, Directions for the Future, at the Jewish Theological Seminary, October 29, 1995.

Bernstein, Carl. *Loyalties: A Son's Memoir*. New York: Simon and Schuster, 1989.

Blaisdell, Thomas. "Education for Parenthood." *The Annals* 67 (September 1917): 47.

Blaszczyk, Regina Lee. "It's a Cinderlla Story: The Home Furnishings Trade, Brides-to-be, and the Construction of Domesticity, 1945–60." Paper presented as part of the symposium on at the Ninth Berkshire Conference on the History of Women, Vassar College, June 11, 1993.

Blewett, Mary. "Good Intentions." *Women's Review of Books* 9, no. 5 (February 1992): 10–11.

Brownmiller, Susan. *Femininity.* New York: Linden Press, 1984.

"Campuses See Revival of Interest in Yiddish as Field of Study." *Chronicle of Higher Education* 42, no. 4, (September 22, 1995): 18(A).

Cobb, Nancy J. *Adolescence: Continuity, Change, and Diversity.* Mountain View, California: Mayfield Publishing Company, 1995.

Coontz, Stephanie. *The Way We Never Were: American Families and the Nostalgia Trap.* New York: Basic Books, 1992.

Cott, Nancy F., ed. *History of Women in America.* Westport, Connecticut: Meckler Press, 1994.

Cyrus, Virginia. *Experiencing Race, Class, and Gender in the United States.* Mountain View, California: Mayfield Publishing Co, 1993.

de Beauvoir, Simone. *The Second Sex: The classic manifesto of the liberated woman.* New York: Random House, 1952; reprint, Vintage Books, 1974.

Deckard, Barbara Sinclair.*The Women's Movement: Political, Socioeconomic, and Psychological Issues.* New York: Harper and Row, 1983.

Dinnerstein, Myra. *Women between Two Worlds: Midlife Reflections on Work and Family.* Philadelphia: Temple University Press, 1992.

Donaldson, Greg. *The Ville:Cops and kids in urban America.* New York: Tickor & Fields, 1993.

Elkind, David. *All Grown Up and No Place to Go.* Reading, Massachusetts: Addison-Wesley Publishing Company, 1984.

Elliott, Stuart. "Advertising." *New York Times,* November 3, 1995, 18(D).

Epstein, Rob, and Jeffrey Friedman. *The Celluloid Closet.* United States, 1995.

Faludi, Susan. *Backlash: The Undeclared War against American Women.* New York: Anchor Books, 1991.

Fein, Richard. *The Dance of Leah: Discovering Yiddish in America.* Cranberry, New Jersey: Associated University Presses, 1986.

Feingold, Henry L. *A Time for Searching: Entering the Mainstream, 1920–1945.* Baltimore: Johns Hopkins University Press, 1992.

"50–Year Retrospective of an All-Girl Class," *New York Times,* May 13, 1994, 4(B).

"Footnotes." *Chronicle of Higher Education* 42, no. 4 (September 22, 1995): 10(A).

Forman, Frieda, Ethel Raicus, Sarah Silberstein Swartz, and Margie Wolfe, eds. *Found Treasures: Stories by Yiddish Women Writers*. Toronto: Second Story Press, 1994.

Freedman, Russell. Review of *Rosie the Riveter: Women Working on the Home Front in World War II* by Penny Colman. *New York Times Book Review*, September 10, 1995: 35.

Freidan, Betty. *The Feminine Mystique*. New York: W.W. Norton, 1963.

Galvin, Herman, and Stan Tamarkin. *The Yiddish Dictionary Sourcebook*. Hoboken: Ktav Publishing House Inc., 1986.

Gilligan, Carol. "On *In a Different Voice:* An Interdisciplinary Forum." *Signs: Journal of Women in Culture and Society* 11, no. 2, (Winter 1986): 304–333.

Gilman, Elizabeth Hale. *Things Girls Like to Do*. Philadelphia: Uplift Vocational Books, 1917.

Glenn, Susan Anita. *Daughters of the Shtetl: Life and Labor in the Immigrant Generation*. Ithaca; Cornell University Press, 1990.

Gluck, Sherna Berger, and Daphne Patai, eds. *Women's Words: The Feminist Practice of Oral History*. New York: Routledge, 1991.

Gonzalez, David, with Garry Pierre-Pierre. "Little Sympathy or Surprise." *New York Times*. November 21, 1993, 44.

Gordon, Mary. *The Other Side*. New York. Viking Press, 1989.

Greenberg, Blu. *On Women and Judaism: A View from Tradition*. Philadelphia: The Jewish Publication Society of America, 1981.

Hartmann, Susan M. *The Home Front and Beyond: American Women in the 1940's*. Boston: Twayne Publishers, 1982.

Harvey, Brett. *The Fifties: A Women's Oral History*. New York: Harper Collins, 1993.

Heller, Scott. "Rescuing Yiddish Books." *Chronicle of Higher Education* 42, no. 4, (September 22, 1995): 11(A).

Heschel, Susannah, ed. *On Being a Jewish Feminist: A Reader*. New York: Schocken Books, 1983.

Howe, Irving. *World of Our Fathers*. New York: Harcourt, Brace, Jovanovich, 1976.

Hymowitz, Carol, and Michaele Weissman. *A History of Women in America*. New York: Bantam Books, 1978.

Jellison, Katherine. "From the Farmhouse Parlor to the Pink Barn: The Commercialization of Rural Weddings in the Postwar Midwest." Paper presented at the Ninth Berkshire Conference on the History of Women, Vassar College, June 11, 1993.

Joselit, Jenna Weissman. *The Wonders of America: Reinventing Jewish Culture, 1880–1950*. New York: Hill and Wang, 1995.

Kaledin, Eugenia. *Mothers and More: American Women in the 1950's*. Boston: Twayne Publishers, 1984.

Katz, Donald. *Home Fires: An Intimate Portrait of One Middle-Class Family in Postwar America*. New York: Harper Collins, 1993.

Kasinitz, Philip. *Caribbean New York: Black Immigrants and the Politics of Race*. Ithaca: Cornell University Press, 1994.

Kaufman, Michael T. "A Labor of Love to Save Yiddish from Extinction." *The New York Times*, July 12, 1995, 3(B).

Klepfisz, Irena. "*Di Mames, Dos Loshen*/The Mothers, The Language: Feminism, Yidishkayt, and the Politics of Memory." *Bridges: A Journal for Jewish Feminists and our Friends* 4, no. 1 (Winter/Spring 1994/5754): 20.

———. "Recognizing Yiddish Literature's 'Nameless Soldiers.'" *Forward* (20 October 1995): 2.

Krause, Corrine Azen. *Grandmothers, Mothers, and Daughters: Oral Histories of Three Genrations of Ethnic American Women*. Boston: Twayne Publishers, 1991.

Krause, David Gonzales, with Garry Pierre-Pierre. "Little Sympathy or Surprise." *The New York Times*, November 21, 1993, p. 44.

Landesman, Alter F. *Brownsville: The Birth, Development, and Passing of a Jewish Community in New York*. New York: Bloch Publishing Company, 1971.

Lee, Felicia R. "Despair Grows in Brooklyn." *New York Times Book Review*, November 28, 1993, p. 25.

Levi, Shonie B., and Sylvia R. Kaplan. *Guide for the Jewish Homemaker*. New York: Schocken Books, 1964.

Magnus, Shulamit. "Out of the Ghetto: Integrating the Study of Jewish Women into the Study of The Jews." *Judaism* 39 (Winter 1990): 28–37.

Mangione, Jerre, and Ben Morreale. *Five Centuries of the Italian American Experience*. New York; Harper Collins, 1992.

May, Elaine Tyler. *Homeward Bound: American Families in the Cold War Era*. New York: Basic Books, Inc., 1988.

McHenry, Robert, ed. *Famous American Women: A Biographical Dictionary from Colonial Times to the Present*. New York: Dover Publishing Company, 1980.

McMurry, Sally. "Getting Married in a Nation of Plenty: Weddings and Consumerism in Postwar America." Paper presented at the Ninth Berkshire Conference on the History of Women, Vassar College, June 11, 1993.

Minnich, Elizabeth Kamarck. *Transforming Knowledge*. Philadelphia: Temple University Press, 1990.

Moen, Phyllis. *Women's Two Roles: A Contemporary Dilemma*. New York: Auburn House, 1992.

Moore, Deborah Dash. *At Home in America: Second Generation New York Jews*. New York: Columbia University Press, 1981.

Murphy, Cullen. "Women and the Bible." *Atlantic Monthly* 272 (August 1993): 39–64.

Oakley, Ann. *The Sociology of Housework*. New York: Pantheon Books, 1974.

Plaskow, Judith. *Standing Again at Sinai: Judaism from a Feminist Perspective*. San Francisco; Harper and Row, 1990.

Rapping, Elayne. "A World Well Lost." *The Women's Review of Books* 10 (September 1993): 11–12.

Robinson, Lillian S. "Foremothers to be proud of." *Women's Review of Books* 11, no. 3 (December 1993): 16–17.

Rosen, Jonathan. "A Dead Languge, Yiddish Lives." *The New York Times Magazine,* July 7, 1996, 25–26.

Rosten, Leo. *Hooray for Yiddish*. New York: Simon and Schuster, 1982.

Rosten, Leo. *Joys of Yinglish*, (New York:McGraw Hill, 1989.)

Roth, Henry. *Call it Sleep*. New York: Robert O. Ballou, 1934.

Roth, Phillip. *Portnoy's Complaint*. New York: Random House, 1969.

Sapiro, Virginia. In *Women in American Society*. Second ed. Mountain View, California: Mayfield Publishing Co., 1990.

Scarf, Mimi. *Battered Jewish Wives: Case Studies in the Response to Rage*. Queenston, Ontario: The Edwin Mellen Press. 1988.

Schneider, Susan Weidman. *Jewish and Female: Choices and Changes in Our Lives Today*. New York: Simon and Schuster, 1984.

Sealander, Judith, ed. *Records of the Women's Bureau of the U.S. Department of Labor, 1918–1965.*

"75th Anniversary: A Woman's Right to Vote." New York: World Trade Center, New York State Division for Women, 1994.

Shapiro, Edward S. *A Time for Healing: American Jewry since World War II*. Baltimore: Johns Hopkins University Press, 1992.

Shepherd, Naomi. *A Price below Rubies: Jewish Women as Rebels and Radicals*. Cambridge: Harvard University Press, 1993.

Shoub, Myra. "Jewish Women's History: Development of a Critical Methodology." *Conservative Judaism* 35 (Winter 1982): 33–46.

Simon, Kate. *Bronx Primitive*. New York: Viking Press, 1982.

Solomon, Deborah. "Alone at Last." Review of Ruth Seidel, *On Her Own: Growing Up in the Shadow of the American Dream*. *The Women's Review of Books* 7 (April 1990): 15.

Sontag, Deborah. "Oy Gevalt! New Yawkese, An Endangered Dialect?" *The New York Times*, February 14, 1993, Section 1, p.1+.

Sorin, Gerald. *The Nurturing Neighborhood: The Brownsville Boys Club and Jewish Community in Urban America, 1940–1990*. New York: New York University Press, 1990.

————. *The Prophetic Minority: American Jewish Immigrant Radicals, 1880–1920*. Bloomington: Indiana University Press, 1985.

————. *A Time for Building: The Third Migration, 1880–1920*. Baltimore: Johns Hopkins University Press, 1992.

"Special Issue: Women's Oral History Two." *Frontiers* (1983).

Stanton, Elizabeth Cady. *The Woman's Bible*. Ann Arbor, Michigan: Northeastern University Press, 1993.

Stein, Leon. *The Triangle Fire*. New York: Carroll & Graf/ Quicksilver, 1962.

Stone, Meg. "The Obstacle That Has No Name." *A Journal of Gender Studies*. Poughkeepsie: Vassar College (Spring 1993): 6.

Tavris, Carol. *The Mismeasure of Woman*. New York: Touchstone Press, 1992.

"The Reconstructionist Movement: Theory and Practice." Wyncote, Pennsylvania: Federation of Reconstructionist Congregations and Havorot, 1988.

Umansky, Ellen M., and Dianne Ashton, eds. *Four Centuries of Jewish Women's Spirituality: A Sourcebook*. Boston: Beacon Press, 1992.

Wagner-Martin, Linda. *Telling Women's Lives: The New Biography*. New Brunswick, New Jersey: Rutgers University Press, 1994.

Weinberg, Sydney Stahl. *World of our Mothers*. New York: Schocken Books, 1988.

White, Lyn. *Educating Our Daughters: A Challenge to the Colleges*. New York: Harper and Brothers, 1950.

Index

Academy of Women Achievers, 110
Adler, Rachel, 52, 185*n14*
advertising, 87, 192*n41*; in Yiddish, 56–57
advocacy activities, 134, 145
affirmative action, 152
African Americans, *see* blacks
American Federation of Teachers, 37
American Jewish Historical Society, 14–15
antinuclear movement, 84, 134
antisemitism, 29, 68
Apter, Al, 2, 4, 5
Apter, Terri, 166, 167
Apter, Terry Guberman, 1–6, 9, 19, 57, 58, 67, 69, 77–78, 105, 107, 112, 134, 153, 160–61
Arbeteringschule, 71
Arendt, Hannah, 192*n47*
armed forces, women in, 75, 113
art: career in, 128; teaching, 155
Ashkenazim, x, 11, 30; *see also* orthodox tradition
athletics, *see* sports
Austria, 48
Austro-Hungarian Empire, 30

Baker, Adrienne, 1, 51–52, 185*n20*, 187*n15*
Baker, Russell, 48
balebostes, 2, 17, 21, 53, 56, 64–65, 86, 100, 133, 136
Bar Mitzvah, 2, 45, 50, 52, 72, 108

Barry sisters, 37
Bat Mitzvah, 45, 72, 92, 142, 144, 145
Baum, Charlotte, x, 48
Beauvoir, Simone de, 191*n30*
Bell, Joe, 30
Benjamin, Bea Gable, 9, 18, 41, 97, 121, 122, 143, 195*n2*
Berman, Ruth Green, 45, 86, 94, 97, 120–21, 127, 134, 140–43, 145
Bernstein, Carl, 89
bet din (domestic courts), 117
Bethesda Naval Hospital, 75
Bible, 21–22, 51, 61, 185*n17*, 187*n15*
birth control, 32–33
blacks, 41–43, 96, 183*n44*, 191*n38*; poverty among, 95; prejudice against, 147; in nursing profession, 99, 121, 137; as working mothers, 162, 197*n10*
Bleckner, Jean Kanowitz, 23–24, 40–41, 60, 70, 71, 107–9, 112, 154, 155, 165
Blewett, Mary, 179*n18*
Bloom, Zena Kusher, 40, 85, 86, 91, 123–24, 134, 155
B'nai Brith, 113, 134
"borscht belt," 72–73
Borough Park, 28, 31
Bowers, Roslyn Wohl, 41, 60, 90, 91, 92, 94–97, 120, 127, 134, 144–45, 150, 152, 153, 155